EARLY CHRISTIANITY IN NORTH AFRICA

Early Christianity in North Africa

Françoıs Decret

Translated by
Edward Smither

James Clarke & Co

James Clarke & Co
P.O. Box 60
Cambridge
CB1 2NT
United Kingdom

www.jamesclarke.co

publishing@jamesclarke.co

ISBN: 978 0 227 17356 5

British Library Cataloguing in Publication Data
A record is available from the British Library

Published by arrangement with Cascade Books,
a division of Wipf and Stock Publishers

First published by James Clarke & Co, 2011

Contents

Translator's Preface

Nearly a decade ago, while working on a Master's thesis on early African Christian theology, I came across François Decret's book *Le christianisme en Afrique du Nord Ancienne*. Appropriately so, I found it at a Christian bookstore run by Kabyle Berbers (from Algeria) in Paris. Since that time, my research on North African Christian history and theology has been greatly aided by Professor Decret's work.

Presently, in my work as a professor of Christian history, students have often asked me about resources for doing research on the early African church. My response has been to ask them if they read French, because Decret's work always came to mind as the best place to start. After some conversations with Decret's publisher Seuil (Paris) and the American publisher Wipf and Stock (Eugene, Oregon), the project to make Decret's work available in the English-speaking world as *Early Christianity in North Africa* became a reality.

Someone has said that *traduction* ("translation") is *trahison* ("treason"). Indeed, the process of translating an author's thoughts and expression from one language to another is quite difficult, if not impossible. My aim has been to be faithful to Professor Decret's words and arguments while making them accessible and readable for an English-speaking audience. I am grateful to Dr. Emily Heady, director of the Liberty University Graduate Writing Center, who carefully proofread each chapter and was especially helpful in working out the "woodenness" of the translation. My hope is that English-speaking students will find this scholarly primer on early African Christianity, something that has previously not existed in English, as a helpful resource in their research.

vii

A final note on style: whenever the reader encounters bracketed comments in the footnotes, please note that these are comments made by the translator

Edward L. Smither, PhD
Assistant Professor of Church History & Intercultural Studies
Liberty Baptist Theological Seminary (Liberty University)

Preface to the English Translation

The African church entered the pages of history on July 17, 180, as twelve martyrs—five women and seven men—from the village of Scilli in Proconsularis (modern Tunisia) were sentenced to death by the Roman Proconsul Vigelius Saturninus. The proconsul had offered the Scillitans a period of thirty days to reflect upon their decision, essentially allowing them to abandon their faith and to return to the official religion. "In a matter so straightforward there is no considering," the accused responded. After the proconsul pronounced his sentence, the Scillitans were tortured and then beheaded. Unlike the first martyrs in Gaul—believers originally from Asia and Phrygia who were put to death in Lyon in 177—the martyrs of Scilli were not Christian immigrants from the East; rather, they were 100 percent African.

In some well-known passages of his *Apology* (ca. 197),[1] Tertullian provides us with the most important indication of Christianity's rapid expansion in Africa. Writing to a pagan audience that was angered over the constant growth of the African church—"the outcry is that the state is filled with Christians"[2]—the polemicist replied:

> If we are enjoined, then, to love our enemies, as I have remarked above, whom have we to hate? If injured, we are forbidden to retaliate, lest we become as bad ourselves: who can suffer injury at our hands? . . . Yet, banded together as we are, ever so ready to sacrifice our lives, what single case of revenge for injury are you able to point to, though, if it were held right among us to repay evil by evil, a single night with a torch or two could achieve an ample vengeance? . . . We are but of yesterday, and we have filled every place

1. [All English quotations of Tertullian are from *ANF* 3–4.]
2. Tertullian *Apology* 1.7.

among you—cities, islands, fortresses, towns, market-places, the
very camp, tribes, companies, palace, senate, forum . . .[3]

Many have reacted to Tertullian's account with skepticism, especially
modern historians who demand more statistical evidence, and his testimony has been dismissed as the exaggerations of an African Christian
lawyer. However, we should recognize the significant growth and dynamic
nature of the African Christian community at the beginning of the third
century, even if the church was still a minority. How could Tertullian,
addressing fellow citizens, a group that included pagans and Christians,
manage to distort a commonly understood reality?

In light of the number of participants, the church councils that
took place in the middle of the third century also attest to the significant growth of the African church. In the fall of 255, thirty-one bishops
from Proconsularis gathered for a council in Carthage and, afterward,
they wrote a letter to eighteen of their Numidian colleagues, stating their
opinion on the issue of baptizing heretics. In the spring of 256, seventy-
one bishops met for a council. On September 1 of the same year, eighty-
seven bishops met. This number did not include those who were absent
due to age, illness, distance, or because a particular church was without a
pastor at that time. Harnack argues that there were 150 bishops in Africa
during this time. When Cyprian was consecrated as bishop of Carthage
in 249, he quickly became one of the most influential leaders in the global
church, and his advice was sought by church leaders from Spain and Gaul.
However, persecution sought its victims. Arrested at his home and taken
to the Proconsul Galerius Maximus, Cyprian was ordered to sacrifice and
give honor to the Roman deities. He replied, "I will not sacrifice . . . do
what you have been ordered to do," and the executioner knew what he
had to do. Hence, the faces of Tertullian, Cyprian, and Augustine become
permanent fixtures in the African Christian story.

Augustine, born in 354 in Tagaste (modern Souk Ahras, Algeria) recounted his disappointing encounter with the Manichean bishop Faustus.
With his spiritual hopes fading, he became completely absorbed in his
career as a rhetor—in Carthage, Rome, and in Valentinian II's court in
Milan—until his baptism in Milan. On the eve of Easter, 387, Augustine
(then thirty-two years old) and his son Adeodatus (fifteen) were baptized

---

3. Tertullian *Apology* 37.4.

by Ambrose, the great bishop of Milan who had played a decisive role in Augustine's conversion. With nothing keeping him in Milan he made plans to return to his homeland. During the return journey to Africa, his mother Monica died at Ostia, and shortly after his return to Tagaste his beloved Adeodatus also passed away.

After returning to Africa, he was ordained as a priest at Hippo (Annaba, Algeria). In 395, he was named co-bishop of Hippo before becoming the city's sole bishop the following year—a role that Augustine would occupy for the rest of his life. Apart from 236 letters (some of which were discovered and edited in 1981) and his sermons, his literary works included ninety-three indexed titles—some of which were considerable in size—that amounted to 252 books. The perspective of Possidius, Augustine's friend and the bishop of Calama (Guelma, Algeria), should be noted:

> So many were the works he dictated and published, so many the sermons he preached in church and then wrote down and revised—whether directed against heretics or devoted to interpreting the canonical books for the building up of the church's holy children—that even a student would hardly have the energy to read and become acquainted with all of them.[4]

Possidius concluded with this remark about his master's work: "I believe, however, that they profited even more who were able to hear him speaking in church and see him there present, especially if they were familiar with his manner of life among his fellow human beings."[5]

In conclusion, scholarship on ancient Africa only continues to increase. For example, in a recent edition of the *Bibliographie analytique de l'Afrique antique*, over 700 books, studies, and reports covering various disciplines were listed. Hence, there is still much time for scholars to investigate the *terrae incognitae* of early Africa. Christians like Tertullian, Cyprian of Carthage, and Augustine of Hippo—now famous in the Mediterranean world and known throughout the world—serve as the skillful narrators who communicate the African Christian story with imagery, severity, and passion. Augustine, originally from the modest village of Tagaste in the High Numidian Plains, sharply reprimanded his country-

---

4. Possidius *Life of Augustine* 18.9.49.
5. Ibid., 31.9.

men for despising Christian martyrs, while taking delight in silly Roman myths: "You have stumbled to the point of forgetting that you are an African!"

François Decret

1   Geographical and Historical Background

ROME'S CONQUEST OF CARTHAGE IN NORTH AFRICA

In the spring of 146 BCE, after victory in its third war against Carthage, Rome established its rule in Africa. Under the orders of Scipio, who faithfully carried out the mission of the warring clan of Marcus Porcius Cato (*Delenda est Carthago,* "Carthage is destroyed"), prestigious Carthage—heir to the legacy of Tyre and Sidon and dominant in the previous centuries in the western Mediterranean world—was destroyed, its walls razed and population exterminated or reduced to slavery. Following a ceremonial salting or cursing of the land, Carthage was deemed eternally cut off from men and doomed to the infernal gods. Yet, this eternity would be brief as twenty-three years after the solemn ceremony, Caius Grachus, tribune of the plebs, boldly founded a large colony on the cursed soil.

Like a well-informed landowner, Rome had been attracted for some time to nearby overseas territories that could become its bread basket. Hence, the Romans first annexed the region of conquered Carthage, an area comprising at least 25,000 square kilometers—which roughly corresponds to the northeast tier of modern Tunisia. Always pragmatic in its approach, Rome had previously been content to take possession of fertile lands and establish colonies for its citizens, including non-land owning military veterans and Italian farmers desiring to migrate in order to acquire and exploit plots of land. However, this first province, *Africa,* would not be developed until the first century CE, as it took Rome nearly one hundred years after taking hold of the remains of Carthage to assimilate the colony politically. This occurred when Caesar made his mark by decisively taking control of the new province, *Africa nova.* From 27 CE, the beginning of Augustus' reign, the two provinces—new and old—were melded together to constitute the large province of *Africa,* later renamed

Africa Proconsularis in honor of its governor, a former Roman consul. In order to be fully efficient, military and political power were placed in the same ruling hands, and the province, invincible for five centuries until the Vandal invasion, was classified as a senatorial province. As a result, this Roman entry into Africa ultimately led to the demise of some of the indigenous Berber kingdoms.

ORGANIZATION OF THE PROVINCES

Though it is not the goal of the present work to deal with all of the developments of Roman colonization, it should be noted that colonization continued through periods of advancement, recoil, and adjustments, leading up to the decisive third-century occupation by the Severans. Indeed, it took Rome more than three and a half centuries to gain control of a region that included mountainous areas and totaled around 350,000 square kilometers.

Not including the new administrative zones organized by the Tetrarchy at various points to manage the growth of the Empire, there were initially four large African provinces that were later increased to eight under Diocletian's reforms:

- Pronconsularis stretched from the west of modern Libya and included all of modern Tunisia. This territory was later divided into the provinces of Byzacena—whose capital was located at Hadrumetum (Sousse, Tunisia)—and Tripolitania with its capital at Lepcis Magna (Al Khums, Libya).

- Numidia, with its capital at Cirta (Constantine, Algeria) stretched from the port cities of modern western Algeria to the southern oasis, to Lambaesis (Tazoult), which was located a dozen kilometers to the east of Batna. Situated at the northern side of the Aures Mountains, Lambaesis was known for its frequent uprisings and, from the time of Trajan, was the base of operations for the Roman African army (*Legio III Augusta*). By the end of the second century, it had become Numidia's leading city.

- Mauretania Caesarea, with its capital at Caesarea (Cherchell, Algeria) covered what is now central and western Algeria. Following reforms in 288, the western part of the province became a new province— Mauretania Sitifien whose capital was Sitifis (Setif, Algeria).

- Further west, Mauretania Tingitane grouped together the districts along the Atlantic coast of present day Morocco from the key city of Tingi (Tangier, Morooco) southward to Sala (Rabat).

Each province was led by an imperially appointed governor who possessed civil authority. The only exception, as noted, was the governor of Proconsularis who was appointed by the Senate and had both civil and military power. The provinces were divided internally into districts or communes that differed according to their administrative status—Roman colonies, *municipia,* or settlements. It should be noted that following an edict by Caracalla in 212, nearly all of the Empire's free inhabitants were granted Roman citizenship.

Africa, despite a full scale Romanization and the development of hundreds of towns, was in reality limited to an area of about 110,000 square kilometers. The region was primarily comprised of Pronconsularis—its two provinces of Byzacena and Tripolitania—and Numidia, which stretched from the coastal regions (including cities like Hippo Regius) to the foothills of the Aures.

If Rome had simply been interested in integrating a "useful" Africa into the Empire, then the venture could be considered successful, at least in regards to what is now the central and eastern Maghreb. It is important, however, to realize that North Africa, whose Arabic name (*Djeziret el-Maghreb*) literally means "island of the setting sun," was spread out over 200,000 kilometers, contained three rivers, and was "anchored" by the Sahara. In all, the vast region totaled some 900,000 square kilometers. Such considerations serve as a reminder that Roman control reached only a portion of Africa. Despite Roman control in the mountainous and southern regions—Numidia and the Mauretanias in particular—there were regular violent uprisings by indigenous tribes against the Roman occupants.

Yet these numbers and figures fail to account accurately for a complex situation. On one hand, almost the entire region of modern Tunisia and the Constantine region of Algeria—stretching from the Mediterranean upper plains to the edge of the Sahara (the Chott al-Gharsa and Chott el-Djerid in Kebili)—were controlled by Rome. It was in this area that soldiers set up military outposts and where church dioceses were eventually created. On the other hand, on the western side of Mauretania Caesarea, the boundaries of Roman civilization stretched from the heights of Pomaria near Tlemcen (Oran) southward to the foot of the high plateaus of the Atlas Mountains—only sixty kilometers or so from the coastline. Hence, despite the difficulties presented by some provinces and regions, Rome capably exerted its authority on the provinces that it was able to occupy.

Certainly the Berber "kingdoms," established progressively in the fifth century as imperial authority had become too weak to carry out its administration, took the mantle of power and established a new type of rule over a diverse population of Romans, Romanized Africans, and Berbers. It was this Roman-African symbiosis that actually provided Roman civilization with a long life in Africa. In spite of the enduring presence of Roman occupation in Africa, in May of 429, Genseric and his armies crossed the Straits of Gibraltar and established a new Vandal rule. The Roman Empire, forced to adapt in light of these circumstances, was still able to conserve the essential *dominium* that stretched back to the glorious reign of Septimius Severus—an African who safeguarded the *pax Romana* with the help of his soldiers.

THE AFRICAN CITY: A KEY TO ROMANIZATION AND SPREAD OF CHRISTIANITY

The indigenous Africans did not expect the Romans to establish cities. Yet this phenomenon of urbanization, which strongly characterized Africa in antiquity, did not originate with Rome's organizing its African provinces. Archaeology has revealed traces of very ancient urban habitations, particularly Punic trading posts. Some of these developed into important cities such as Hadrumetum, Tacape (Gabes, Tunisia), and Mogador (Essouara, Morocco)—cities that were scattered along the modern Tunisian Mediterranean coast and stretched to the Moroccan Atlantic side. The fact remains that African urbanization was a key factor in Romanization as well as in the establishment of Christianity. Thus, urbanization was a phenomenon that would profoundly integrate Africa into the process of transformation occurring in a Roman controlled Mediterranean region. Urbanization developed over several centuries from the second century until the reign of the Severans, a period also marked by particular efforts in urbanization. While African cities were indeed diverse in terms of their physical design, that discussion will not be addressed in this study.

How many cities were there and what was the proportion of urban dwellers to the total population of the African provinces? From ca. 150 to the middle of the third century—the period of the Antonins and Severans and arguably the height of Roman Africa—historians estimate that there were between four and six or seven million inhabitants, with the latter figures being the most accepted. Nearly 500 cities could be counted, an enormous number indeed, with at least 200 situated in what is now Tunisia. The inhabitants of the cities comprised one-fourth to one-third of the entire population.

Regard for the importance of the African cities varies as much as the population estimates. It is likely, however, that Carthage—which according to the third-century historian Herodian competed with Alexandria as the second most prominent city in the empire after Rome—could have by conservative estimates numbered 150,000 people, including its urban center and suburbs. Moreover, upon considering the surface area of the urban areas at their broadest limits as determined by archaeology, as well as conjectures about the average urban population—conjectures based on how the territory was actually used—other arguments have been put forth. Thus, Lepcis Magna in Tripolotania, the favored homeland of Septimius Severus, may have numbered as many as 80,000 inhabitants. A number of key towns probably contained some 20,000 residents: Hadrumetum, Utica, Hippo, Cirta, Mauretania Caesarea, and Volubilis. Finally, the small towns, some of which surely numbered more than 10,000, contained modest urban centers and were at times stretched out over vast rural areas—often the property of city-dwelling bourgeoisie— that were linked administratively to the provincial districts.

Whatever we conclude about these statistics—always a hypothetical enterprise when dealing with the ancient world—at least one thing is certain: the urban network was dense and rich enough to spread out over the African territory, though it did not occur in uniform fashion in the various provinces. It was in these privileged localities that an African– Roman amalgamation took place. Certainly, the accelerated process of urbanization in Africa contributed to the success of the Empire and was an essential factor in the expansion of what has been rightly termed "Romanization."

For its part, the Christian movement also benefited from this urban expansion. The limits of imperial power also determined the limits on Christian expansion. In fact, none of the known dioceses had its episcopal seat located beyond the provincial boundaries and the regions controlled by military detachments, at least at the time of the great Roman expansion in Africa. It was in this period that the *fossatum Africae,* a line of defense formed by a deep ditch measuring four to ten meters wide and consolidated by fortified works, solidified the frontier at the southern Aures against the incursions of nomadic tribes. With that, the farthest military outposts stretched into the Saharan region to places like Castellum Dimmidi (Messad, Algeria), which is to the west of the modern route linking Djelfa and Laghouat. Moreover, it should be noted that with the exception of the diocese of Numidia, which spilled over into that of Proconsularis, the administrative boundaries and organization of the North African church essentially coincided with that of the empire in Roman Africa. This organizational structure became evident at the council of Carthage in 258, where "several bishops gathered together from the provinces of Africa, Numidia, and Mauretania . . ."

Within the context of this urban and rural matrix, a number of religions were being propagated in Africa. Passionately committed to the "gods made in their image," the pagans were just as "religious" as the Christians in their belief and just as fervent in their practices. Indigenous African cults were joined by other pagan religious expressions that came from the East, Egypt, Greece, and Rome.

In the interior of the country, the ancient local deities were honored through sacred practices that were often performed in caves. As the cave walls were covered with magical and religious designs, they were probably centers of worship. Also, certain wells, rivers, trees, rocks, venerated animals, and even the sun and moon had regular followings of worshippers who offered sacrifices and sought their protection. In Mauretania, one finds structures honoring the Maure deities such as *dea Maura,* who possessed its own temple, as well as *Diana Maurorum* and the *dii Mauri* who were grouped together under one name within the venerated Libyan pantheon. Throughout the centuries, the ancient kings, including Hiempsal and Juba, also erected pagan altars.

In addition to the Berber religions, the two most popular deities in the African religious mosaic were imported by the Carthaginians, yet they continued to gain a popular following after the Roman conquest. The first deity, Ba'al Tanit (Juno Caelestis in Latin), was the goddess of fertility and "assistant" to the second, the great Carthaginian god Ba'al Hammon who originated from Phoenicia. Taking the name Saturn of Africa, this god of land and sky was held in much higher regard than all of the previously honored local deities and thus, the cult of Ba'al extended to all of Roman Africa. Later, Tertullian, attempting to argue for monotheism in the context of the pantheon, would draw parallels between the Christian God and Saturn. Here we have a particularly characteristic example of Romanization: a Punic deity, undoubtedly Africanized before the arrival of Rome, which sustains the religious fallout of a foreign presence on African soil.

Against this backdrop of traditional deities, other pagan cults, originating from all around the Mediterranean world, were added. They included: Mithras, a symbol of eternity; Serapis, who came from Egypt and would have adherents as far as the villages of the interior; and the goddess Ma (Bellona), the grandmother of the gods, who originated from Phrygia in Asia Minor and had followers from Proconsularis to Mauretania Caesarea and even to Lambaesis in southern Numidia. Each cult had its own temples, altars, priests, and circles of devotion, some of which gathered in specific locations that honored Mars, Venus, Ceres, and Ma. These cults arrived in Carthage with their adherents— merchants, soldiers, civil servants, and settlers. Within the African pantheon, the greatest prominence was given to the Capitoline Triad: Jupiter, the master of the Roman pantheon, Juno, and Minerva. The three could be typically found alongside one another in one temple or were assigned their own temples in the same vicinity. That the gods were grouped in a pair or trio actually reflected the multiple aspects of a single deity—just as the goddess Tanit functioned as the "face of Ba'al." In the majority of the most important African cities, the Capitol stood as the most opulent and prestigious building in the city. Finally, the official cult of the divine emperors should be mentioned within this religious mosaic. The emperors (*Divi*) had their own temples in the cities and worship practices overseen by a *flamen*, a priest who was a member of the local aristocracy.

Hence, long before the arrival of Christianity, the Africans were already deeply religious. Though some foreign deities, particularly those of Egypt and Phoenicia, were initially more prominent, all of the pagan cults would become mutually accommodating. Though we are unable to discuss the sedimentary levels that resulted as new religions replaced older ones, the past and present were able to co-exist despite different dates of arrival in Africa and juxtaposition in belief and practice. This reality, consistent throughout the history of religious people in antiquity, constitutes one of the strongest aspects of the African religious tradition.

Inasmuch as they were able to appeal to the richness of their traditions and their own genius, the Africans contributed to the changes in civilization that characterized the centuries of Roman domination in the western Mediterranean. Further, in the context of bitterly defending its uniqueness against Roman attempts to organize and standardize African society, African Christianity (*catholica*) would also lay hold of a major place in the history of the early church.

ADDITIONAL RESOURCES

Birot and Dresch, *La Méditerranée et le Moyen-Orient.*
Decret and Fantar, *L'Afrique du Nord dans l'Antiquité: Histoire et civilization—des origins au V siècle.*
Despois and Raynal, *Géographie de l'Afrique du Nord-Ouest.*
Février, *Approches du Maghreb romain: Pouvoirs, differences et conflicts* (2 vols).
Julien, Courtois, and LeTourneau, *Histoire de l'Afrique du Nord.*
Picard, *La Civilisation de l'Afrique romaine.*
Romanelli, *Storia delle province romane dell'Africa.*
Salama, *Les Voies romaines de l'Afrique du Nord.*
Warmington, *The North African Provinces from Diocletian to the Vandal Conquest.*

2 Origins of the African Church

On July 17, 180, twelve Christians from the region of Scilli appeared before the governor's tribunal in Carthage. Undoubtedly, this process put into practice Trajan's rescript of ca. 112, which set a precedent for formally charging Christians with apostasy and prescribing torture if charges were brought by a known accuser. The *Acts of the Scillitans,* which have survived in several Latin manuscripts as well as another Greek version, recount the rather dry administrative process of interrogation carried out by the proconsul Vigelius Saturninus. We observe the proconsul's promise of pardon if the prisoners would abandon their faith to return to the official Roman cult. The Scillitans responded, "Honor to Caesar as Caesar: but fear to God."[1] When called upon to swear by the genius of the emperor, one of the believers, Speratus, confessed: "The empire of this world I know not; but rather I serve that God whom no man has seen, nor with these eyes can see." Despite the governor's proposed recess for the accused to reflect upon their plight, they responded: "In a matter so straightforward there is no considering." As these responses succeeded in halting the judicial process, the magistrate pronounced his sentence, which also brought the *Acts* to a close:

> Saturninus the proconsul read out the decree from the tablet: Speratus, Nartzalus, Cittinus, Donata, Vestia, Secunda and the rest having confessed that they live according to the Christian rite, since after opportunity offered them of returning to the custom of the Romans they have obstinately persisted, it is determined that

---

1. [All English quotations of the *Acts of the Scillitan Martyrs* are taken from Roberts et al., *The Ante-Nicene Fathers,* hereafter referred to as *ANF.*]

they be put to the sword. They all said: Thanks be to God. And so they all together were crowned with martyrdom.

The *Acts of the Scillitan Marytrs* is the earliest document in the collection of African hagiography. This account, the execution of five women and seven men, also serves as African Christianity's official entry into history. It is remarkable that the names of some of the martyrs were typically African names (Cittinus, Felix, Nartzalus, Speratus, Veturius). In contrast to the first martyrs of Gaul—who originated from Asia and Phrygia and were put to death in Lyon in 177—the martyrs of Scilli, a village in Proconsularis, were not members of a community that had migrated from the East; rather, they were of pure African stock.

The opening pages of North African Christianity seem to have no connection to the apostolic period. Nor is there a great episode of a golden legend, a great saint, or an apostle arriving on the African shores to convert the unbelievers. Rather, this history opens through the testimonies of blood.

To be sure, the "new religion" was known publicly in the African provinces well before the martyrdoms of 180. The Scillitans themselves declared in the course of the interrogation that their faith had already offended the sensitivities of their fellow citizens long before their arrest and trial: "We have never done ill, we have not lent ourselves to wrong, we have never spoken ill, but when ill-treated we have given thanks; because we pay heed to Our Emperor."

SECOND CENTURY CHURCH EXPANSION

A number of factors indicate that Christianity was spreading on "Barbarian" soil from an early date. In 197–198, Tertullian addressed the imperial authorities and their pagan constituency in his *Apology*: "We are but of yesterday, and we have filled every place among you—cities, islands, fortresses, towns, market-places, the very camp, tribes, companies, palace, senate, forum . . ."[2] Around fifteen years later, he lashed out again—this time to the proconsul Scapula:

> . . . What will you make of so many thousands, of such a multitude of men and women, persons of every sex and every age and every rank, when they present themselves before you? How many fires,

2. Tertullian *Apology* 37.4. [All English quotations of Tertullian are from *ANF* 3–4.]

how many swords will be required? What will be the anguish of
Carthage itself, which you will have to decimate, as each one recognizes there his relatives and companions, as he sees there it may
be men of your own order, and noble ladies, and all the leading
persons of the city, and either kinsmen or friends of those of your
own circle? . . . We are an immense number, probably the majority
in each city.[3]

Allowances should surely be made for the polemicist's exaggerations, and
we should avoid venturing into a risky and ultimately unhelpful game
of statistics and percentages. The modern critic should nevertheless ad-
mit the considerable importance of the African church at the beginning
of the third century—a church comprised not only of the lower classes
in the cities and countryside, but also influential members of the upper
class—even if the Christian communities, dynamic and prospering, were
still only a small minority of the population. How could Tertullian have
effectively distorted the situation of the church when his Carthaginian
audience—imperial authorities, Christians, and pagans—were quite
aware of the realities of the Christian presence?

Other documentation also lends support for an early African
church. Before addressing the first church councils held at Carthage, let
us first consider the catacombs of Hadrumetum (Sousse)—underground
caves stretching over five kilometers where some fifteen thousand graves,
dating from the second to fourth centuries, have been counted. Many
of these contain motifs and inscriptions that were characteristically
Christian, including images of the Good Shepherd, a dove, and a fish.
Well before Christians were buried in the catacombs around 150, a local
church had certainly been planted and had experienced growth. It is also
quite evident that before the Gospel reached Hadrumetum—150 kilometers south of Carthage—it had reached the capital of Pronconsularis.
Hence, there was probably a church in Carthage before the end of the
first century.

CARTHAGE: MOTHER OF THE AFRICAN CHURCH

While assigning a precise date for the advent of Christianity in Africa is
quite difficult, another challenging issue should also be raised—the prov-

---

3. Tertullian *To Scapula* 5.

enance of the Gospel into Roman Africa. As noted, there is no basis for a pious tradition that would trace the founding of African Christianity to the apostolic period. Neither Tertullian, Cyprian, nor Augustine made such claims. So, did the new faith come from Rome or directly from the East? It should first be affirmed that Carthage, situated on the shores of North Africa, was undoubtedly the first city to be touched by Christianity. Open to Hellenistic influences in all its forms, the capital of Proconsularis was also the first center for Latin literature in this period.

A vast Mediterranean crossroads where African, Egyptian, Greek, and Eastern religions confronted its cosmopolitan population, Carthage had a direct relationship with Rome; yet, the city was also connected with all of the important economic centers of the East. The organization of the Empire's maritime transport—its fleets and port systems—were directly tied to Rome's economic and political role. Indeed, Rome (more specifically Puzzuoli) was where all of the principal sea routes converged and the African route was the most important one in the western Mediterranean. It stretched from Carthage, where Caesar and Augustus had rebuilt a commercial port, and during the summer months (between the spring and autumn equinox) linked the provincial capital to the eastern coast of Sardinia before continuing to the Italian ports. Carthage was equally connected to Ephesus (Asia Minor) and to the great cities of Alexandria (Egypt) and Antioch (Syria), and thus ranked among the most populated cities of the Empire—cities that through their energy and enterprise controlled most of the Mediterranean's commerce. Of course, Alexandria and Antioch were also the two principle centers of the church and evangelization at this time.

CARTHAGE, ROME, AND THE EASTERN CHURCHES

So, did Christianity come to Africa from Rome or the East? While no documentation provides a clear response to this question, it is likely that the Gospel converged on Africa from both locations at the same time. When speaking of the "Roman" origins of the African church, this should not be taken to mean the intervention of the ecclesiastical hierarchy of the church in the empire's capital, particularly the pope, as some later hagiography has claimed. For example, an early fifth-century letter from Pope Innocent I to Decentius of Gubbio seems to make this claim. Even if the pope had written that Rome—where the Christian community itself included many believers from the East—had established churches in Africa, this does not mean that African Christianity originated in Rome. Actually, the key agents who spread the Gospel in the Africa provinces were Italian immigrants who came as settlers, as well as merchants and soldiers. Still, they were not alone in their evangelization and were probably not the first to serve in this capacity.

Augustine reminded his listeners of the antiquity, importance, and prestige of the church at Carthage—an authority received because of the city's proximity to overseas countries. In confronting the Donatist stubbornness, he reiterated that the Carthaginian bishops had a constant relationship not only with the Roman church but also with "all of the other regions from whence the Gospel came to Africa."[4] In this way, he accused the schismatics of severing relationships that united the African catholic church to the eastern churches—the region where the African church received its beginnings.

If Tertullian was correct, the African church experienced a very rapid expansion. Let us now examine the factors that account for this growth.

THE ROLE OF THE DIASPORA IN THE ORIGINS OF THE AFRICAN CHURCH

When considering the establishment of the first Christian groups in Africa who in turn contributed to early evangelization, the role of the Jewish Diaspora should be considered. A large number of Jews, mostly of Palestinian origin, could be found in Africa during the Roman period. Based at least on epigraphic evidence, the majority of Jews made up the lower classes though there was a small bourgeoisie who possessed some economic power. Before the end of the third century BCE, some noteworthy Jewish settlements had been formed in Carthage, Cirta, Sitifis, Auzia (Sour el-Ghozlane in southern Algeria), and toward Volubilis in Mauretania Tingitane. Though archaeological evidence is limited apart from the necropolis at Djebel Khaoui, which will be treated later, two synagogues should be mentioned here. The first was located in Naro (Hammam Lif, Tunisia), possibly dating back to the third century BCE.

---

4. Augustine *Letter* 43.7 [unless otherwise noted, all English translation of Augustine's *Letters* are from Augustine, *Works of Saint Augustine*, hereafter *WSA*].

The second, in Lepcis Magna, was a structure that eventually became an adjoining room to the Catholic basilica. It is alleged that the synagogue and church were linked together by settlers in Cyrene in the period of the Ptolomies. From very early on, the Jews began to migrate in successive waves toward the Berber regions and settle there.

Moreover, Jewish Christians, perhaps those who were part of the original Christian movement, would have come to Africa with the Diaspora at the end of the first century CE. We should also note the presence of nominal Jews, later mocked by the Bishop Commodius: "Why do you run to the synagogue and divide yourselves? . . . Then, you leave the synagogue and go again to the temples . . . Well! To want to be half Jew and half pagan . . . You were blind and you go enter the house of the blind; the blind leading the blind into a ditch." By the second century CE, there were numerous Jewish settlements in Roman Africa, particularly in the coastal cities, but also on the high plains and in the confines of the desert. It appears that they had even organized themselves into tribes. In his *History of the Berbers,* Ibn Khaldoun makes mention of several Berber tribes that professed to be Jews.

Since Tertullian[5] had accused the Jews of directing their jealous hostility toward the young church, it is possible to conclude that African Christianity developed within the local Jewish Diaspora. For some time the importance of the Jewish necropolis of Djebel Khaoui has been considered by scholars. Located in the center of Gamarth a few kilometers north of Carthage, the cemetery contained one epitaph and some fragmentary inscriptions, indicating the presence of Christian tombs. From this we may conclude that the earliest African Christians, undoubtedly from Jewish origins, must have maintained good relations with the synagogue in order to be buried next to their former fellow believers. Hence, this was a sign of some agreement or harmony between the two communities. However, the reservations of Père Delattre—who carried out his archaeological digs in an otherwise anarchical context—ought to be considered. He argues that "the ruins are insufficient to determine what is here" and that if Christians were buried in the Jewish necropolis, which cannot be confirmed, it would have only been an exception.[6]

---

5. Cf. *Apology.*
6. See Delattre, *Gamart ou la nécropole juive de Carthage,* 49–50.

Whatever is to be made of the uncertain origins of African Christianity, the fact remains that from the end of the second century the Christian community experienced a significant and bitter opposition from the Jews, probably on account of the rapid growth of the church. Throughout his *Apology*, Tertullian consistently argued that the synagogues had become "sources of persecution."[7] It should be noted, however, that this argument seems based on similar New Testament polemics against the Jews. Thus, Tertullian was not challenging a particularly African Jewish attitude toward Christians. Nevertheless, a fierce controversy was sparked in which the two parties demonstrated an uncommon aggressiveness. Though early Christianity in North Africa was understood in reference to Judaism and characterized by the older faith in its initial worship forms—including a more favorable African reading of the New Testament—we should not forget that it would have also been affected by other influences.

DID PUNIC BELIEFS CLEAR THE WAY FOR CHRISTIANITY?

It has been argued periodically that ancient Punic traditions—a henotheism (belief in one deity) or even a Semitic monotheism affirmed and refined over time—must have cleared the way for Christianity in Africa. It remains to be proven that the transition to the new religion began with a belief in a single deity that over time resulted in the God of the New Testament. The development of a traditional pagan deity into a god of creation and order, which then evolves into a single God, is not merely characteristic of the Punic legacy in Africa. It seems to correspond to the slow social and economic changes apparent in the entire Mediterranean world. In the mid-third century, during a church council presided over by Cyprian, the Bishop Saturninus remarked: "Even as they worship idols, the pagans recognize and worship a sovereign God who is both Father and Creator." It does not seem, however, that this transformation in belief could have truly occurred to any significant extent or on a popular level until the rise of Christianity in the first two centuries CE. The following examples will be advanced to support this argument.

Between 162 and 166, Fronton, the famous polemicist from Cirta, delivered his diatribe, *Against the Christians*. Apuleius, another African

---

7. Tertullian *Apology* 7.

from Madauros (Mdaourouch, Algeria), who wrote in the middle of the second century, was quite aware of the religious tradition of his region. In a passage in his *Metamorphosis*, he did not hesitate to stigmatize Christian monotheism and the eucharistic liturgy, likening them to a corrupted woman in love with an ass and indulging in her vices:

> Then despising and trampling on the divine powers, instead of the true religion, counterfeiting a nefarious opinion of God, whom she asserted to be the only deity [to the exclusion of other Gods who proceed from, and are rooted in, the first God] devising also vain observances, and deceiving all men, and likewise her miserable husband, she enslaved her body to morning draughts of pure wine, and to continual adultery.[8]

These "intellectuals" (Fronton and Apuleius) obviously had no interest in seeing a change in the religious traditions and political situation of their day—from which they benefited.

At the end of the fourth century, the African Manichean Faustus of Milevus gained renown for making a direct connection from his ancestors' faith to the Christian faith. Also, Honoratus and Nebridius, close friends of Augustine, both came from families in which traditional paganism was quite alive. Yet such paganism was also very influenced by the deeper metaphysical speculations of Plotinus and other Platonic philosophers.

It should further be noted that from the first decade of the third century, the new religion had extended beyond the regions of Punic influence. The Christian presence reached into the areas inhabited by the Getulian peoples—a group of nomadic tribes that moved about on the edge of the Sahara from the south of modern Morocco to the Gulf of Syrte. The Getulians saw at least part of their land come under Roman control during the colonial expansion. Again, according to Tertullian, the Christian movement expanded significantly in the African interior, particularly in the high plains region, where it would have impacted numerous Getulian tribes. It also moved west where it touched the nomadic populations of Mauretania Caesarea and Mauretania Tingitane.[9]

---

8. Apuleius *Metamorphosis* 9.14.5 (201–2).

9. Tertullian *Against the Jews* 7.4.

ORGANIZATION OF THE EARLY CHURCH AT CARTHAGE

Under Roman law, slaves had the same right to a burial plot as a free citizen. In fact, in the face of death, the pagan cults did not disown slaves; rather, their graves, like those of free men, became a sacred place (*locus religiosus*). This concern for an honorable burial, which resulted in a funeral cult, often meant that slaves, liberated slaves, free citizens from lower classes, and imperial slaves were buried in the same location in a cemetery. Similarly, average citizens were placed alongside those of a similar profession. These funerary societies, protected by Roman law, offered a proper burial to all, regardless of class, and guaranteed that homage to the deceased could continually be offered. Allowed only in Rome initially, these societies eventually became authorized in all of the provinces through a decree from Septimius Severus from which time the movement became widespread. In spite of these accords offered to slave and free alike, the situation for Christians was still unsettled. Though churches were authorized to serve as funerary societies, their individual members still lived under the grip of imperial laws that treated them as a forbidden religious sect.

It seems that from a very early date the church at Carthage had formed a community whose meetings took place in the *areae,* open-air cemeteries where only Christians could be buried. For Cyprian, it was inconceivable that Christians could be buried beside pagans. As prescribed by Roman law, Christian cemeteries, like other cemeteries, were situated outside the confines of the city so that the living would not be "soiled" through contact with the dead. Situated near the suburb of Megara, the Christian *area* in Carthage adjoins the pagan *areae.* Though indistinguishable from the outside, fences inside separate the Christian and pagan burial areas. Cyprian was buried "in the cemetery of procurator Macrobius Candidianus, which is in the 'Huts' Road (*Via Mappaliensis*) near the baths."[10] Probably, the private property on which the cemetery was established was later donated to the church by the owner. This cemetery, where Cyprian was venerated, was also where deceased Christians, including those who were born far from Carthage, were buried. Over a two-week period in 295, the martyr Maximilian and the devout ma-

---

10. [All English citations of the *Acta proconsularia* are taken from "The Martyrdom of Cyprian" at http://www.philthompson.net/pages/martyrs/cyprianmart.html.]

tron Pompeiana, both of Tebessa (near Constantine), were brought to Carthage for burial.

The cemeteries also served as places for worship assemblies. For this purpose, a chapel was erected on the tomb of Cyprian. This *cella*, where believers gathered for worship, probably also housed the tombs of some key personalities or privileged members of the community. The *area,* however, served as the burial ground for all believers and their gravestones included diverse Christian symbols—the cross, Christian emblems, a dove, an anchor, and the words *in pace.*

During times of persecution, these cemeteries, still tolerated by the government as Christian funerary societies, became key centers for Christian worship. This explains the pagan war cry against the Christians: "*Areae non sint!* No more cemeteries!" That is, the funerary societies and the Christian community should no longer be protected by the law. Indeed, during this period the funerary society was the only legal way that the church at Carthage could meet for worship or collect offerings for the poor. Thus, it was in the graveyard in the midst of burying a martyr that the church celebrated the Lord's suffering through the Eucharist, with a slab of stone serving as the Lord's table (*mensa*).

Apart from the *cella,* the church at Carthage also possessed a locale, most certainly an entire house, which would have been located outside of the city proper. Tertullian referred to this structure as a church (*ecclesia*). While *ecclesia* should surely be understood metaphorically, there were also multiple architectural references to the structure—thresholds, doors, roofing—that indicate that there was an actual building dedicated for worship. These house meetings would have been known to all as Tertullian responded to the accusation that Christians were having secret meetings: "Our manner of life has become better known; you know the very days of our assemblies; therefore we are both besieged, and attacked, and kept prisoners actually in our secret congregations."[11]

CHRISTIANITY CONFRONTING AFRICAN SOCIETY

The progress of Christianity in Africa was certainly challenged by imperial edicts. However, prior to any official opposition and perhaps even afterwards, Christianity experienced more real opposition from other

11. Tertullian *Ad Nationes* 1.7

levels in African society. Deep religious feelings could be found at the heart of the pagan devout, and the masses had for some time been deeply influenced by mysticism. Because the Africans had always demonstrated a welcome attitude toward various religions coming from Rome, Greece, Egypt, Asia, and the East, they were intolerant of a new religion that made exclusive claims. In the same sense, the Africans had risen up against the deities throughout the provinces that had their own special cult or band of followers. As a result, the ancient deities Ba'al Hammon and Tanit continued to be venerated without opposition after being cloaked in Roman "dress" and becoming Saturn of Africa and Juno Caelestis.

Christianity had not come simply to revive the ancient cults; rather, it wanted to destroy all other worship forms and become the only religion. Thus, Christians were required to renounce an all-too-recent past and destroy the objects and images venerated in worship. This claim to one unique religion and a resulting uniformity in belief from East to West was not only insulting to pagans whose gods and long-standing worship would be reduced to the level of superstition, it also touched upon an inherent African aversion to particularism and to becoming aligned to any ideological system.

Worse still, by planting itself in the midst of the masses, the new religion began to tear at the tightly woven African social fabric. As paganism penetrated every aspect of daily life, it was necessary for Christians, desiring to remain faithful to their convictions, to cut themselves off from their fellow citizens. They were essentially removed from family life and its traditional veneration of ancestors. Unable to participate in weddings and funerals with pagan rituals, African family life was becoming threatened. Christian convictions also proved to be a serious attack against social life in Roman Africa. Town council sessions typically opened with some act of pagan homage. Public festivals and ceremonies—gladiator games in the arena, chariot races around the circus, and plays that depicted mythological characters—were all inaugurated with sacrifices to the chief gods. All of these festivities—quite familiar to Tertullian, who was a great admirer before denouncing them as morally incompatible with the Christian life in his work *On the Shows*—included passions and excesses that the new religion rejected.

Was such moral severity merely a façade and in reality a form of hypocrisy? Two Africans, Fronton and Apuleius, quite aware of the thoughts and sympathies of the masses, used their pens to accuse the

Christians of indecent and disgraceful acts—accusations that were quite welcome within pagan contexts. The rumors circulated that members of the new sect, despite claims to purity and choosing to remove themselves from the city and look down upon the rest of society, actually indulged in mysterious, dark communal rites that included evil plots, incest, ritual murders, child sacrifice, and cannibalism.[12]

These libelous rumors and vile stories, disregarded by Roman authorities and pagan intellectuals alike, managed to gain a popular hearing and resulted in a verbal campaign against the Christians. Tertullian wrote:

> In however wide a circuit a report has been circulated, it must needs have originated some time or other from one mouth; afterwards it creeps on somehow to ears and tongues which pass it on and so obscures the humble error in which it began, that no one considers whether the mouth which first set it going disseminated a falsehood—a circumstance which often happens either from a temper of rivalry, or a suspicious turn, or even the pleasure of feigning news.[13]

The people of the towns and countryside were unable to let such charges against the Christians go without a response. For, in their minds, Christian corruption had resulted in natural disasters, floods, and draughts—which ruined the African soil and their livelihood—as well as epidemics and general bad luck for the populace. Alleged nocturnal Christian practices deemed magical could only unleash formidable evil powers. Christian impiety toward the traditional pagan deities had certainly stirred up their anger. As a result, the entire population was forced to suffer the consequences. "If the Tiber rises as high as the city walls, if the Nile does not send its waters up over the fields, if the heavens give no rain, if there is an earthquake, if there is famine or pestilence, straightway the cry is, 'Away with the Christians to the lion!'"[14] When a plebeian, stirred up by skillful ringleaders, shouted "death to the Christians," the shrewd governor, charged with the task of maintaining order in his province and not terribly concerned with legal due process, rarely opposed the passionate outcry of the mob.

---

12. See Tertullian *Apology* 3; 7–8; 16; 35; *Ad Nationes* 1.1; 7; 17.

13. Tertullian *Ad Nationes* 1.7.

14. Tertullian *Apology* 40.

Because of their own religious law, the Jews had always found it difficult to integrate into African pagan society. With the arrival of Christianity in North Africa, they thought they had found a new scapegoat. Thus, they went to great lengths to distinguish themselves from the Christians, affirming that there was nothing in common between Jewish and Christian belief, which caused great confusion for some time for the Roman magistrates. Tertullian regarded the Synagogue as a hostile force against the church, one that quietly incited persecution against the Christians.[15] However, as already noted, the question must still be raised whether Tertullian's accusations have a historical basis in the church at Carthage, or if they refer back to Christian-Jewish conflict in the apostolic period or early first century.

Pagan aggression toward the Christians was not merely limited to verbal insults or clashes, it affected Christian cemeteries. Despite the dictates of Roman law that, for religious reasons, protected the sanctity of burial grounds, some Christian tombs were ransacked and destroyed by angry mobs. Tertullian wrote in his *Apology:*

> How often, too, the hostile mob, paying no regard to you, takes the law into its own hand, and assails us with stones and flames! With the very frenzy of the Bacchanals, they do not even spare the Christian dead, but tear them, now sadly changed, no longer entire, from the rest of the tomb, from the asylum we might say of death, cutting them in pieces, rending them asunder.[16]

Five years later, the procurator Hilarianus, serving as interim governor, was quite slow to address the problem of the Christian *areae* as the population pushed for distinctively Christian cemeteries to be removed. During this time, the burial grounds were again vandalized, and the perpetrators were apparently never arrested.[17] Among the causes for renewed persecution against the African church at this time, which drove the political decisions of the emperors, was the hostility of the angry masses.

However, in this context, the African provincial governors were not only less severe with the Christians when compared to their colleagues in the rest of the empire, there were even times when some governors,

---

15. See Tertullian *Scorpiace* 10.10; *Apology* 16; 21.25; *Ad Nationes* 1.14; *Against the Jews* 13.26.

16. Tertullian *Apology* 37.

17. Tertullian *To Scapula* 3.

though not without risk, extended favor to the Christians. Tertullian, who was not inclined to sing the praises of the magistrates, recognized the kindness of certain proconsuls who began serving around 191. In his writings, he cited several positive examples. Vespronius Candidus, who vigorously stood behind the wording of some imperial edicts, refused to hear a case against a Christian pushed into his tribunal by an agitated mob. Julius Asper also sent away a similar case, declaring that he would not get involved in such matters. Valerius Pudens searched carefully in the law for language supporting the accused and rejected the accusations of a pagan who had used intimidation to extort money from a Christian. The case of Cincius Severinus is perhaps more characteristic of the merciful spirit at work in some of the proconsuls: he handed down an ambiguously worded decision against the accused Christians, which allowed the interrogator to save face and the defendants to go free. For Tertullian, who wrote in ca. 212 against the rather zealous governor Scapula, to make a point to cite these kind examples among the proconsuls—civil servants named by the Senate for one-year terms that were potentially renewable—indicated that benevolent examples were surely the exception.

Despite the criticisms of some extremists, the African church responded to both existing and potential persecution by adopting strategies for stalling. Those who did not feel strong enough in their faith to face interrogation and other legal procedures were encouraged to avoid the temptation to lapse by fleeing to another town where they were less known and therefore at less risk. "It would be better to flee from town to town than to deny Christ in prison or during torture. However, the most blessed are those who depart this world with the martyr's crown." To avoid problems, the faithful were also encouraged, according to the old tradition of purchasing the silence of tax officials through bribes, to pay a ransom to the *beneficiarii* or *curiosi*—uniformed or civil police that were investigating the forbidden religion.

Tertullian later wrote the treatise *On Fleeing in Times of Persecution* (ca. 212) in order to chastise those believers taking flight—individuals regarded by Tertullian as cowards and traitors. Tertullian argued that purchasing complicity from local officials was just as bad as fleeing:

> As regards your feet, you have stood; in respect of the money you
> have paid, you have run away. Why, in this very standing of yours
> there was a fleeing from persecution, in the release from persecu-

tion which you bought; but that you should ransom with money a man whom Christ has ransomed with His blood, how unworthy is it of God and His ways of acting, who spared not His own Son for you, that He might be made a curse for us.[18]

He adds in irony, "Perhaps, if you pay well enough you may request a martyr's crown?" Indeed, in advocating this unswerving position, Tertullian does identify himself with Montanist sentiments; yet these were also his convictions prior to joining the Montanists. In his work *Ad Nationes*, addressed to a pagan audience around 197, he declared: "It is therefore against these things that our contest lies—against the institutions of our ancestors, against the authority of tradition, the laws of our governors, and the reasonings of the wise; against antiquity, custom, submission; against precedents, prodigies, miracles,—all which things have had their part in consolidating that spurious system of your gods."[19]

THE TIME OF PERSECUTION: PERPETUA, FELICITAS, AND THEIR FRIENDS

In 197 a new persecution broke out in Carthage as officials appealed to previous anti-Christians laws, particularly Trajan's rescript, and Christians found themselves in very difficult circumstances. According to Tertullian's *Apology*, Christians were appearing before the tribunal on a daily basis. Punishments included pre-trial torture, exile to nearby islands, decapitation, being thrown to the beasts in the amphitheatre, being torn to shreds by iron hooks, being burnt alive, and crucifixion. A large number fled the city at the beginning of this wave of persecution.

In 202, the Emperor Septimius Severus traveled to Palestine to inspect the empire's borders that were being threatened by the Parthians. Needing to mobilize all of the empire's forces against this threat, Severus placed a ban on all Jewish and Christian proselytizing. Though Tertullian generally had a favorable view of the emperor, this edict, which did not come in the context of a general persecution against Jews and Christians, seemed more aimed at Christian evangelism. Thus, as the Roman leadership in Africa sought to put the order into effect, complete with investigations and legal actions, another wave of persecution was unleashed.

18. Tertullian *On Fleeing in Times of Persecution* 12.
19. Tertullian *Ad Nationes* 2.1.

Churches were ordered to close their doors and discontinue their meetings, while believers were subject to interrogation from the authorities. Tertullian informs us that Christians were forced to register with the police and came under constant surveillance as they became identified with prostitutes and those associated with the underworld. Given the corruption in the Roman administration, some Christians paid out sums of money to avoid registering their names and thus avoided potential danger.

It is unknown exactly how the edict of 202 was carried out in order to stop the growth of the Christian community. However, it does not seem likely that the new measures were modified in any way for the sake of the Christians. Though simply being a Christian did not automatically justify legal action, the old laws still had not been repealed. Thus, those born Christians remained subject to Trajan's laws, which meant that they could be denounced or condemned. Others who failed to register with the police yet joined the church were subject to the 202 edict and the magistrates' actions. In light of this "double legislation," it was too confusing to distinguish between those being prosecuted by Trajan's edict of 112 or Severus' new law. Nevertheless, a great number of African Christians suffered during this period.

In the context of Severus' edict of 202, a group of African believers was martyred. The details of their suffering have been preserved through a masterpiece of hagiography—*The Martyrdom of Perpetua and Felicitas and their Companions*. The work is composed of three diversely important elements. The first part features Perpetua's rather long autobiography, which recounts her stay in prison, her impressions, her painful discussions with a pagan father who wanted to save her from executions, and her visions. The second part includes the testimony of the condemned deacon Saturus who also experienced a vision. The final portion is written by a narrator—often identified as Tertullian though the evidence is inconclusive—who after a long introduction recounts the torture and executions of these martyrs.

The authenticity of this *Passion* had never been seriously doubted. The Latin text, undoubtedly the original, includes an appended version of the *acta* as well as a Greek version. Despite the apparent complexity associated with these texts, the three elements serve as an ordered account. While the Latin text says nothing about the origins of Perpetua, Felicitas, and their friends, the accompanying texts indicate that they came from

Thuburbo Minus (Tebourba, west of Carthage)—a tradition that has never been disputed.

The five young catechumens arrested included: Revocatus and Felicitas, both slaves; Saturninus and Secundulus who were free men; and Perpetua, a twenty-two year old woman of noble birth, educated in the liberal arts, married according to the rules of the matrons, and still nursing a son at her breast. Though surely kept under close watch by the Carthaginian authorities following their arrest, the five were allowed enough freedom to receive baptism. Afterward, they were transferred to the military prison where, prior to receiving their sentences, Secundulus died. Saturus, who had led the group to faith and served as their teacher and had been absent at the time of their arrest, turned himself in to the authorities in order to join the others in martyrdom.

Afterward they were brought to the *praetorium* where the Procurator Hilarianus tried in vain to convince them to sacrifice to the traditional gods. They remained firm in their refusal, which left the magistrate with no choice but to sentence them to death by wild beasts in the coliseum. In the days that followed, Felicitas, who was pregnant and close to delivering her baby, feared that she would not be able to join her companions in martyrdom as Roman law forbade pregnant women from being executed. So it was a blessing for her when she gave birth prematurely, which permitted her to be tortured with her friends.

On March 7, 203, as games honoring the anniversary of Geta's ascension to emperor were underway, the condemned were thrown to the beasts in the Carthage arena. The tribunal wanted to dress the men in the robes of Saturn's (Ba'al Hammon's) priests and the women in those of the priestesses of Ceres (Tanit) in an effort to identify the Christians—already accused of committing ritual murders—with these practitioners of human sacrifice who had recently undergone harsh punishment. Yet they adamantly refused: "We have come thus far of our own accord, for this reason, that our liberty might not be restrained."[20] The officer in charge, understanding that being a Christian for this group meant performing the ultimate sacrifice, gave in to their protests regarding the pagan clothing. They were then thrown several times to the wild beasts—a sight that actually aroused the crowd's pity to some extent, especially toward the two young women—until they were horribly wounded and crushed. Until

20. *The Martyrdom of Perpetua and Felicitas* 6.1

the panting bodies were disposed of in the *spoliarium,* where the arena's dead were typically discarded, the crowd requested that the martyrs be brought back into the arena again so "that as the sword penetrated into their body they might make their eyes partners in the murder."[21]

Though this journey to martyrdom was certainly tragic, optimism prevailed for the Christians as they desired to live up to their baptism. The *Martyrdom* reconstructs well these feelings: condemned to the beasts, Perpetua and her friends rendered their prison cell joyful; the day of martyrdom was a "day of victory"; the condemned entered the arena with "joyous and brilliant countenances"; Perpetua entered with a "placid look, and . . . gait as a matron of Christ" while singing Psalms; and after their initial scourges, they "rejoiced that they should have incurred any one of their Lord's sufferings." These reflections raise the issue of how "Montanist" Perpetua and her friends were. The prophetic visions, which played a strong role in this account, and the rather eastern apocalyptic dreams of Saturus manifested a clear Montanist tendency. Indeed, an ongoing cult to Perpetua and her friends could be found in the church at Carthage, Rome, as well as the church at large. While the *Martyrdom*'s narrator, particularly in the preface and conclusion, emphasizes some Montanist ideas—exaltation for the martyr, a manifestation of the Spirit, and a new Pentecost—there is no compelling evidence to confirm that Perpetua and fellow martyrs were part of this movement.

Indeed, other Christians were condemned to death for having defied the imperial edict. Besides Perpetua and her companions, the *Martyrdom* recognizes the names of four other Christians: Jucundus, Artaxius, and Saturninus, who were burned alive; Quintus, who died in prison; "and many other martyrs." The hunt for Christians would continue for another two years until the administration of Julius Asper, who brought a reprieve. Yet an even more severe period of persecution—driven by informants wanting to satisfy their personal hatred—would take place from 211 to 213, during the reign of Scapula Tertullus, the governor of Proconsularis. Tertullian wrote a letter to Scapula, one of his finest works to be sure, demanding that Christians be accorded freedom of conscience:

> It is a fundamental human right, a privilege of nature, that every man should worship according to his own convictions: one man's religion neither harms nor helps another man. It is assuredly no

21. *The Martyrdom of Perpetua and Felicitas* 6.4.

part of religion to compel religion—to which free-will and not force should lead us—the sacrificial victims even being required of a willing mind.[22]

Persecution also stretched into Numidia and Mauretania, though it was generally less brutal and only implicated Christians impacted by Severus' edict.

Around 211, probably in the camp of Lambaesis in the south of Numidia where the administration of the Roman African army was headquartered, "bonuses" (*donativa*) were given to the soldiers on the occasion of the new emperor's rise to power. As the soldiers who were crowned with laurels—a practice associated with the imperial cult—advanced to receive a monetary gift, a Christian soldier refused to wear the crown, announcing that he could not serve two masters (the emperor and Christ). In the same blow, he rejected the institution of the army where pagan rites were present everywhere. Tertullian dedicated his work *De Corona* (*The Chaplet*) to this soldier who, after this confrontation, was brought before the tribunal, placed temporarily in a cell, and then executed after being judged by a Roman court.

The incident of the Christian soldier's bold declaration threatened a very fragile peace, and, as Tertullian related with his usual biting mockery, nominal Christians were quick to condemn such conviction.

> It is plain that as they have rejected the prophecies of the Holy Spirit, they are also purposing the refusal of martyrdom. So they murmur that a peace so good and long is endangered for them. Nor do I doubt that some are already turning their back on the Scriptures, are making ready their luggage, are equipped for flight from city to city; for that is all of the gospel they care to remember. I know, too, their pastors are lions in peace, deer in the fight.[23]

It was against this prudent and fearful attitude that Tertullian protested:

> What have you in common with the flower which is to die? You have a flower in the Branch of Jesse, upon which the grace of the Divine Spirit in all its fullness rested—a flower undefiled, unfading, everlasting, by choosing which the good soldier, too, has got promotion in the heavenly ranks.[24]

22. Tertullian *To Scapula* 2.
23. Tertullian *De Corona* 1.
24. Tertullian *De Corona* 15.

These dissensions illustrate well the tensions present within the church between "hardliners" and moderates—a conflict that continued to develop and would not disappear even after the persecution had subsided.

The persecution, which began with the Scillitans in 180, lasted nearly thirty years and manifested itself in various forms through periods of intense crisis as well as times of relative peace. This period of persecution seems to have subsided during the administration of Scapula in the second year of Caracalla's reign. In the decades that followed, leading up to the accession of Decius in 249, the church experienced a long period of peace in which it was able to recuperate its losses and organize its institutions.

EARLY WORSHIP PRACTICES IN THE AFRICAN CHURCH

Worship in the church at Carthage during Tertullian's lifetime was not organized in a systematic fashion. This was largely due to the need to adapt constantly during persecution. Worship assemblies and their accompanying practices were not directed by a liturgical calendar; rather, they varied according to the circumstances facing the church. Christian gatherings were initially comprised of a *synaxis* (liturgical assembly), which had at its core the celebration of the Eucharist and commemoration of the Lord's Supper. In addition, the believers' assembly featured Scripture reading, with the Gospels occupying the most prominent place; public and private prayers; chanting of the Psalms; and a homily. Fellowship was also a key aspect. Tertullian, who provides little information on the liturgical elements, mentions only the readings, singing of Psalms, and alludes to the homily. He wrote: "The church is prepared with water, clothed by the Holy Spirit, and nourished by the Eucharist."

Though by the middle of the third century the Eucharist was celebrated each morning of the week, we have no clear indication of how frequently it was celebrated in the early years of the African church. Undoubtedly following the Jewish tradition, it appears that the liturgical assembly with its readings, prayers, sermon, hymns, Eucharist, or breaking of bread, lasted from the evening of the Sabbath evening until dawn Sunday. The churches maintained this worship schedule, yet as the Eucharist developed and individual church practices became more autonomous, some churches felt free to celebrate this rite in the morning while others did so in the evening. At the end of the second century, when the church broke with the Jewish calendar and practices, the Sabbath was abandoned and Sunday was adopted as the Lord's Day (*Dominicus dies*) around which the Christian week was organized. Similarly, the annual liturgical calendar was developed around Easter and the celebration of the Lord's resurrection.

The Easter celebration (*pascha*), whose translation shows the influence of the Jewish Passover (*pessa'h*), was probably initiated very early in the life of the African church while there were still harmonious relations with the Synagogue. Easter, preceded by the Lenten period and a night vigil, was observed fifty days after the Passover celebration. During this fifty-day period, which culminated at Pentecost, all penitential acts were suspended. On the other hand, both Tertullian and Cyprian seemed to be unaware of the Christmas and Ascension celebrations.

It is difficult to determine the origins of days of fasting and abstinence. Two days of the week, Wednesday and Saturday, were set apart for these disciplines and thus designated "stations." It is unclear whether this form of weekly penance was influenced by Montanism. While giving instruction on these days, which are never mentioned by Cyprian, Tertullian urged believers to wait until just after the fast was broken to celebrate the Eucharist.

What was the liturgical language of the African church prior to the third century? It would certainly seem fanciful to imagine that the diverse churches—in towns and cities, along the coastlines and in the interior, and communities established in the Sahara—would have spoken the same language in their worship assemblies. Greek was spoken widely in North Africa well before Roman colonization. It was the language of the cultivated classes, and from the second century it was commonly spoken in Carthage and the large urban centers such as Mauretania Caesarea. The Numidian Prince Juba II, an ardent Hellenist who was granted the kingdom of Mauretania by the Emperor Augustus in 25 BCE, had made plans to transform Caesarea into a Greek city. Tertullian himself composed four of his works in Greek, while others such as *The Martyrdom of Perpetua and Felicitas and their Companions*, originally written in Latin, were translated into Greek.

With the expansion of Roman power in the provinces, including its army and administration, Latin prevailed over time as the primary language in Africa. Though Greek was not completely abandoned as the liturgical language of the church at Rome until the second half of the fourth century, Latin, which represented the culture at large, had become the official language of the African church by the third century. Through Cyprian, we learn about a portion of a dialogue between the priest and the people at the beginning of the Eucharist.[25] Latin manuscripts of the Gospels and Psalms were indeed quite numerous in Africa, as Augustine alluded to "the translations of the Scriptures from Hebrew into Greek can be counted, but the Latin translators are out of all number."[26] Thus, there is no evidence for the view that there was an official African translation—the so called *Vetus Afra* that later served as the basis for the early Italian *Vetus Itala* translation. Though various Latin translations were circulating in Africa, some more accepted and known than others, there was never one officially agreed upon Bible. The bishops appeared to demonstrate much freedom in which text they used. We may simply conclude that Augustine preferred the *Vetus Itala*—an Italian text that was widely used in Africa—for its precise language and clarity of expression.

To be sure, the colloquial Latin used in African society and in the church was not the Latin of Tacitus, but rather that of soldiers, veterans, merchants, and Italian peasants who had come to Africa as colonists in search of their fortune. "Roman" speech, had it continued in this manner, would have certainly developed into several dialects reflecting the different regions of North Africa. The majority of inscriptions, most notably the thousands of epitaphs, were written in this type of Latin with its "Africanisms" and "Berberisms" spoken by the lower classes in Berber regions. The populations of Italy, beginning with the inhabitants of Rome, as well as those in Spain and Gaul, also had their own "street" Latin. However, Roman Africa did not merely possess a popular language. Rather, it was in Africa, as opposed to Rome, that the Christian Latin literary tradition got its start through prolific writers like Tertullian, Cyprian, and Augustine. As a key force in "Latinization," Christianity was also an important means of Romanization in Africa.

Though Latin was imposed on Africa with the organization and administration of the provinces, traditional languages were still spoken. This included Libyan or Berber—spoken in the interior and mountainous regions hardly impacted by the Roman presence—and especially

---

25. Cyprian *On the Lord's Prayer* 30. [English translations of *On the Lord's Prayer* are from *ANF* 5.]

26. Augustine *On Christian Doctrine* 2.11.16. [English translations of *On Christian Doctrine* are from *NPNF* 1.2.]

Punic, which was continually spoken in the market towns and villages surrounding the ancient Carthaginian trading posts. This reality was strongly illustrated through Augustine's embarrassing ordeal of trying to find a qualified priest for the Punic speaking church at Fussala, a *castellum* located only forty miles from Hippo. In the end, Augustine was forced to settle for a *lector* named Antoninus, the only Punic speaker among his clergy in Hippo. A dozen years earlier, the bishop of Hippo had refused to send one of his deacons, Lucillus, to serve with Bishop Novatus of Sitifis who had requested Lucillus' service. According to Augustine the only reason for refusing this request was that Lucillus was a Punic speaker: "But since he is conversant with the Punic language, through want of which the preaching of the gospel is greatly hindered in these parts."[27] It is likely that such clergy assigned to the Punic speaking areas were responsible for preaching and presiding over the liturgy for these churches.

In the course of the first half of the third century, as the number of believers grew and churches multiplied, church leadership also developed, though it generally mirrored the leadership structure outside of Africa. Bishops presided over the worship assemblies and were assisted by priests and deacons, though the latter served the church mostly in practical matters. The *collegium* of bishops was already quite developed, and around 220 Bishop Agrippinus of Carthage gathered his colleagues from Proconsularis and Numidia for a church council. That the council was held in Carthage was an indication of how the capital of Proconsularis was becoming the leading center of African Christianity. From this very first council, we observe the superior rank attributed, almost by rights, to the bishop of Carthage. His growing stature, when compared to that of the other African bishops, was certainly due to Carthage's significance as the oldest Christian community in Africa, not to mention Carthage's place as the political capital of Roman Africa. Tertullian would refer to his bishop as *Pontifex Maximus* ("supreme Pontif"), a pagan title traditionally reserved for the emperor, yet applied here to a bishop who had assumed leadership. Tertullian also addressed the bishop of Carthage as *benedictus papa* ("blessed father") and *episcopus episcoporum* ("bishop of bishops").

Observed exclusively in the African church, one original aspect of church leadership and practice should be noted—*seniores laici* ("lay

27. Augustine *Letter* 84.2.

elders"). This referred to faithful, proven believers being set apart for leadership—not through paying for the honor—but by being chosen for it.[28] In providing a measure of accountability, their particular role was presiding over church meetings. It has been argued that this practice originated from the synagogues, revealing Christianity's strong connection to Palestinian Judaism. The Sanhedrin, which had functioned as a court of justice, was linked to a system of elder rule where leaders were selected from prominent aristocratic families in the city. It is important to remember, however, that African Christianity had also been impacted by other influences. For instance, in the African epigraphic texts there is mention of *seniores locorum*—a council of sorts that served the magistrates in the period of the Tetrarchy by administering villages and small towns that lacked a full municipal statute.

In one of her visions, Perpetua made mention of a bishop, a priest, and worship assemblies. As the Christian movement benefited from such ecclesiastical organization in the last quarter of the second century, it is clear that the church had existed in North Africa for several decades, perhaps even from the end of the first century. The church's origins, however, remain quite discreet and modest. Neither Tertullian, Cyprian, nor Augustine offer the slightest historical insight on this point. The development of the church at Carthage, as presented by Tertullian, leaves no doubt that there was an early Christian presence in Africa.

ADDITIONAL RESOURCES

Delattre, *Gamart ou la nécropole juive de Carthage.*
Frend, "Jews and Christians in Third Century Carthage."
LeJay, *Les Origines de l'Église d'Afrique et l'Église romaine.*
Mesnage, *Le Christianisme en Afrique: Origines, developpement, extension.*
Saxer, *Saints anciens d'Afrique du Nord.*
Shaw, *The Passion of Perpetua, Past and Present.*

---

28. See Tertullian *Apology* 39.

3 Tertullian: the "Master"

AN AFRICAN FOR HIS TIME

Tertullian's life, his dates of birth and death, as well as the chronology of his writings, cannot be known with certainty. It is generally accepted that Quintus Septimius Florens Tertullianus was born at Carthage around 160. Both of his parents were pagans and, according to Jerome, his father was a centurion or proconsul probably attached to the troop appointed to Carthage. He carried out his command in the garrison that served the governor of Proconsularis. As a youth, Tertullian was a devoted pagan who led a rather free life that included frequenting the "cruel games" of the arena. He seemed particularly drawn to the bloody combat of the gladiators and later wrote: "I would prefer not to recount everything so as to revive those memories." Around his thirtieth year and the time of his conversion to Christianity (ca. 190–195), he wrote, "a man becomes a Christian, he is not born one."[1]

Like Apuleius, his countryman of the previous generation, Tertullian studied rhetoric and law. His thorough training in theoretical law (*juris consultus*) not only prepared him to practice law, which he may have done for a time, but exposed him to a world of knowledge imparted by poets, philosophers, and Greek and Latin historians. Indeed, he made an effort to understand everything. Tertullian's close friendships with the powerful of his day—friendships probably established in school—later protected him in a very militant pagan context. This protection, perhaps offered without his knowledge or against his will, allowed him to flaunt a passionate commitment to Christ and to attack with a violent polemic those persecuting the church. Hence, he seemed to carry out his work without the fear of torment that had impacted so many others in the

---

1. Tertullian *The Soul's Testimony* 1.

church. Though Jerome wrote that Tertullian was set apart as a priest in Carthage, Cyprian, Augustine, and Tertullian himself made no mention of this ordained status.

Far from meriting the reputation for misogyny that some have alleged, Tertullian was married and actually wrote a treatise dedicated to his wife. *Ad Uxorem* (*To His Wife*) is a passionate and lyrical work that celebrates human love. Following the Apostle Paul's example, he also offered his wife some advice to follow after his death, specifically regarding remarriage. While warning her about the dangers of remarriage, he urged her that if she could not remain single, then she should marry a Christian of humble social stature.

Tertullian's prominent place in the history of the church is due to the fact that, more than any of the leaders who came after him, he aptly represented his context and provided great evidence for the African Christianity of his day. His unique contribution to the African church, still young and developing at this point, was based more on what he took from the African spirit. Through his genius and weaknesses, boldness in the midst of battles, revolt in the face of injustices, excesses, affinity for provocation, preference for paradox, quibbling spirit, and appetite for brilliant and subtle formulas, Tertullian represented an entire people. It was neither the homilies of his bishop—full of doctrinal points—nor the speculations of philosophers, that could convert the African heart. He wrote that "the philosophers were the patriarchs of heretics . . . poor Aristotle who had taught them dialectics."

Previously, proselytism, Jewish-Christian conflicts, and Tertullian's regard for the Jews have been discussed. Indeed, Tertullian's *Against the Jews* included a discussion between a Christian and a Jewish proselyte. Yet it was primarily in his battles with the so-called Gnostics—a movement that first appeared in Asia and later Carthage, where it was a threat to the church—that Tertullian first distinguished himself as a polemicist. Around 200, he unleashed his *Prescription Against Heretics,* arguably his most complete work, in which he declared his opponents' thoughts utterly baseless and all discussion with them useless: "We want no curious disputation after possessing Christ Jesus, no inquisition after enjoying the gospel!"[2] In his fight against heresies, which spanned nearly a dozen years, special mention must be made of his campaign against Marcion,

2. Tertullian *Prescription Against Heretics* 7.12.

in which Tertullian wrote five books to combat Marcion's teachings and those of his disciples. To be sure, Tertullian proved to be an ardent defender of the "great church."

DEFENDER OF MARTYRS ON THE BASIS
OF FREEDOM OF CONSCIENCE

Refusing to engage in futile discussions with those who did not have the Scriptures, Tertullian was a practical realist. Placing his confidence only in indisputable testimonies, this revealed his great need for truth—a quest that became an almost fanatical obsession. He was fascinated by martyrs, their heroic testimonies, and their "demented stubbornness." In his letter *To Scapula*, he wrote: "For all who witness the noble patience of its martyrs, as struck with misgivings, are inflamed with desire to examine into the matter in question; and as soon as they come to know the truth, they straightway enroll themselves its disciples."[3]

Tertullian was an apologist, theologian, moralist, and satirist, as well as a distinguished writer and rhetorician. Indeed, he was one of the most original writers of his day and left behind a large and significant corpus of writings. Of his forty or so works, thirty have survived. It is impossible in the present work to discuss fully his literary output; rather, a word about his innovation will suffice. Prior to Tertullian, the church had no shortage of martyrs and often included those quite eager to face torture. "We give thanks to God. Today we are martyrs in heaven," said the Scillitans. Martyrs like these simply accepted the judge's decision without any defense, seeming to respect the law that was condemning them.

Despite his refusal to demand tolerance for Christians, Tertullian broke with this passive submission by appealing to the humanity of the magistrates, those responsible for condemning the accused. Also, he taught Christians no longer to view themselves as sheep gently marching toward the slaughter—an approach that ultimately led to the demise of paganism. Clearly against believers submitting to wicked laws, he wrote: "But go zealously on, good presidents, you will stand higher with the people if you sacrifice the Christians at their wish, kill us, torture us, condemn us, grind us to dust; your injustice is the proof that we are innocent

---

3. Tertullian *To Scapula* 5.4.

. . . The oftener we are mown down by you, the more in number we grow; the blood of Christians is seed."[4]

As magistrates enforced laws that dismissed the natural rights of men and women—itself a "legal crime"—Tertullian demanded that the universal entitlement of individual conscience be respected. In defending these freedoms, he had already challenged the Proconsul Scapula over "human rights and natural law."

> For see that you do not give a further ground for the charge of irreligion, by taking away religious liberty, and forbidding free choice of deity, so that I may no longer worship according to my inclination, but am compelled to worship against it . . . Every province even, and every city, has its god . . . In, fact, we alone are prevented having a religion of our own. We give offence to the Romans, we are excluded from the rights and privileges of Romans, because we do not worship the gods of Rome.[5]

In *Ad Nationes,* he denounced the condemnation of the innocent: "Your sentences, however, import only that one has confessed himself a Christian. No name of a crime stands against us, but only the crime of a name."[6]

Drawing attention to the absurd procedure in which the magistrates applied Trajan's rescript—condemning only those Christians denounced by a known accuser—Tertullian added:

> O miserable deliverance, under the necessities of the case, a self-contradiction! It forbids them to be sought after as innocent, and it commands them to be punished as guilty. It is at once merciful and cruel; it passes by, and it punishes . . . If you condemn, why do you not also inquire? If you do not inquire, why do you not also absolve? . . . You condemn the man for whom nobody wished a search to be made when he is presented to you, and who even now does not deserve punishment, I suppose, because of his guilt, but because, though forbidden to be sought, he was found . . . in the case of others denying, you apply the torture to make them confess—Christians alone you torture, to make them deny . . . "I am a Christian," the man cries out. He tells you what he is; you wish to hear from him what he is not . . . Why do you torture me

4. Tertullian *Apology* 50.12–14.
5. Tertullian *Apology* 24.6–10.
6. Tertullian *Ad Nationes* 1.3.2.

to sin? I confess, and you put me to the rack. What would you do if I denied? Certainly you give no ready credence to others when they deny. When we deny, you believe at once.[7]

AN "ANTI-ESTABLISHMENT" CHRISTIAN

While revolting against an intolerant Roman paganism that denied Christians their civil rights, Tertullian also waged another battle. This time it was against the church's hierarchy, which he deemed too reasonable, too human, and guilty of misusing its power and thus compromising with the world. Passionate and unwilling to compromise, Tertullian refused to accept his church's attempt to adapt to the non-believing world—the "earthly city."

Tertullian's passion, observed in his ardor as a theologian and near fanaticism as a combatant for the faith, also had a Stoic ring to it. In the face of persecuting officials and the highest ranking church leaders, his castigating and aggressive rhetoric was both sincere and bitterly ironic. Having become acutely aware of the shortcomings of the Carthage church, he began to place his hopes elsewhere, as he, by his own admission, was "a man of no goodness . . . most miserable, ever sick with the heats of impatience."[8] Tertullian preferred the tempest in the open sea to the calm port waters; yet was he in danger of becoming shipwrecked?

TERTULLIAN AND MONTANISM

Around 207–208, while continually fascinated by martyrs and, according to Jerome, disgusted by the attitudes of Roman clergy, Tertullian began to distance himself more and more from the Catholic church where, in his estimation, he had been a voice crying in the wilderness. In 213–214, he broke with the *catholica* (or at least its authority structure) completely. While not completely convinced of all of Montanus' ideas—though he was drawn to Montanus' eschatological teachings—Tertullian embraced the spirit of the passionate prophets who had ignited the movement. The Montanist movement was constituted in Carthage in a chapel that resembled the Catholic churches in the city, and its meetings were char-

---

7. Tertullian *Apology* 2.8–9, 10–13.
8. Tertullian *Of Patience* 1.5.

acterized by a religious enthusiasm, a quest for prophecies, and ecstatic experiences that would confirm the members' "favored" status. Thus, they boasted about the illumination they had received, a point that especially worried the Catholic clergy, while exhorting their followers to exercise great moral rigor that included new forms of penance and fasting. In anticipation of an imminent end of the world, the Montanists also advocated absolute abstinence.

Initiated in Asia Minor through Montanus' preaching, the Montanist movement was widespread in this region reaching its highest point around 172. It was further propagated in the East, Lyon, and at Rome where it was condemned by the Bishop Eleutherus (174–189). Also called Phrygians in reference to Montanus' home province, the Montanists believed that the arrival of the heavenly Jerusalem would be the next great earthly event. This millenarian view held that Christ would soon be returning in triumph to establish his reign on the earth for one thousand years as foretold by the book of Revelation. Thus, prophecy occupied a central place within the movement. When Montanus delivered his messages in the self-proclaimed role of "the Parclete's prophet," he believed that the Holy Spirit spoke directly through the prophecy and provided guidance for the "spiritual ones."

Tertullian allowed himself to be seduced by this charismatic church's teachings ("the church of saints") where the prophet replaced the priest, and where the Holy Spirit gave direction to a Christian community free of worldly minded, cowardly leaders. For Tertullian, Christian doctrine was in no way shaken by the new teaching; on the contrary, it was confirmed and upheld. In his work on fasting, he remarked: "not that Montanus and Priscilla and Maximilla preach another God, nor that they disjoin Jesus Christ (from God), nor that they overturn any particular rule of faith or hope."[9] In another work, he attacked a fierce opponent of Montanism:

> We, however, as we indeed always have done and more especially since we have been better instructed by the Paraclete, who leads men indeed into all truth believe that there is one only God, but under the following dispensation, or *oikonomia,* as it is called, that this one only God has also a Son, His Word, who proceeded from Himself, by whom all things were made, and without whom nothing was made.[10]

9. Tertullian *On Fasting* 1.
10. Tertullian *Against Praxeas* 2.

It is possible that despite assenting to Montanus' teachings, Tertullian, who never had any contact with eastern Montanists or those in Rome, may not have fallen into heresy himself. Considering that the Holy Spirit, understood as God in his notion of the Trinity, is real and that sanctification is the same as "spiritualization," Tertullian did not betray the ancient faith.

Also, in proclaiming that the church was the Spirit's "spiritual body" (*ecclesia spiritus*) that experiences unity in this spiritual dimension, Tertullian could not be charged with being a schismatic. In his mind, the purpose for an established ecclesiastical leadership was to allow the community of believers, the true church, to have a known presence in society and history. Thus, even disagreements over spiritual disciplines, the liturgy, and even points of doctrine—though in his day "orthodoxy" was far from being settled—were not enough to divide the church. Ultimately, Tertullian's personal feelings and perhaps subjective view of ecclesiology should not be given priority over his view of the "rule of faith" (*disciplina fidei*), a guide for insuring orthodoxy that was greatly employed by Tertullian in his writings against heretics.[11]

The fact remains that like certain reformers in the eastern church— such as Tatian, who advocated some system of penance in his *Diatesseron* (ca. 175–180)—Tertullian's vision for Christianity was both traditional and reactionary. Undoubtedly, his ardent monotheism, articulated in the face of dualistic heresies that opposed the God of the Old and New Testaments,[12] was firmly in the mainstream of catholic teaching. Yet his ideal of church—the "little troop" of the Gospel composed only of the elect whose faith was strengthened, inspired, and renewed through rigorous asceticism—flew in the face of traditional teaching. In addition to this view of the church, Tertullian also addressed moral issues in his writings. Convinced that the end of the world was imminent, he urged believers to be abstinent and disapproved and even forbade second marriages.[13] In short, by holding and defending these rigorous views, Tertullian succeeded in alarming believers while dissuading others who were in search of a more "human" church.

11. Tertullian *Prescription Against Heretics* 19.
12. See Tertullian *Against Marcion, Against the Valentians.*
13. See Tertullian *On Exhortation to Chastity; On Monogamy.*

By highlighting the conduct of a rebellious Christian soldier,[14] he put the entire Christian community in a precarious position with the imperial authorities. Also, through condemning believers who took flight in persecution, he further embarrassed the church leadership. So, what was Tertullian's expectation for the bishops?

In the same violent and sincere manner that characterized his fight against the political establishment persecuting the church, Tertullian waged a new battle against the practices of the Catholic church and its leaders fighting for supremacy. He demanded that Pope Calixtus give an account for the spiritual authority he possessed:

> I now inquire into your opinion, (to see) from what source you usurp this right to "the church." If, because the Lord has said to Peter, "Upon this rock will I build my church," "to you have I given the keys of the heavenly kingdom;" or, "Whatever you shall have bound or loosed in earth, shall be bound or loosed in the heavens," you therefore presume that the power of binding and loosing has derived to you, that is, to every church akin to Peter, what sort of man are you, subverting and wholly changing the manifest intention of the Lord, conferring (as that intention did) this (gift) personally upon Peter? "On you," He says, "will I build my church;" and, "I will give to you the keys," not to the church; and, "Whatsoever you shall have loosed or bound," not what they shall have loosed or bound ... "the church," it is true, will forgive sins: but (it will be) the church of the Spirit, by means of a spiritual man; not the church which consists of a number of bishops. For the right and arbitrament is the Lord's, not the servant's; God's Himself, not the priest's.[15]

Thus, he reaffirmed the spiritual charter of the church over and against unwarranted institutions and power structures adopted by the Catholic church. Ultimately, Tertullian's "libertarian" approach resulted in his being ostracized by the overall Christian community.

A pagan in his youth, then a faithful Catholic, and finally attracted by Montanus' *ecclesia spiritus,* Tertullian truly desired to follow the straight path. Nevertheless, this third step was also a temporary one. Tertullian became opposed to the Montanist view of the Paraclete, which for him did not conform to the orthodox doctrine of the Trinity in which the Holy

---

14. See Tertullian *De Corona.*

15. Tertullian *On Modesty* 21.9–10, 16–17.

Spirit shared indivisible unity with the Father and the Son. As a result, he initiated a schism within the Montanists. As Tertullian had broken with the Catholic church over the "new prophecy" and "Spirit church" issues, his break with the Montanists was just as significant. It should be noted that Tertullian's trinitarian doctrine was a decisive contribution to orthodox theology, as he was the first Latin writer to use the term *trinitas* to refer to the three persons of the godhead. Thus, he broke with the movement over his disagreement with the Montanist understanding of the Spirit.

The "Tertullianist" community that he initiated after leaving the Montanists had an obscure existence in Carthage. At the beginning of the fifth century, they possessed one basilica in Carthage and their worship assemblies greatly resembled those of the Catholic church: including readings from Scripture, singing Psalms, sermons, and prayers. The major difference in worship was that time was allowed for visions and expressions of charismatic gifts.

Augustine, after thoroughly studying Tertullian's thought, exonerated him and his followers from all charges of heresy. Though Augustine mentioned Tertullian in his work *On Heresies*,[16] Augustine was careful to distinguish between Tertullian and the "Phrygians," whom he regarded as heretical. When Tertullian passed away, the movement dwindled significantly. Augustine reported that the final members of the Tertullianist community were ultimately reconciled to the Catholic church and gave up its basilica in Carthage.

Augustine's favorable view of Tertullian was shared by Cyprian, who upheld Tertullian's prestige in Carthage and benefited by reading a few pages from Tertullian each day. Whenever he asked his secretary for a volume of Tertullian's works, Cyprian habitually said, "hand me the master." The bishop of Carthage described the genius of his fellow African Christian as "severe and passionate" (*acris et vehementis ingenii*).

TERTULLIAN AND THE AFRICAN CITY

In light of his embattled career, can Tertullian be regarded as the proper representative of an African church in constant political and social conflict from the end of the Antonin dynasty to the empire's third-century crisis? Though it is hardly possible to offer a definitive answer here, it will

16. See *On Heresies* 86.

suffice to raise a few points to highlight some of the ambiguity that stands out in Tertullian's views—attitudes that certainly represented a current of thought in African Christianity.

In his shortest treatise *On the Pallium* (ca. 209–211), he defended the argument that the *pallium*, a Greek woolen coat, should replace the Roman toga as the official dress for Christians. It was not because Tertullian had a particular love for Greece or its culture; rather, this change symbolized for the Christian, a citizen of Rome, a conversion to a new and superior Christian philosophy. Tertullian thus addressed a central theme of a larger problem: the place of Christians within the progress of Romanization and their role in the life of the Roman city.

In his *Apology* and letter *To Scapula,* Tertullian identified the Emperors Tiberius, Marcus Aurelius, and Septimius Severus as protectors of the Christians. He also offered prayers for the prosperity of Rome and its leaders: "We pray for life prolonged; for security to the empire; for protection to the imperial house; for brave armies, a faithful senate, a virtuous people."[17] The emperors, ignorant of the world's imminent end, were also in need of the Christians' prayers.[18] Some years later, perhaps between 203 and 206, he again wrote that it was appropriate for Christians to honor kings and emperors, "so long as we keep ourselves separate from idolatry."[19]

Tertullian did not hide his enthusiasm over the Roman Empire's success, an excitement shared especially by his privileged contemporaries who benefited from the *pax Romana.* He composed a veritable hymn to the *felicitas* of the emperors who were victorious over the "Barbarians"— which in Africa referred to nomadic tribes pushed back beyond the borders of Roman control. The emperors were thus directing the human race on the path of progress.

> But antiquity is by this time a vain thing (to refer to), when our own careers are before our eyes. How large a portion of our orb has the present age reformed! How many cities has the triple power of our existing empire either produced, or else augmented, or else restored! While God favors so many Augusti unitedly, how many populations have been transferred to other localities! How many peoples reduced! How many orders restored to their an-

17. Tertullian *Apology* 30.4.
18. See Tertullian *Apology* 32.1.
19. Tertullian *On Idolatry* 15.7.

cient splendor! How many barbarians baffled! In truth, our orb is the admirably cultivated estate of this empire; every aconite of hostility eradicated; and the cactus and bramble of clandestinely crafty familiarity wholly uptorn; and (the orb itself) delightsome beyond the orchard of Alcinous and the rosary of Midas.[20]

After this tribute to the glory of the caesars—a treatise that some have regarded as a call to being Roman (*romanitas*)—one would expect that Tertullian would personally enlist in the service of the empire and call Christians to unite together with pagans for the glory of Rome. On the contrary, this new philosopher, in the same book, preached on the virtues of political and social disengagement:

> I, it says, owe no duty to the forum, the election-ground, or the senate-house; I keep no obsequious vigil, preoccupy no platforms, hover about no praetorian residences; I am not odorant of the canals, am not odorant of the lattices, am no constant wearer out of benches, no wholesale router of laws, no barking pleader, no judge, no soldier, no king: I have withdrawn from the populace. My only business is with myself: except that other care I have none, save not to care. The better life you would more enjoy in seclusion than in publicity. But you will decry me as indolent. Forsooth, we are to live for our country, and empire, and estate. Such used, of old, to be the sentiment. None is born for another, being destined to die for himself.[21]

This rhetoric characterized Tertullian's attitude during his "Tertullianist" stage. As Tertullian had remained consistent in his views toward government, it is impossible to conclude that Montanism had caused him to develop a more tolerant attitude toward political authorities. Fifteen years earlier, he had written in the *Apology*, "only one thing in this life greatly concerns us, and that is, to get quickly out of it."[22] In his brief work *On Prayer* (ca. 198–200), he haughtily declared that he had not put his hope in Babylon, the symbol of this world; rather, in affirming his millenarian view, he longed for the inauguration of Christ's kingdom. He added that the Christian is "a foreigner in this world, a citizen of Jerusalem, the city above."[23] In order to hasten the fulfillment of this hope,

20. Tertullian *On the Pallium* 2.7.
21. Tertullian *On the Pallium* 5.4.
22. Tertullian *Apology* 41.5.
23. Tertullian *De Corona* 13.4.

"the consummation of the age," Tertullian prayed "your kingdom come" (*veniat regnum tuum*) and "our wish is, that your reign be hastened, not our servitude protracted."[24]

In Tertullian's day, the Christian movement did not integrate into the life of the African city or pursue social justice. The church perfectly tolerated the Roman Empire and the African society to which it belonged and managed to focus effectively on its interests, which did not include challenging the political order. Thus, a spirit of autonomy that would characterize the Donatists in the following centuries cannot be detected during this period. Without a doubt, Tertullian would not have recognized the Donatist church with its rival clans battling for the upper hand in church matters and seeking to control key episcopal positions.

Hence, the harsh polemicist of Carthage failed to be innovative and certainly did not initiate a Christian society—a third century Lamennais.[25] In fact, Tertullian was not convinced that the organization of Roman society was evil, and thus he never proposed even one social reform. Finally, in his writings, there is no revolutionary theory that posed a threat to the established political institutions.

Tertullian did not seem interested in promoting mankind's earthly development, as he was convinced that the Day of the Lord or final judgment was near. Yet, because he was already living in Rome's final days, his teaching, which advocated a systematic abstention from the world and complete disinterest in the earthly city, contained the deadly germs that could contribute to a breakdown of society. In light of this protesting attitude, where he advocated the age to come while renouncing the present world, Tertullian and his followers who held to this anachronistic view of Christianity could have been regarded as dangerous, anti-establishment types. As anarchists and foreigners to the political and social order, their convictions and actions effectively undermined the family, the army, and the social structure—in short, they undermined Rome.

As noted, in his final work *On Modesty*, he revolted against the office of the Roman bishop, whose claim to power was based on inheriting Peter's keys to the kingdom. Also, he protested against the church's penitential discipline and its ability to forgive sins. With this treatise, which

24. Tertullian *On Prayer* 5.1.

25. [Decret is, of course, referring to Hugues Felicité Robert de Lamennais (1782-1854), a French priest, philosopher, and political commentator who ultimately separated himself from the Roman Catholic Church]

dates to around 222, he completed nearly a quarter of a century of defending and defining the church. At this point, we lose track of Tertullian, who probably died not long after writing this final work.

"The first writer of Christian Latin," Tertullian made an enormous contribution through his corpus of writing—"the first monument in the Latin Christian literary tradition." Along with Apuleius, he best exemplified the African spirit in writing. Today, he is not only one of the most read Latin writers—not so much for his ideas but for his literary style—but one who elicits the most research and continual scholarship. The "master" should be placed in the highest ranks of the church fathers and in the history of Christianity. In the estimation of the German Protestant historian Harnack, Tertullian was "the founder of western theology."

ADDITIONAL RESOURCES

Aziza, *Tertullien et le judaïsme.*

Barnes, *Tertullian: A Historical and Literary Study.*

Braun, *Approches de Tertullien. Vingt-six études sur l'auteur et son œuvre (1955–1990).*

Daniélou, *Les Origines du christianisme latin.*

Fredouille, *Tertullien et la conversion de la culture antique.*

Guignebert, *Tertullien: Étude sur ses sentiments à l'égard de l'Empire et de la société civile.*

Powell, "Tertullianists and Cataphrygians."

Saxer, "Mort et culte des morts à partir de l'archéologie et de la liturgie d'Afrique dans l'œuvre de saint Augustin."

Saxer, *Morts, Martyrs, Reliques en Afrique chrétienne aux premiers siècles: Les témoignages de Tertullien, Cyprien, et Augustin à la lumière de archeology africaine.*

4 Mid-Third-Century Persecution and Crisis in Africa

In the forty years that followed the persecution and subsequent death of Septimius Severus, the African church grew and developed considerably. This development was particularly evident through the African church councils—the habitual synodal gatherings of the African church leaders—which increased in frequency especially during Cyprian of Carthage's episcopate (249–258). Synods and councils are synonymous terms—the first is taken from the Greek, while the second is derived from the Latin *concilium*. These gatherings afforded sister churches the opportunity to meet and study common problems facing their respective communities. At the September 1, 256, council of Carthage, the bishops—referring to themselves as "beloved colleagues"—stated that they had "come together as one body" from their varying provinces "with priests, deacons, and the greater part of the people being present likewise." Thus, the church councils, which saw a regular increase in the number of bishops attending (a direct result of new bishops being set apart to respond to the needs of a growing church), provide the best indication of the Gospel's expansion across the African provinces. As noted, the number of Roman African cities numbered as high as 500 by this point.

Mention has already been made of the first known African council, convened in Carthage in 220 under the leadership of Agrippinus. There, "a great number of bishops" from Proconsularis and Numidia gathered to learn about Bishop Calixtus of Rome's penitential legislation for adulterers. Between 236 and 240, there was certainly another gathering under Donatus, Cyprian's immediate predecessor. The main business of this council, attended by eighty-four bishops, was the dismissal of Bishop

46

Privatus of Lambaesis, the Numidian primate, on account of his "numerous and serious offences."

The "synodal tradition" strongly manifested itself during Cyprian's ten years as bishop of Carthage. From 251 to 254, four councils took place in Carthage (April 251; May 15, 252; spring of 253; and fall of 254) to address the problem of the lapsed—those who denied their faith during the Decian persecution, yet desired re-entry into the church. Three other councils met (fall of 255, spring of 256, September 256) to decide the fate of those who had been baptized in a schismatic or heretical church, yet also desired communion with the Catholic church. It is possible that another council may have met at the beginning of 257.

Often depending on the nature of the issue being addressed, councils could fall into three categories: local, reserved for the region of Carthage; provincial, which included Numidian bishops; and plenary councils, those involving the entire African church. In a typical local council, around forty bishops met. The councils of 252, 254, and 255 included forty-two, thirty-seven, and thirty-one bishops respectively. Cyprian listed the bishops present at the 255 gathering in *Letter* 70, a collectively written post-council letter addressed to eighteen Numidian colleagues. Provincial councils typically numbered sixty bishops with around forty from Proconsularis and twenty from Numidia. The gatherings of 253 and the spring of 256 included sixty-seven and seventy-one bishops respectively. Finally, plenary councils usually involved around eighty-four bishops, coming from various provinces or wherever an episcopal see existed. This was the case in the council convened under Donatus (ca. 236–240). In September of 256, Cyprian called together eighty-six of his fellow bishops to address the rebaptism issue. As the decision of the 255 council—refusing fellowship to those baptized in heresy—contradicted Bishop Stephen of Rome's verdict on the matter, Cyprian felt it necessary to gather even more bishops than normal to affirm the African position prior to communicating it to Rome. It should be noted that bishops were also motivated to attend councils to discuss particular circumstances facing their individual churches. Finally, as bishops traveled to Carthage for councils, they were typically accompanied by a priest or a deacon, which brought even more out-of-town guests to the provincial capital.

As Carthage was important enough to host many church councils, the church in the metropolis bore some extra financial burdens; yet it never seemed to be lacking in financial means. Thus, let us consider here the development of the church treasury, one of Cyprian's key innovations as bishop and an important aspect of church administration, as evidenced by his letters. Cyprian repeatedly mentioned expenses and receipts, while the beneficiaries, recipients of food and clothes, included the poor, widows, orphans, and the sick. Finally, the church also cared for the confessors—those placed in prison or in work camps—as well as those in exile.

Charitable gifts and financial contributions were not limited to caring for the needs of just the poor in Carthage. In 253, following an appeal from eight Numidian bishops, Cyprian took up an offering and sent five thousand sesterces to ransom a group of believers taken hostage by a rebellious tribal group.[1]

In the second half of the third century, the rapidly growing African church began to adopt a vision for ministering to social needs. The Christian Scriptures had certainly advocated that "faith without works is dead" (Jas 2:17); yet prior to Cyprian, this aspect of Christianity was hardly noticeable in church life, nor was it a priority for the church leadership. Tertullian, as noted, had been too preoccupied proclaiming the Day of the Lord. He also regarded poverty as a blessed state. Hence, this new emphasis on charitable giving surely strengthened relationships between the different social classes within the church. In the case of the lapsed, some were interested in reintegrating into a church that promised them not only forgiveness and eternal life, but also earthly, material aid.

If the church at Carthage, radiant and well-organized, had not ceased to grow during the peaceful decades between 212 and 249, it probably would not have been regarded as a pillar of the greater society as it was by Cyprian's time. Thus, the uncompromising rigor advocated by Tertullian was now little more than a distant memory.

In his treatise *On the Lapsed* (ca. 251), in which he praised the example of confessors whose conduct earned them "the highest title of glory," Cyprian also painted a less-than-flattering picture of his flock. On the verge of facing Decius' persecution, he wrote:

> Each one was desirous of increasing his estate; and forgetful of
> what believers had either done before in the times of the apostles,
> or always ought to do, they, with the insatiable ardor of covet-
> ousness, devoted themselves to the increase of their property.
> Among the priests there was no devotedness of religion; among

1. Cf. Cyprian *Letter* 72.3.1.

the ministers there was no sound faith: in their works there was no mercy; in their manners there was no discipline. In men, their beards were defaced; in women, their complexion was dyed: the eyes were falsified from what God's hand had made them; their hair was stained with a falsehood. Crafty frauds were used to deceive the hearts of the simple, subtle meanings for circumventing the brethren. They united in the bond of marriage with unbelievers; they prostituted the members of Christ to the Gentiles. They would swear not only rashly, but even more, would swear falsely; would despise those set over them with haughty swelling, would speak evil of one another with envenomed tongue, would quarrel with one another with obstinate hatred. Not a few bishops who ought to furnish both exhortation and example to others, despising their divine charge, became agents in secular business, forsook their throne, deserted their people, wandered about over foreign provinces, hunted the markets for gainful merchandise, while brethren were starving in the Church. They sought to possess money in hoards, they seized estates by crafty deceits, they increased their gains by multiplying usuries.[2]

Despite the moralist's certain exaggerations, Cyprian's depiction of the lax state of his own congregation and that of the broader church is difficult to dismiss. In denouncing the inferior morals of believers as well as the serious infractions and depravity of the clergy, Cyprian leaves no doubt that he was deeply affected by these fallen ones who had hardly put up a fight. Over the years, believers and pastors alike had forgotten the old lessons learned during persecution, and divisive factions began to spring up within the church. In order to reach his goals and rally the hearts of his people, Cyprian not only demonstrated great pastoral skills, but he also became politically shrewd.

DECIUS' PERSECUTION AND ITS IMPACT IN AFRICA

In September of 249, Decius, the deeply pagan Illyrian general and commander of the army in the Danube region, was proclaimed emperor by his soldiers. During this period of crisis in Rome, his primary objective was to restore traditional morals. That is, through a popular movement, he sought to rally Rome's citizens to a renewed devotion to the imperial

2. Cyprian *On the Lapsed* 6. [Unless otherwise indicated, English quotations from Cyprian's works are from *ANF* 5.]

authorities and Roman gods. Undoubtedly, he also wanted to destroy the leadership of the church—particularly the bishops—which, through its development and organization, had become regarded as a rival power and threat to the Roman state. Desiring to diminish the authority gained by clergy who cast a shadow on his own power, Decius wanted to institute an "official" church and thus subjugate Christianity to a place within the Roman pantheon—all of which were under the *imperium* of Decius, the *Pontifex Maximus*.

Though probably issued sometime at the end of 249, Decius' first edict cannot be dated with certainty. Though the text of the edict has not survived, its merciless content, which combined shrewd and persuasive tactics with violence and torture in suppressing those who did not comply, can clearly be discerned in how the edict was carried out. All of the inhabitants of the Roman Empire were to participate in a general sacrifice to the Roman deities. Caracalla's edict had of course functioned in a similar manner and thus served as a precedent for Decius' edict. The emperors essentially communicated that there was no more fitting action for a Roman citizen than to offer homage to the pantheon's worthy objects. Failing to comply with the order signified a denial of one's citizenship and a deliberate affront to the emperor. Beginning in December of 249, Christians in Rome who refused to sacrifice were imprisoned, and on January 20, 250, Bishop Fabian of Rome was put to death. As Cyprian wrote, Decius hoped that Fabian would not have a successor: "that savage tyrant [Decius] was menacing bishops of God with dire and dreadful horrors, at a time when news that a rival emperor was being raised up against him he would receive with far greater patience and forbearance than word that a bishop of God was being appointed in Rome."[3] As a result, the office of bishop at Rome remained vacant for fifteen months.

Mindful of these same threats in Carthage, Cyprian was convinced that, in order to best continue his ministry at bishop, he needed to leave the city. After making this controversial decision, he went into hiding somewhere far from Carthage accompanied by a group of clergy and some laymen as well. Though a warrant for his arrest was issued, he was not seriously pursued except that his belongings in Carthage were confiscated. From hiding, he continued to care for the needs of the church

---

3. Cyprian *Letter* 55.9. [All English quotations from Cyprian's *Letters* are from Clarke, *Letters of St. Cyprian of Carthage*, Ancient Christian Writers 43, 44, 46, 47, hereafter referred to as *ACW*.]

initially by delegating leadership responsibilities to a group of his clergy. Later, he appointed a special commission of two bishops and two priests, to whom instructions were directly addressed. During his fifteen month absence from Carthage, there was no shortage of critics and his position and authority became threatened, especially as the imprisoned confessors began to acquire a sort of spiritual authority. Rallying around a certain Novatus, a group of priests who had already opposed Cyprian's election as bishop endeavored to hinder his authority as bishop. Eventually, they appealed to Rome to block his return to Carthage, denouncing him as a pastor who had abandoned his flock. Despite these plots against Cyprian, the majority of believers in Carthage remained faithful to their bishop.

During Cyprian's absence, the imperial edict was carried out with much vigor in Carthage. Though adherence to the imperial cult was required of everyone, it could be fulfilled in various ways. As sacrificial fires were started each morning, the rich or the most zealous could offer an animal sacrifice—a goat, lamb, or even a cow. The poor were allowed to pour out a drink offering or to burn incense in front of a statue of the emperor, demonstrating homage to the emperor's divinity. Decius presented an impossible situation for the Christian movement, which of course forbade believers from taking part in any form of worship outside of the church. While Decius sought to rally Roman citizens around his personality cult, Christians who complied became apostates in the eyes of the church. Thus, the fallen began to be recognized by the infamous title of the *lapsi* (fallen, renegades, apostates), which included grades of infractions and resulting punishments. Those who offered sacrifices (*sacrificium*) were dubbed *sacrificati* ("sacrificers"), while those who had burned even a handful of incense (*thus*) were called *thurificati* ("incense burners").

The official ceremony took place in front of the Capitol temple, erected in honor of the Triad of Jupiter, Juno, and Minerva. Appearing before the altar with head veiled in a sacrificial gesture, the individual recited a religious formula that for a believer, understanding Christianity's requirements, amounted to a public renunciation of the faith. In every place, from the cities to the smallest villages, the entire population was required to appear before a commission of magistrates, assisted by five notaries, responsible for overseeing the sacrifices. Those who sacrificed had their names recorded, and received a certificate (*libellus*) attesting that they had complied with the edict. Again, this served as a statement of blasphemy for professing Christians, who were immediately denounced as apostates. The ceremony was at times followed by a sacred meal that included wine offerings and meat sacrificed to the gods. Conforming to the ancient custom of bribing government officials, some Christians with connections or financial means managed to avoid offering the sacrifice—and thus guarding their conscience and personal security—by purchasing the *libellus* from local officials. Despite their efforts, this group was also condemned by the church and became known as *libellaciti* ("certificate buyers").

Christians felt directly targeted by the imperial order. Though the sacrifice was imposed in order to promote national unity and to prove loyalty to the emperor, for Christians it set off an imperial persecution. While the government's fundamental goal was submission to the edict, the church saw it as a means of tempting prisoners to deny their faith. Cyprian observed this in the case of the lector Celerinus, a young African who after standing firm under torture in a Roman prison was released for no apparent reason: "For a period of nineteen days he was shut up in prison under close guard, in chains and irons. But though his body was in bondage, his spirit remained unfettered and free. His flesh grew emaciated by prolonged hunger and thirst, but his soul striving by faith and courage, God nourished with spiritual sustenance."[4]

It has been argued that the Decian persecution had two phases. The first dealt solely with church leaders—bishops and clergy—who through their compliance would influence their flocks to follow suit. This hypothesis is difficult to support simply because the universal order to sacrifice was not limited to Christians. Nevertheless, thanks to Cyprian's rich accounts, the different stages of the edict, especially related to the plight of Christians, can be observed. For instance, those who did not appear for the first public ceremony received a personal invitation from the magistrate. At this meeting, if they failed to produce a *libellus*, the individual was asked to renounce faith in Christ and perform the sacrifice or appear before the tribunal for violating Rome's ancient laws. Those who were still at large and had not sacrificed were sought out, arrested, and ordered to comply. If they did not sacrifice, they were brought before the proconsul's tribunal and convicted for refusing to obey the edict. At this point, they were placed in prison and tortured with iron nails—"legal torture" according to the Roman judiciary—which the authorities hoped would

4. Cyprian *Letter* 39.

force at least the pretence of submission to the edict. If they continued to refuse, Christians had their belongings confiscated and faced banishment or exile.

At Carthage the number of apostates was considerable. This was not so much on account of fearing torture, as was the case in previous persecutions; rather, Christians complied with the edict out of apparent respect for the government and to avoid the jeers and insults of their pagan neighbors. According to Cyprian, entire Christian families could be seen walking toward the forum, their arms filled with flowers, animal sacrifices, or incense. Similarly, leading members of society left their houses and were followed by their clientele to the place of sacrifice:

> Immediately at the first words of the threatening foe, the greatest number of the brethren betrayed their faith, and were cast down, not by the onset of persecution, but cast themselves down by voluntary lapse . . . They indeed did not wait to be apprehended ere they ascended, or to be interrogated ere they denied. Many were conquered before the battle, prostrated before the attack. Nor did they even leave it to be said for them, that they seemed to sacrifice to idols unwillingly. They ran to the market-place of their own accord . . . as if they had formerly wished it, as if they would embrace an opportunity now given which they had always desired. How many were put off by the magistrates at that time, when evening was coming on; how many even asked that their destruction might not be delayed![5]

Cyprian added:

> But to many their own destruction was not sufficient. With mutual exhortations, people were urged to their ruin; death was pledged by turns in the deadly cup. And that nothing might be wanting to aggravate the crime, infants also, in the arms of their parents, either carried or driven, lost, while yet little ones . . .[6]

Ordinary believers were not the only ones to submit to the pagan rite. In fact, a number of clergy in Carthage, including bishops, went down and sacrificed with their entire congregations following behind. Cyprian cited the case of several church leaders who fell: Jovinus and Maximius, whose places of ministry are unknown; and Fortunatianus, bishop of Assuras

---

5. Cyprian *On the Lapsed* 7–8.

6. Cyprian *On the Lapsed* 9.

(Zanfour, Tunisia).[7] Another bishop from Pronconsularis, Repostus of Saturnuca, directed his assisting clergy to lead "the vast majority of his people"[8] to apostatize.

While such lamentable cases of apostasy offered a great blow to the churches, the examples of believers who stood firm in their faith, at times heroically, should also be noted. Condemned for refusing to sacrifice, clergy, laymen, women, and children alike, were thrown into prison and held in solitary confinement in small, dark cells that could hardly hold them. Under such intolerable pressure and destitution, they had only the churches to care for their needs. Cyprian exhorted believers to provide for those in prison:

> I ask that there be nothing wanting in furnishing supplies to those who have confessed the Lord with words of glory and who are now to be found in prison, as equally to those who are suffering from need and want but yet continue faithful in the Lord. For all the funds collected have been distributed amongst the clergy precisely to meet emergencies of this kind, thus putting a number in the position to ease individual cases of hardship and necessity.[9]

He insisted, however, that prison visits should be done with the utmost discretion, avoiding excessive zeal, so that the prisoners' suffering would not be aggravated.

Several confessors—the name given to those who suffered or gave their lives for the faith—died in their jail cells from starvation or as a result of torture. Orders, however, were not given to torture a prisoner to death; rather, the goal was to wear them down through repeated questioning so that they would eventually give in and sacrifice. Cyprian wrote of "tortures which do not readily let their victims go to their crown but which wrench for as long as it takes to break a man."[10] Hence, the persecutor endeavored to make apostates—not martyrs. This was the case for three Christians in particular—Ninus, Clementianus, and Florus:

> These brothers of ours had previously been arrested during the persecution, and stoutly confessing the name of the Lord had withstood the violence of the magistrates and the attacks of the

7. Cf. Cyprian *Letter* 65.

8. Cyprian *Letter* 59.10–2–3 [English translation my own].

9. Cyprian *Letter* 5.1.

10. Cyprian *Letter* 11.1.3.

frenzied mob. Subsequently, however, while being subjected to savage tortures before the proconsul, they gave way under their extreme torments, and through those protracted agonies fell from the heights of glory which they were scaling in the vigor of their faith.[11]

According to the Carthage church's official list from April 250, twenty believers died during this wave of persecution; the majority starved to death, while the rest died from torture.

THE PROBLEM OF THE "LAPSED" (*LAPSI*)

Legal proceedings against "rebellious" Christians came to a halt at the end of 250 as the empire was forced to deal with a renewed Vandal attack on the provinces in the Danube region. The following year, after Decius' death, efforts to carry out the emperor's edict were abandoned. Nevertheless, the African bishops had already been and were now faced with an even greater challenge—dealing with those who had succumbed to the pressure and sacrificed (*lapsi*), yet now requested readmission into communion with the church.

Regardless of the details of individual cases, the lapsed were excluded from fellowship and, according to the African tradition, only a perpetual state of penance could insure their re-entry into communion. While many desired to regain the spiritual and moral blessings of church membership, others, as noted, were interested in what the church offered materially. Many were convinced that the number of fallen believers alone would oblige the church leadership to accept everyone back. Thus, these *lapsi* refused to perform any type of penance and threatened to riot the churches of those clergy who refused to readmit them. The bishop's authority was certainly put to the test through these events.

Since well before the end of persecution, priests in Carthage, as well as some confessors, assumed a more prominent role. Confessors, in light of their near "martyrdom," took on a sort of priestly status and began to issue certificates of reconciliation (*libelli pacis*), offering immediate pardon for the lapsed. This judgmental role they assumed was normally limited to bishops. As a result, a parallel hierarchy between bishops and confessors developed—the latter receiving their authority not from the church, but from the Holy Spirit. The lapsed would visit the confessors in

11. Cyprian *Letter* 56.1.

prison, shower them with thoughtful words, and return with a precious certificate that granted peace and immediate re-entry into communion with the church. Sometimes a certificate was not even written to a particular beneficiary, but was addressed to a group of *lapsi*. At other times the paper was acquired by proxy and granted in the name of an already deceased confessor. Generally speaking, the generous and rash confessors would grant forgiveness to a group without examining each individual case. A certain Lucianus, who had previously spent time in prison for his faith, handed out certificates in the name of some of his illiterate friends who had also suffered for being a Christian. Finally, five renegade priests and their spokesperson Novatus further undermined the bishops' authority by forming a group that advocated leniency toward the *lapsi* and a hasty reintegration into church.

Once aware of these excesses and the subsequent ecclesiastical anarchy, Cyprian wrote three pastoral letters from his place of hiding. At first he advised the confessors to issue certificates only to those who had completed a period of penance. At the same time, he appealed to the clergy to respect the ecclesiastical hierarchy, especially the bishop's authority. He also urged church members to be prudent, warning them that their impatience could ultimately harm the process of church discipline. Regardless, in the face of such circumstances, the bishop was forced to offer a compromise and abandon the African church's traditional rigor toward apostates. In the spring of 251, a council met in Carthage and formally decided that those clearly guilty of apostasy—the *sacrificati* and *thurificati*—would be subject to an indefinite period of penance, except for those on the verge of dying. The *libellatici*, though also required to perform penance, were immediately readmitted to fellowship. At a follow-up council in 252, the bishops extended forgiveness and reconciliation to all of the *lapsi* who had continued in their penance since the time of their fall. On the other hand, clergy who had sacrificed were forever banished from the priesthood.

When Trebonius Gallus came to power, the church feared another wave of persecution. However, between 252 and 254 an even greater calamity—a plague from Ethiopia and Egypt—wreaked havoc on Carthage. These unfortunate events, which actually did more harm to the church than Decius' edicts, marked the end of a sad period for the lapsed. However, this also set off a new crisis that would result in schism in the church.

A group of clergy—those who initially opposed Cyprian's consecration as bishop and later became entangled in the controversy of the confessors offering reconciliation certificates—rose up against Cyprian's authority and succeeded in delaying his return to Carthage. The party's leaders included Novatus, who would soon go to Rome in search of support, and Felicissimus, a layman who had recently been ordained a deacon. Felicissimus was the predominant leader in the schism and claimed to have instituted a "church on the mountain." He proclaimed that "those following Cyprian would have no communion in this mountain fellowship."[12]

This split in the Carthage church was a direct result of the chaos perpetrated by the persecution in Africa in which rebellious clergy refused to give up the authority they acquired while the bishop was absent from his diocese. From the beginning of 251, while still in hiding, Cyprian, denouncing such schemes, wrote:

> For the spite and treachery of certain presbyters has made it impossible for me to reach you before Easter day. They have not forgotten the plots they laid, they have not lost all their old venom against my episcopate, or rather against the votes you cast and the judgment of God. Accordingly, they are renewing their former attacks upon us, they are starting up afresh with all their habitual craftiness, their sacrilegious schemings.[13]

Felicissimius, who would soon be excommunicated along with his five colleagues, merged his group with a similar group led by Bishop Privatus of Lambaesis, who had also been denounced by a church council. Along with four of his partners, Privatus ordained Fortunatus—one of the five priests who had opposed Cyprian and who had just been excommunicated—as bishop of Carthage, thus forming a rival communion. Departing for Rome to have the new bishop recognized, Felicissimus ultimately failed in his efforts as the pope became aware of the situation while Felicissimus was still en route.

Still desiring to overthrow Cyprian, these schismatic Africans, who had rivaled Cyprian by showing lenience in the whole *lapsi* affair, made common cause with another faction—a rigorist group that greatly resembled the Montanists. In the spring of 251, after a long vacancy,

---

12. Cyprian *Letter* 43.1 [English translation my own].
13. Cyprian *Letter* 43.1.2.

Cornelius was consecrated bishop of Rome after being elected by a majority of church members. Yet a schism was instigated by the well-known priest Novatian, a writer and distinguished theologian, who had also functioned as spokesperson for the church when Rome had no bishop. Desiring to maintain that power, Novatian had himself elected bishop by a small minority of church members and through the influence of a group of priests and confessors that rallied around him. Novatus, who had already conspired with Felicissimus in Africa and had been in Rome for over a year, also joined this faction in the Roman church split.

Like the Marcionites, Novatian's followers quickly multiplied in Italy, Gaul, the East, and in Africa, where a bishop had already been set apart. Thus, in 252 Carthage had three rival bishops: Cyprian for the Catholic church; Fortunatus, who represented Felicissimus' party; and Maximus, the Novatianist. Though these schismatics, at times joined by Montanists, continued to survive in Asia Minor and Syria until the seventh century, they were reduced to little more than minor sects in Africa as Cyprian tirelessly confronted them. By 255 the Novatianists relented and requested permission to re-enter the Catholic church.

According to Catholic church leaders—in Africa as well as at Rome—such conflicts could easily be attributed to factions wanting to sow seeds of discord, or to certain parties frustrated by their inability to gain power. Though these considerations should certainly be factored into our analysis, schisms also revealed, once again, two notions of church present in Africa. The *collegium* of bishops, led by Cyprian, believed that the church should remain open to everyone—from the spiritual elite pursuing monastic discipline to the masses of Christians with only slight regard for the Gospel's teachings. On the other hand, following Tertullian's tradition, which viewed church hierarchy with hostility, the schismatics viewed the church as a small group of saints or "pure ones." Such ideals were crystallized by groups like the Cathars that developed later in the East. Hence, this more rigorous church movement strived to be a community of martyrs and confessors living in conflict with the "earthly city." In light of that, Novatian, regarding the apostasy of the *lapsi* as highly scandalous, advocated a severe measure of penance. Allowing no compromise with the Catholic church on this matter, he required Catholics joining the Novatianist communities to be rebaptized.

The African church, unified in both its organization and its institutions, was also unified in spirit and thus too solid to be shaken at this stage. Moreover, Cyprian possessed the ability to gather bishops from all over North Africa. Though the schismatics had certainly labored in vain, their failure actually prompted another, more intense controversy—one in which Carthage and the African church would confront the leadership of the church at Rome.

THE BAPTISMAL CONTROVERSY BETWEEN THE AFRICAN CHURCH AND THE ROMAN CHURCH

The African church's independent spirit, one of its key characteristics, could be observed repeatedly throughout the early church period. Though the African church was intimately connected to Rome, the bishop of Carthage enjoyed a position of increasing authority in the eyes of the entire African church and even beyond—an influence that none of the Carthaginian bishops desired to diminish. This influence, however, was diluted somewhat in the fourth century as provincial primates were set apart, beginning first in Numidia. The developing conciliar tradition regularly gathered bishops from various provinces under the leadership of the Carthaginian bishop, which only added to his influence. Each year the bishop of Carthage visited various provinces where his presence was requested. He ratified episcopal elections and oversaw the transfer of clergy from one diocese to another. Though bishops like Cyprian were mindful to lead with moderation and in deference to their colleagues, some of Cyprian's successors tended to abuse their authority. As a result, measures were put into place to counter this tendency.

The canons of the African church councils—though largely referring to a later period—provide some helpful insight into the subject of discipline and church leadership. The canons expressed without ambiguity the church's pride in defending its right to deal with disciplinary matters in Africa. This was in contradistinction to those clergy who preferred to have their case decided in Rome, despite the fact that the Roman bishop's judgment might not be acceptable to the African church leadership. Thus, if clergy felt the need to complain about a course of action taken by their bishop, they could, with their bishop's consent, appeal the matter to neighboring bishops or even have the issue addressed by a council of bishops in Carthage. The bishops later decided—in an effort to put a stop to clergy traveling outside of Africa—that priests or other clergy who appealed to an overseas tribunal would be excommunicated in Africa. To be sure, the African church's tendency to take offense at Rome's intervention should not be understood as a very spiritual reaction. In fact, it was this "African autonomy" that also characterized violent resistance movements and tensions between the diverse elements of African society, a tendency that continually shook up the imperial authorities.

Though misunderstandings sometimes occurred between Cyprian and Cornelius of Rome, they were quickly resolved because of the close, harmonious relationship that existed between the two bishops. The two had, of course, worked together in the long and bitter battle against Novatian. Following Cornelius' death in exile and Lucius' brief episcopate, Stephen was set apart as bishop of Rome and served in that capacity from 254 to 257. Right away, a number of conflicts arose between Stephen and Cyprian. For instance, Stephen authorized the appointment of two Spanish bishops, both of whom had purchased certificates (*libelli*) in order to escape persecution under Decius. These appointments, of course, went against the decision of the fall 251 council of Carthage. As a result, the Spanish churches appealed to the African bishops for direction on the matter, which revealed Carthage's ecclesiastical influence on the western church. The African bishops responded by convening a council in Carthage in 254 in which they countered Stephen's decision. They ruled that the Spanish bishops were disqualified for church leadership and should be removed from their places of ministry.

Carthage's prestigious position in the western church was further affirmed in 254 when Bishop Faustinus of Lyon wrote several letters to Cyprian in which he shared some recent problems in the Gallic church. In collaboration with the Roman church, Cyprian intervened to put an end to the scandal in the church at Arles—a church whose bishop, Marcianus, had left and joined the Novatianists.

A more serious question would arise and bring division between the Roman and African churches. In late 254 or early 255, Cyprian responded to a certain Bishop Magnus' queries: "You ask whether it is obligatory that those who come over to us from Novatian ought to be included in the company of other heretics and that after his profane washing they are to be baptized within the Catholic church by means of the one, true, and lawful baptism, that is to say of the church."[14] Cyprian quickly responded that in Africa, the tradition was to reject the validity of baptism

14. Cyprian *Letter* 69.1.

performed by heretics; thus, those coming to the Catholic church from a heretical communion were required to be baptized. However, those who were baptized as Catholics prior to falling into heresy or schism were allowed to return to communion after a simple penance and imposition of hands by the church leadership. In his treatise *On the Unity of the Church,* Cyprian passionately presented the African church's position on heresy: "Although there can be no other baptism but one, they think that they can baptize; although they forsake the fountain of life, they promise the grace of living and saving water. Men are not washed among them, but rather are made foul; nor are sins purged away, but are even accumulated."[15] While Tertullian had previously defended this thesis,[16] Cyprian added that the first known council of Carthage, convened by Agrippinus and including bishops from Numidia and Proconsularis, had ruled this way too.[17] However, at Rome, as well as Alexandria and Palestine, former heretics were admitted to fellowship simply after a period of penance and the imposition of hands.

As heresies and schisms multiplied, the matter of granting reconciliation to heretics became one of the biggest challenges facing the church. In 255, eighteen Numidian bishops wrote a letter addressing the issue. The council of Carthage, which convened in the fall of 255 and brought together the bishops of Proconsularis, met to decide the issue and offered a definitive response for their colleagues: "In this judgment we are in harmonious agreement with you, being of the same opinion and holding it as certain that no one can be baptized outside and away from the church, on the grounds that there is only one baptism that has been appointed and that is in the holy church."[18] Shortly after the gathering, Bishop Quintus of Mauretania, previously undecided in his view, received his copy of the council's decision.

Cyprian argued that appealing to tradition alone was insufficient for settling the matter. He urged bishops not to be governed by their stubbornness, but rather to be compelled by reason. Cyprian added that, in the circumcision controversy, St. Peter had not arrogantly appealed to his position as a church leader to decide the matter; instead, he humbly

15. Cyprian *On the Unity of the Church* 11.
16. Cf. Tertullian *On Baptism* 15.
17. Cf. Cyprian *Letter* 74.4.1.
18. Cyprian *Letter* 70.1.2.

yielded to Paul: "He [Peter] has thus given us an object lesson in harmony and forbearance, showing that we must not stubbornly cling to
our own ideas; rather we should adopt as our own any beneficial and
salutary suggestions that are from time to time made by our brethren
and colleagues."[19] It is not impossible to conclude that Cyprian, through
these words, was directly challenging Stephen's approach to the matter.
For from an African standpoint, the Roman bishop was arrogantly in-
voking the primacy of his see to settle the matter. Perhaps the bishops of
Mauretania, not as directly aligned to Carthage, had consulted Stephen,
who had in turn sought to win them to his view. Cyprian's letter was clear:
for Stephen, the Roman practice of admitting heretics into communion
ought to be followed by all churches because of Rome's antiquity and relationship to Peter.

   Around the same time, Cyprian was again consulted on the "re-
baptism" question by another Mauretanian bishop, Jubaianus, and responded by sending him two conciliar letters addressing the issue. In his
own long and argumentative response, Cyprian refuted certain aspects of
the Roman position raised by his correspondent. Jubaianus observed that
baptizing heretics or schismatics who desired entrance into the Catholic
church would be like adopting the Novatianist practice of baptizing
Catholics entering their sect. Cyprian retorted that the African tradition was not new and went back to the time of Agrippinus. In correcting Jubaianus, who seemed quite taken by Novatian, Cyprian cautioned
against attributing too much innovation to the schismatic: "Novatian was
like a monkey. Though not a man, he imitated men's actions, and laid
claim to the authority of the Catholic church."

   In the spring of 256, a provincial council of seventy-one bishops
from Proconsularis and Numidia upheld the existing position of the
African church. In a very firm letter—a masterpiece by the council's key
diplomat—Cyprian communicated to Stephen the council's decision. He
did not fail to assert that the African bishops were making a decision
for African churches, a decision that could not be imposed on other
churches:

> We bring these points to your notice, dearly beloved brother, in
> a spirit of mutual respect and sincere affection. We believe that
> these matters which conform to piety and truth will recommend
> themselves to you also, knowing as we do your true piety and

19. Cyprian *Letter* 71.3.1.

faith . . . We are not forcing anyone in this matter; we are laying down no law. For every appointed leader has in his government of the church the freedom to exercise his own will and judgment, while having one day to render an account of his conduct to the Lord.[20]

When Stephen learned of the African council's decision, he stipulated, under threat of excommunication, that the African church conform to the Roman tradition. He responded with his customary excess and uncompromising posture, which he justified because of his stature as bishop of Rome. Though we possess only a fragment of Stephen's letter, Cyprian referred to the Roman bishop's arguments as "arrogant, irrelevant, self-contradictory, ill-considered, and inept" and accused him of "endeavoring . . . to champion the cause of heretics in opposition to the followers of Christ and the church of God."[21] In the end, Cyprian rejected Rome's orders to receive heretics back into the Catholic church without baptizing them again:

> Truly this is a noble and authentic tradition which is being placed before us by the teaching of our brother Stephen and what suitable authority for it he presents to us! . . . The church of God, the bride of Christ, has fallen on such evil days that she is now to follow the example of heretics! . . .What blindness of soul can this be, what perverseness, to refuse to acknowledge the unity of faith which proceeds from God the Father and the tradition of our Lord Jesus Christ our Lord and God.[22]

In the context of this controversy, which was only worsening and moving toward a split between the two churches, the African bishops sent a delegation to Rome. However, Stephen refused to meet them, refused them food and shelter, and ordered his congregation not to welcome the Africans into their homes. Finally, he referred to Cyprian as "a bogus Christ, a bogus apostle, and a crooked dealer."[23]

In the midst of such tension, Cyprian called a plenary council in Carthage on September 1, 256—a gathering attended by eighty-six bishops from various provinces who were accompanied by priests, deacons,

---

20. Cyprian *Letter* 72.3.
21. Cyprian *Letter* 74.1.
22. Cyprian *Letter* 74.4.
23. Cyprian *Letter* 75.25.

and even some laymen. This was, without a doubt, the most important church council of Cyprian's career. By way of introduction, Cyprian made note of the conciliar letter that he had previously sent to Stephen as well as the correspondence he had exchanged with other bishops on the matter. He then asked that each of his colleagues take responsibility for making a decision on this issue. In the surviving *acta,* Cyprian communicated:

> It remains, that upon this same matter each of us should bring forward what we think, judging no man, nor rejecting any one from the right of communion, if he should think differently from us. For neither does any of us set himself up as a bishop of bishops, nor by tyrannical terror does any compel his colleague to the necessity of obedience; since every bishop, according to the allowance of his liberty and power, has his own proper right of judgment, and can no more be judged by another than he himself can judge another. But let us all wait for the judgment of our Lord Jesus Christ, who is the only one that has the power both of preferring us in the government of His Church, and of judging us in our conduct there.[24]

In this opening speech, Cyprian did not merely speak to his colleagues in this manner to remind them of their independence; rather, he was primarily addressing the bishop of Rome—the "bishop of bishops." As the central issue came up for a vote, the African pastors unanimously moved to uphold their tradition—baptizing those entering the Catholic communion from heresy. This, of course, did not apply to those who were already baptized in the Catholic church prior to a season of heresy.

After the council, Cyprian quickly dispatched one of his deacons to carry the news to Bishop Firmilian of Cappadocian Caesarea—a significant leader in the eastern church, who, along with his colleagues in Asia Minor, agreed with the African church on this issue. Firmilian responded with a long letter comparing Stephen to Judas Iscariot while also referring to the Roman bishop in a harsh manner:

> This is a fine example of preserving the unity of the Spirit in the bond of peace: to cut himself off from the unity of charity, to alienate himself from his brethren in everything, in a frenzied fit of quarreling to rise in rebellion against the sacred bonds and obligations of peace. With such a person can there possibly be one

24. *The Seventh Council of Carthage under Cyprian.* [All English references are taken from *ANF* 5.]

body, one Spirit, seeing that perhaps there may not be even one soul, so slippery is it, so inconstant, so unstable?[25]

Despite his strong rhetoric, there is no official indication that Firmilian initiated an effort to excommunicate Stephen. It should be noted, however, that when Stephen refused to receive or extend hospitality to the African bishops visiting Rome ("they were refused peace and communion"), Firmilian accused Stephen of treating the Africans as if they were excommunicated. Despite his attitude toward the Africans, it is uncertain whether his threats to Cyprian[26] were ever followed up with a formal canon decreeing excommunication. Neither Cyprian's letters nor his biography provide any additional insight on this development.

We can certainly conclude that during his long and heated conflict with Stephen, Cyprian, who enjoyed the full support of his African colleagues, never gave in to the Roman bishop. Though Stephen was resolved to condemn the "rebel bishops," Valerian's persecution would not allow him the opportunity, and Stephen's death put an end to any intended action. In the end, the African church won its case in this heated theological dispute and maintained an autonomous posture prior to relinquishing it suddenly at the 314 council of Arles—a completely different context. These theological battles had a considerable impact on the church in the Mediterranean world, and the church at Carthage found itself on equal footing with the churches in Asia Minor and Syria—those that had their origins in the apostolic period.

PERSECUTION UNDER VALERIAN

In June of 251, after Decius was killed in battle, Valerian emerged as the victor following a bloody contest with his opposing Vandal general. Sharing the title Augustus with his son Gallienus, Valerian inherited the Roman Empire. The pro-Christian sympathies demonstrated by Gallienus' wife probably explained the emperor's favorable attitude toward the church in the early years of his reign. Furthermore, Denys of Alexandria's portrayal of Valerian as a protector of the Christians should be regarded as rhetorical exaggeration.

25. Cyprian *Letter* 75.25.2.
26. Cf. Cyprian *Letters* 74–75.

Certainly influenced by his minister Macrian, an adherent to the Roman pantheon's eastern religions and self-declared enemy of the Christians, Valerian issued an initial edict against the church in 257. As we will see, however, ideological reasons were not the only factors for Valerian's actions. Though the text of the edict has not survived, its provisions were transmitted through Carthage's *Acta proconsularia* and essentially amounted to a citation recorded by a clerk and delivered to those summoned to the Proconsul Aspasius Paternus' office on August 30, 257. In fact, Cyprian was called to answer questions related to bishops, priests, and deacons in response to this imperial order.

Though not requiring non-pagans to sacrifice to the traditional deities, the emperor ordered them at least to recognize the ceremonies—a "recognition" that implied attendance. Though freedom of conscience was permitted, participation in the rites promoted solidarity among Rome's citizens. Also, higher ranking Christian clergy were required to submit to the edict or face exile. The proconsul added: "We also forbid anyone taking part in any religious gathering or entering the cemeteries. All who disobey this excellent order will incur the death penalty." The Christian movement was thus considered an illegal entity.

Cyprian opposed any form of participation, even passive, in the official cult. Born and reared in paganism, he was quite aware that even the simplest act of deference to the authorities constituted a compromise—including being present or making the simplest gesture. He declared: "I am a Christian and a bishop. I know no other gods but the one, true God . . . to whom we pray night and day for ourselves and all men, and even for the salvation of the emperors."[27] Aware of the official legislation, which from the time of Trajan had not accepted unfounded accusations, Cyprian refused to denounce his fellow Carthaginian clergy against the hopes of Aspasius Paternus.

In fact, Cyprian's initial appearances before the tribunal were characterized by a sense of mutual respect between the governor and the bishop. Carefully emphasizing from the beginning that he was not acting out of personal interest, the proconsul gave an account of the imperial order and how "the holy Emperors Valerian and Gallienus had seen fit to make known their will." Cyprian brought his brief hearing to an end by telling the proconsul: "Do as you have been commanded." The magistrate made known his intended sentence: "Therefore, following the order of

27. *Acta proconsularia.*

Valerian and Gallienus, will you accept exile and leave for the town of Curubis?" Cyprian simply responded, "I will go," and he spent around a year in the small town of Curubius (modern Korba on the southern Cap Bon). Cyprian was accompanied to this rather bearable "exile" with friends and colleagues, including his eventual biographer Pontius. There, he continued a ministry of correspondence, particularly to fellow clergy who had been arrested and were suffering much more than Cyprian.

Also during this period, the presiding official in Numidia arrested some Numidian clergy who refused to cease their worship meetings and sentenced them to hard labor in the mines, a form of capital punishment. From Curubis, Cyprian maintained a relationship through letters with these men—a dozen bishops and priests who were apparently divided into three groups. One group worked in the copper mines at Sigus, a town probably near Sicca Veneria (Le Kef, Tunisia). Cyprian's *Letter* 77 in particular provides much insight into the harsh treatment endured by the confessors.[28]

In 258, a second edict was given ordering all clergy who persisted in resisting the imperial order to surrender or face the death penalty. Like the first edict, the original text of the second edict has not survived. What we do know about it comes indirectly through Cyprian, who commented on it in one of his letters. Though details of "persecution" under Decius and Valerian were probably exaggerated by some writers, as these accounts fail to be corroborated elsewhere, it cannot be doubted that a bloody suppression of Christianity was happening empire-wide.

It seems that several crises during this period also influenced the emperor's religious policies. The greatest challenge facing the empire was inflation and the state's treasury was nearly bankrupt. The seemingly bottomless pit of public debt, resulting from a rapid increase in prices as well as the bills accumulated by war (against the Goths on the Danube and in Asia Minor, and against the Persians), pushed the currency to near collapse. A significant revolt, initiated by the Berber chief Faraxen that shook up Numidia and Mauretania Caesarea between 254 and 260, also succeeded in getting the emperor's attention.

In the midst of these circumstances, Valerian and his minister of finance proposed several strategies to replenish the treasury. Wide scale confiscation of church property probably figured into this political strat-

---

28. Cf. Cyprian *Letter* 77.3.

egy to reverse the empire's economic crisis. Thus, beginning in Rome around 258, the church's rather considerable resources began to be assimilated into the imperial accounts.

After a group of Cyprian's emissaries returned to Curubis from Rome and briefed him on the situation, Cyprian wrote the following letter to his colleague Successus:

> For there have been rife a wide variety of unconfirmed rumors. The truth of the matter stands as follows. Valerian has sent a rescript to the Senate, directing that bishops, presbyters, and deacons are to be put to death at once but that senators, high-ranking officials, and Roman knights are to lose their status as well as forfeit their property, and that if, after being so dispossessed, they should persist in remaining Christians, they are then to suffer capital punishment as well. Furthermore, that matrons are to be dispossessed of their property and dispatched into exile and that any members of Caesar's household who had either confessed earlier or should have done so now, are to have their possessions confiscated and are to be sent in chains, assigned to their imperial estates . . . I request that you make these matters known to our other colleagues.[29]

In the case of senators, high-ranking officials, Roman knights, and even members of Caesar's household, renouncing the Christian faith did not mean that confiscated property would be restored. This "economic" aspect of Christian persecution in 258 indeed merits further consideration. Despite this tendency, there is no compelling evidence to show that the emperor's definitive goal was to dismantle a Christian ruling class. Nevertheless, the fact remains that Valerian's persecution affected large numbers of the population, including Bishop Sixtus II of Rome and Cyprian, the "pope" of Carthage.

ADDITIONAL RESOURCES

Demoustier, "Episcopat et union à Rome selon saint Cyprien."
Duquesne, Chronologie des lettres de saint Cyprien.
Marschall, Karthago und Rom.
Saumagne, "La persécution de Dèce à Carthage d'après la correspondence de saint Cyprien."
Saxer, "Autonomie africaine et primauté romaine de Tertullien à Augustin."

29. Cyprian Letter 80.

5   Cyprian, the "Pope" of Carthage

A COMMITTED LIFE

When referring to Cyprian, Jerome simply called him an African (*Cyprianus Afer*), which meant that he came from the Roman province of *Africa*, later renamed *Africa Proconsularis* because it was governed by a proconsul. Based on other evidence from Lactantius, Augustine, Jerome, and Cyprian's own writings, a great deal is known about Cyprian's life—much more than what we know about his contemporaries. Considered the Cicero of Latin Christianity, Cyprian was the first bishop to contribute to the African literary tradition.

Cyprian's writings include a corpus of eighty-four letters, which provide rich detail about his work as a bishop and his relationships with other clergy. Sixty-five of these letters—six of which were conciliar letters in which he was the primary author—were written by Cyprian while another sixteen letters came from Roman clergy like Novatian and Cornelius, and were addressed to Cyprian or the Carthaginian clergy. While unfortunate that none of these letters was dated internally, it is nevertheless helpful that each letter, except for two, included the name of its recipient. Cyprian's correspondence, full of insights into his theology, is complimented by thirteen small treatises written to the church at Carthage, some of which were essentially sermons. This collection of letters and treatises not only provides important evidence for understanding African church history, it also serves as an important milestone in Latin Christian literature. To be sure, Cyprian remained one of the most popular Christian authors well into the medieval period, and his works have survived to the present day via numerous manuscripts.

In addition to these primary sources, our understanding of Cyprian's life is strengthened by other key secondary sources from the period. First, the *Acta proconsularia* is a very valuable document highlighting official actions of the Roman authorities toward Cyprian, including his court appearances, interrogations, the judgments rendered by the Carthaginian governors, and his martyrdom. Secondly, the *Life of Cyprian*, the first work of its type in early Christian Latin literature, was written by a certain Pontius, a deacon from Carthage who lived with Cyprian during his exile until the time of his execution. Though Pontius was Cyprian's contemporary and offers an important eye witness account, his work seems to lose some historical value because of its devotional and edifying purpose. Hence, the work functions as a panegyric to honor Cyprian's holy example—that "this incomparable and lofty pattern may be prolonged into immortal remembrance."[1]

While these sources provide an accurate understanding of Cyprian's life during his ten years as bishop (249–258), his pre-conversion life is quite unknown. Though named Caecilius Cyprianus, he also went by Thascius. While it cannot be confirmed with certainty, Cyprian was probably born in Carthage. According to Pontius, he lived in a villa with gardens in Carthage—a home that he owned—which gives the impression that he had always lived there. Though his date of birth is unknown—even Augustine was unaware of it—we can plausibly suggest that it was sometime around 210. Finally, Cyprian does not seem to have had a personal relationship with Tertullian, his "master" who probably died around 222.

A man of great financial means, Cyprian certainly belonged to the rich and cultivated bourgeoisie in Carthage. Jerome recorded that Cyprian, born into paganism, was initially "a defender of idolatry." After receiving a comprehensive education, Cyprian was on the path to success, and his background and training gave him access to the pomp and splendor of the highest ranks of the Roman administration. A brilliant communicator who had mastered the rules of rhetoric and eloquence, Cyprian developed quite a reputation in Carthage, where he may have practiced law for a time. It is also likely that he held a position in the civil or municipal administration. Though not possessing Tertullian's legal mind, Cyprian's writings do reveal a level of judicial expertise that he would put to use in his career as a bishop. Cyprian also enjoyed an elegant lifestyle

---

1. Pontius *Life of Cyprian* 1. [All English translations of *Life of Cyprian* are from *ANF* 5.]

with fine food, luxury, and pleasure, and his circle of friends included the leading pagans of Carthage. He probably maintained these friendships after his consecration as bishop, which perhaps explains the respect he commanded from police and magistrates during his arrests and periods of interrogation. To be sure, the conversion of this rich member of the social elite came as a shock to Carthage's high society.

Jerome, commenting once more on Cyprian's life, added: "It was under the influence of the priest, Caecilius, from whom he received his name, that Cyprian became a Christian and donated his wealth to the poor."[2] Cyprian was probably baptized around 246. Setting a precedent for Augustine's later confessional-style autobiography, Cyprian recounted the steps in his conversion at the outset of his treatise to his friend Donatus, probably one of Cyprian's former colleagues in the legal profession:

> While I was still lying in darkness and gloomy night, wavering hither and thither, tossed about on the foam of this boastful age, and uncertain of my wandering steps, knowing nothing of my real life, and remote from truth and light, I used to regard it as a difficult matter, and especially as difficult in respect of my character at that time, that a man should be capable of being born again . . . These were my frequent thoughts. For as I myself was held in bonds by the innumerable errors of my previous life, from which I did not believe that I could by possibility be delivered, so I was disposed to acquiesce in my clinging vices; and because I despaired of better things, I used to indulge my sins as if they were actually parts of me, and indigenous to me.[3]

Upon his conversion, Cyprian took a vow of celibacy, renouncing the worldly pleasures that had characterized his previous life, and donated his earthly belongings to the poor and to the church. He probably paid a greater price by breaking with his worldly "masters," the classical authors of Greek and Latin literature. From this point on, he had but two masters that he consulted daily—the Bible and Tertullian. Though occupying a place of prominence and authority as bishop of Carthage, Cyprian lived and conducted himself quite humbly. Despite this simplicity, he was still very much a man of action, which propelled the African pastor to a place of renown among the leaders of the Christian movement of his day.

2. Jerome *Lives of Illustrious Men* 67 [English translation my own].

3. Cyprian *To Donatus* 3–4.

Shortly after his baptism in 246, he was set apart to the priesthood by Bishop Donatus, his predecessor in Carthage. In early 249, Cyprian was consecrated as bishop and became the "pope" of Carthage—a title signifying the bishop's fatherly and spiritual care for the flock entrusted to him. Not reserved uniquely for the bishop of Rome, this distinction was also used to address bishops in Asia Minor and Alexandria. Cyprian was called pope not only by his congregation, but also by some Roman clergy.[4] In a letter denouncing Felicissimus and the five priests who led a schism during the Decian persecution, Cyprian referred to his own episcopal election and this fatherly authority of a bishop: "there is a man who is appointed bishop in the place of a deceased bishop; he is chosen in time of peace by the vote of the entire congregation . . . it can only be the adversary of Christ and the enemy of his church who is hounding the appointed leader in the church with his attacks."[5]

Due to his abilities as an administrator and theologian, Cyprian was a solid spiritual leader for the church at Carthage, to which he gave himself first and foremost. He was also an influential advisor to churches in Spain and Gaul, who addressed their problems to the African church councils overseen by Cyprian. As an administrator, Cyprian tirelessly gave himself to the clergy and people of Carthage. He also left a corpus of important theological writings, which on one hand, were written in clear and sober pastoral manner, yet on the other, possessed all of the passion of Tertullian and the African tradition. Thus, by often alluding to military imagery in his writings, he influenced African theology toward a "militant spirituality."

A CHAMPION OF UNITY

Cyprian's treatise On the Unity of the Church was probably published in the spring of 251. The most influential of all of his works, it was read aloud at the council of Carthage in 251. It is also the work that best captured Cyprian's personality. The schisms set off by Novatus and Felicissimus, which had succeeded in dividing the Carthage church, gave Cyprian the occasion to write this exhortation. Addressed not only to Cyprian's clergy and flock, its recipients also included confessors in Rome who were still

---

4. Cf. Cyprian Letters 30, 36.
5. Cyprian Letter 59.6.

following Novatian. Like *On the Lapsed,* which had confronted apostasy during the Decian persecution, *On the Unity of the Church* was prompted by the circumstances surrounding schism and written in the context of several church councils dealing with this issue.

Cyprian believed that unity, a value that he championed until his own martyrdom, ought to be a bishop's chief concern, because unity was the primary characteristic of the Christian faith. Cyprian wrote, "Can he who is not bound to the unity of the church, believe himself to be bound to the faith? Can one who opposes the church be certain that he is also in the church? One cannot even be a martyr if he is not in the church." Cyprian was convinced that outside of the church, falsehood and impiety reigned, and that salvation could only be experienced within the context of the church: "We cannot have God for our father without the church as our mother. He, who does not maintain unity, fails to keep God's law and rejects faith in the Father and the Son."[6] As signs pointing to the Lord's imminent return abounded—a millenarian position already defended by Tertullian—those outside of the fold were urged to return immediately to communion or risk perishing. Cyprian argued that church unity should be affirmed on several levels.

First, during the Decian persecution, Cyprian asserted that Christian unity (*concordia*) was expressed through corporate prayer. He wrote to the priests and deacons of his diocese:

> Every one of us should pray to God not for himself only, but for all his brothers, just as the Lord taught us to pray. His instructions are not for each of us to pray privately but he bade that when we pray we should do so with united hearts in communal prayer for everyone. If the Lord shall observe that we are humble and peaceable, joined in union together, fearful of his wrath, chastened and amended by the present sufferings, He will make us safe from the assaults of the enemy.[7]

These arguments are also supported in Cyprian's treatise *On the Lord's Prayer,* a work written as Cyprian was going into hiding during the Decian persecution. He refers to the apostles' practice of corporate prayer: "They continued with one accord in prayer, declaring both by the urgency and by the agreement of their praying, that God, 'who makes

---

6. [English translation my own.]

7. Cyprian *Letter* 11.7.3.

men to dwell of one mind in a house,' only admits into the divine and eternal home those among whom prayer is unanimous."[8]

In *On the Unity of the Church,* Cyprian specified further that unity was not dependent upon the number of believers gathered together:

> When, therefore, in His commandments He lays it down, and says, "Where two or three are gathered together in my name, I am with them," He does not divide men from the church, seeing that He Himself ordained and made the Church; but rebuking the faithless for their discord, and commending peace by His word to the faithful, He shows that He is rather with two or three who pray with one mind, than with a great many who differ, and that more can be obtained by the concordant prayer of a few, than by the discordant supplication of many.[9]

This practice does not simply refer to a prayer gathering of a few Christians; rather, Cyprian alludes to the united "Catholic prayer" of the entire church.

As Novatian worked to attract more believers into his schismatic movement in 251, another aspect or level of church unity (*concordia*) was raised—the unity of the bishops. In dealing with the problem of the lapsed, Cyprian had already requested that the clergy demonstrate their unity by adopting a united stance on the issue. In a letter to priests and deacons at Rome, he wrote: "You should read these same letters also to any of my colleagues who may be present with you or who may come later. In this way, we may act in unison and harmony, adhering to the same health-giving measures for healing and curing the wounds of the fallen."[10] Cyprian constantly urged the bishops to be united so they could speak with one voice for the universal church. For instance, Cornelius' election as bishop of Rome over Novatian was legitimized because of the "testimony of his episcopal colleagues, all of whom were in unanimous agreement."[11] Hence, the church's universality and catholicity was determined by the unity of its bishops.

A difficult question is raised in the fourth chapter of *On the Unity of the Church*—a chapter that exists in variant manuscripts, itself an unre-

---

8. Cyprian *On the Lord's Prayer* 8.

9. Cyprian *On the Unity of the Church* 12.

10. Cyprian *Letter* 34.31.

11. Cyprian *Letter* 8.1 [English translation my own].

solved controversy. In what is probably the oldest manuscript—or at least, as some argue, a text unaffected by later "additions"—Cyprian speaks of "the chair of Peter" and of the "primacy of Peter." The text in question continues: "Although Christ gave all of the apostles the same authority, he nevertheless established but one episcopal chair. Set apart on account of Christ's authority, this chair is the heart and reason for unity." In founding his church on Peter, Jesus clearly and concretely presented a case for unity—the essential quality and greatest goal for the church. That said, though the bishop of Rome in some respects served as a communication link between bishops and "personified" the unity of the church, he had no official delegation to speak or decide on his behalf.

While the mission to teach, signified by the notion of "chair" (*cathedra*), was first given to Peter, it was also conferred with the same authority on all of the apostles: "The other apostles were the same as Peter except that Peter occupied a primal place of authority (*primatus*). This shows that there is but one church and one seat of authority. All of the apostles are good shepherds, yet there is one single flock that is led in one accord out to pasture. This unity must be firmly defended, especially by those of us who are bishops."[12] On the basis of the earlier text of *On the Unity of the Church*, Peter's primacy emerges as a symbol of and exhortation to unity. While Rome's privileged position could be likened to the rights of a firstborn, or conferred due to its ecclesiastical seniority, it did not mean that the Roman bishop had authority and jurisdiction over his episcopal colleagues.

In a later redaction of *On the Unity of the Church*—regarded by some as the only text written by Cyprian—the term "primacy" does not appear and more emphasis is placed on the apostle's equality. The following citation from John's Gospel shows the apostles on equal footing: "'As the Father has sent me, even so I am sending you.' And when he had said this, he breathed on them and said to them, 'Receive the Holy Spirit. If you forgive the sins of any, they are forgiven them; if you withhold forgiveness from any, it is withheld'" (John 20:21–23). Peter's powers are declared identical to those of the other apostles, in content as well as importance: "Assuredly the rest of the apostles were also the same as was Peter, endowed with a like partnership both of honor and power."[13]

---

12. Cyprian *On the Unity of the Church* 4–5 [English translation my own].

13. Cyprian *On the Unity of the Church* 4.

Certainly, both versions of the text could have been written by Cyprian, under different circumstances. The harsh conflict over the re-baptism of heretics that took place between Cyprian and Bishop Stephen could provide an explanation in the changes to *On the Unity of the Church*. Nevertheless, it should be noted that neither text asserts that Peter or his successors have authority and jurisdiction over the universal church.

According to Cyprian, next to Christ's eminent authority, the Catholic church's greatest source of authority was the united *collegium* of bishops speaking with one voice in Christ's name. This notion of collegiality was especially developed among the African church leaders as bishops were elected by the clergy and laity and were later consecrated by other key provincial bishops. Hence, the bishop of Rome was not empowered with the authority to single-handedly make doctrinal or disciplinary decisions for the entire church. Firmilian's harsh words regarding Stephen have been noted: "to cut himself off from the unity of charity, to alienate himself from his brethren in everything."[14] The Holy Spirit should serve as the ultimate guide and judge for the universal church, not the church at Rome. Thus, if the Roman bishop cut himself off from the church, which speaks through its unified body of bishops, it is imperative for the sake of unity that he be shown the error of his ways. In condemning Marcianus of Arles, Cyprian had already written: "it is plainly evident that a man does not hold the truth of the Holy Spirit with the rest of his colleagues when we find that his opinions are different from theirs."[15]

Despite consistently affirming the rights of bishops from outside influences, Cyprian showed some inconsistency in this area as he solicited Rome's intervention at times on certain matters. For instance, indignant over Novatus and other Carthaginian schismatics attempting to win the Roman bishop to their view, Cyprian wrote: "they now have the audacity to sail off carrying letters from schismatics and outcasts from religion even to the chair of Peter, to the primordial church, the very source of episcopal unity."[16] While turning to Stephen for help in confronting the Novatianist Bishop Marcianus, Cyprian actually gave the Roman bishop directions for how to proceed in the matter: "I exhort you, therefore, to direct letters to that province and to the faithful who dwell at Arles, urging that after Marcianus has been excommunicated, a successor be appointed

14. Cyprian *Letter* 75.25.2.
15. Cyprian *Letter* 68.5.
16. Cyprian *Letter* 59.14.

in his place."[17] Though Cyprian appealed to the pope in this matter, he never asked him to get involved with an issue facing the African church.

As the apostles were considered Peter's equals—"endowed with a like partnership both of honor and power"—bishops also shared the same episcopal authority. Cyprian wrote: "In his [Christ's] view the church consists of the people who remain united with their bishop, it is the flock that stays by its shepherd. By that you realize that the bishop is in the church and the church is in the bishop, and whoever is not with the bishop is not in the church."[18] Thus, it appears that Cyprian became the leading voice for episcopal authority in the church. Following the two significant church crises that also raised theological questions—the problem of the lapsed and the rebaptism of heretics—the bishop's role increased significantly in Cyprian's mind, especially as the African church leadership clashed with that of Rome.

Cyprian continued to affirm a bishop's autonomy within the context of the leader's diocese. Writing to the Numidian Bishop Antonianus at a time when apostasy was dividing the church, Cyprian asserted: "Provided that the bonds of harmony remain unbroken and that the sacred unity of the Catholic church continues unimpaired, each individual bishop can arrange and order his own affairs, in the knowledge that one day he must render an account to the Lord for his own conduct."[19] Cyprian communicated similarly in letters to his Roman counterparts, Cornelius and Stephen. After their decision concerning the rebaptism of heretics at the council of Carthage in the spring of 256, Cyprian and the African bishops wrote to Stephen: "For every appointed leader has in his government of the church the freedom to exercise his own will and judgment, while having one day to render an account of his conduct to the Lord."[20]

Cyprian's words to Antonianus ("provided that the bonds of harmony remain unbroken") further signified that a bishop's autonomy must be exercised in the context of ecclesiastical unity. Thus, it was not permissible for a bishop to act in a manner contrary to the decisions of church councils. The frequent African councils, prompted by issues facing the church and the need to establish rules and policies for the churches, succeeded

17. Cyprian *Letter* 68.2–3.
18. Cyprian *Letter* 66.8.
19. Cyprian *Letter* 55.21.
20. Cyprian *Letter* 72.3.

in unifying the bishops in their respective work. Hence, an individual bishop's freedom to lead could not prevail over *concordia*—a recurring theme in *On the Unity of the Church*—and dissident bishops were urged to return to unity with their colleagues. In short, a bishop's freedom and autonomy was derived from his membership in the *collegium* of bishops. Cyprian summarized: "The episcopate is one, each part of which is held by each one for the whole."[21]

In light of these theological convictions concerning church leadership, Cyprian publicly scorned the bishop of Bulla Regia (Hamman Daradji, Tunisia). Opposing the decisions of church councils from the spring of 251 and May of 252, which prescribed measures for readmitting the lapsed to communion, this bishop prematurely reconciled a priest who had sacrificed during the Decian persecution. Cyprian wrote: "Our colleague Therapius with rash and precipitate haste granted him reconciliation though the time for this was still premature. This action has seriously disturbed us, for it marks a departure from the authority of our decree."[22] In the same letter, Cyprian urged Bishop Fidus to abide by the decision of a recent church council from the end of 253 that dealt with the baptism of infants—a decision that Fidus opposed. Hence, in Cyprian's view, unity and agreement among church leaders were distinguishing characteristics of Christ's church.

Whenever Cyprian confronted one of his colleagues, he always made reference to an appropriate conciliar decision and acted as an advocate for episcopal unity. In a letter to the Mauretanian Bishop Jubaianus, Cyprian reminded him of the judgments rendered at the councils of 255 and the spring of 256:

> We have written this brief reply to you . . . we do not wish to prevent any bishop from doing what he thinks right, for he is free to exercise his own discretion . . . we do our very best to refrain from quarreling over this question of heretics with our colleagues and fellow bishops . . . charity of spirit, the honor of the episcopal college, the bond of faith, the harmony of the episcopate, these we preserve in patience and gentleness.[23]

These words summarized perfectly Cyprian's episcopal theology.

21. Cyprian *On the Unity of the Church* 5.
22. Cyprian *Letter* 64.1.
23. Cyprian *Letter* 73.26.

THE MARTYR

In a letter written at the end of August of 258 to his colleague Successus, Cyprian informed him of a recent imperial rescript targeting the church. As the edict singled out members of the clergy who would face capital punishment, Cyprian made a final reference to his Roman colleague Sixtus: "You should be further informed that Sixtus was put to death in the cemetery on August 6, and, along with him, four deacons." Apparently briefed by messengers returning from Rome, Cyprian added: "Moreover, the Emperor Valerian has added to his address a copy of the letter which he has written to the governors of the provinces concerning us. We are daily awaiting the arrival of this letter, resolved as we are to stand in all firmness of faith ready to endure a martyr's suffering."[24]

This letter and the *Acta proconsularia* are the only texts that provide any detail about Valerian's edict. However, there is no evidence to support a firm date for its implementation in Africa. We do know that upon the arrival of the new proconsul Galerius Maximus, Cyprian was summoned from exile in Curubis and ordered to appear before the tribunal. Following the governor's orders, Cyprian returned to his villa in Carthage and waited to be arrested. In the meantime, he resumed his pastoral ministry. According to Augustine, Cyprian's return to Carthage occurred in August of 258 and corresponded to an apparent massacre in nearby Utica. In the so-called *Massa Candida*, a large number of Christians from Utica—estimates vary between 150 and 300—were put to death. Bishop Quadratus, the head of the church at Utica, was executed also on August 21. Later, the basilica at Hippo Diarrhytus (Bizerte) was named in his honor.

Already present in Utica for these events, Galerius Maximus issued a warrant for Cyprian's arrest. Warned that imperial agents were en route to arrest him, Cyprian, apparently not wanting to experience martyrdom at Utica, probably followed the advice of friends and went into hiding again. From there, he wrote his final letter to the priests, deacons, and all of the faithful at Carthage: "It befits a bishop to confess his faith in that city where he has been placed in charge over the Lord's flock, it is proper that the appointed leader in the church should bring glory upon all his people by making his confession in their midst."[25] While refusing

24. Cyprian *Letter* 80.3.
25. Cyprian *Letter* 81.1.

to accept martyrdom under Decius, Cyprian embraced it under Valerian at the time and place of his choosing. Indeed, there is something rather aristocratic about his actions and like a *patronus*, he chose to die in his church. As the proconsul returned to Carthage, Cyprian also returned to his villa.

The circumstances of Cyprian's arrest and interrogation have been preserved in the *Acta Cypriani*, a text included in the larger *Acta proncon-sularia*—the governor's official document that justified the legalities of his judicial process. The short transcript prepared by an assistant present at the execution ably captured the interaction between Cyprian and the proconsul and serves as one of the most famous texts in the history of martyrdom.

On September 13, two of the proconsul's senior officers, flanked by an escort of soldiers, appeared at Cyprian's villa, where he greeted them with a smile. The bishop was then transported to a place called the *Ager Sexti*, the location of Galerius Maximus' vacation home. Upon arrival, the interrogation was put off until the following day because the proconsul was ill. Cyprian spent the night at the home of a military officer and was treated with much respect—including enjoying a final meal with some of his companions. From the time of his arrest, the Carthaginian Christians had gathered in mass and kept vigil outside of where Cyprian was staying.

The next day, the proconsul ordered Cyprian brought in to the *Atrium Sauciolum* and began the formal process by identifying the accused: "Are you Thascius Cyprianus? . . . Are you the one who has presented himself as the leader of a sacrilegious sect?" He then called upon Cyprian to submit to the laws of Rome: "The most holy emperors bid you to sacrifice . . . think it over." Cyprian flatly refused and said: "Do what you have been ordered to do. In such a just cause there is nothing to think over."

The *Acta* continue:

> Galerius Maximus, after conferring with the college of magistrates, with difficulty and unwillingly pronounced this sentence: "You have long lived sacrilegiously and have gathered many in your criminal sect, and set yourself up as an enemy of the Roman gods and of their religious rites. The pious and most holy Augusti emperors Valerian and Gallienus, and Valerian most noble Caesar, failed to bring you back to the observance of their religious ceremonies."

"Therefore, since you have been seen to be the instigator of the worst of crimes, we shall make an example of you before those whom you have associated with yourself in these wicked actions. The respect for the law will be sanctioned by your blood." Having said this he read out in a loud voice from a tablet the decree: "I order that Thascius Cyprianus be punished by being beheaded." Bishop Cyprian said: "Thanks be to God."

Surrounded by soldiers, the condemned bishop departed for the place of torture and execution. As he walked, a crowd of Christians accompanied him and formed a procession of sorts. The *Acta proconsularia* close with the final eyewitness account:

Thus Cyprian was led into the countryside of Sexti (*Ager Sexti*), and there he took off his cloak and hood, knelt on the ground and prostrated himself in prayer to the Lord. He then removed his dalmatic and gave it to the deacons, leaving himself only in his linen garment, and so waited for the executioner. When the latter arrived, the bishop ordered his own followers to give the executioner twenty-five gold pieces. Meanwhile his brethren held out pieces of cloth and handkerchiefs to receive the blood as relics. Then the great Cyprian with his own hands bandaged his eyes, but since he could not tie the corners of the handkerchief, presbyter Julian and subdeacon Julian went to help him. Thus bishop Cyprian was martyred and his body, because of the curiosity of the pagans, was placed in a place nearby where it was hidden from their indiscreet eyes. It was then carried away at night with lighted flares and torches and accompanied as far as the cemetery of procurator Macrobius Candidianus, which is in the "Huts" Road (*Via Mappaliensis*) near the Baths. A few days later, proconsul Galerius Maximus died. The holy bishop Cyprian was martyred on September 14th under emperors Valerian and Gallienus, but in the reign of our Lord Jesus Christ, to whom all honor and glory be forever.

ADDITIONAL RESOURCES

Daniélou, *Les Origines du christianisme latin*.
Demoustier, "L'ontologie de l'Église selon saint Cyprien," *Recherches de science religieuse*.
Monceaux, *Saint Cyprien*.
Sage, *Cyprian*.
Saumagne, *Saint Cyprien, évêque de Carthage, "pape" d'Afrique (248–258): Contribution à l'étude des "persecutions" de Dèce et de Valérien*.

6 Organization and Life of the Third-Century African Churches

Cyprian's correspondence certainly documents well the church councils that took place at Carthage between 220 and 256. More importantly, his letters give the names of bishops present at the councils—an indication of the development of the churches and the overall expansion of Christianity in Africa at this time. Any numbers from Cyprian's letters pertaining to the African episcopal dioceses, however, should be accepted with caution, as precise statistics are impossible to determine. As a result, varying numbers have been proposed due to the difficulty of knowing the precise geographic location for each bishop and church. Nevertheless, in a recent work, a list of episcopal sees from Cyprian's period has been generated from church council documents and Cyprian's correspondence. Also, recent success in identifying ancient names of places has resulted in determining the location of dioceses across the African provinces, especially in Proconsularis where they experienced the most significant multiplication.

In light of the number of bishops absent from church councils due to age, illness, or some other cause, as well as the number of vacant churches at the time of the African church councils, there were probably 100 African bishops in 256. Harnack estimates that there were 150. The dioceses were probably established primarily in centralized areas. By contrast, during this period, few churches could be counted in Gaul, including cities like Lyon and the region around Narbonne. At the council of Arles in 314—nearly 100 years after the 220 council of Carthage and following Constantine's peace to the church—only sixteen Gallic churches were represented, twelve of which had a bishop.

By the mid-third century, the African dioceses were already significantly large. In light of this, the September 256 council of Carthage
proves quite interesting. The council's *acta* were signed by the eighty-
seven bishops in attendance, and for the first time the names or locations of their churches were also identified. In addition to this evidence,
some other dioceses are also mentioned in Cyprian's letters. The churches
were apparently distributed quite unevenly throughout the provinces and
regions, while Proconsularis had the highest concentration of churches.
Moving westward from Carthage, and from the coastline to the African
interior, the number of churches diminished—generally in proportion
to the decreased Romanization in this region. Of the eighty-seven bishops mentioned in the *acta* (twenty of whom are not identified), around
sixty were probably from Proconsularis, twenty from Numidia, and three
from Mauretania Caesarea. At this point, it would be helpful to list those
dioceses whose location was identified. In some cases, the churches were
established in ancient centers that are now modern towns and cities (the
modern city name will be specified), or that have been located based on
compelling archaeological evidence.

In Proconsularis, fifteen dioceses have been identified along the
coastline from the Gulf of Syrta to the border of Mauretania. They include Lepcis Magna, Oea (Tripoli), Sabratha, and Girba (Djerba) in the
region of Tripolitania; Leptis Minor (Monastir), Hadrumetum (Sousse)
in Byzanena; Neapolis (Nabeul) and Carpis (Henchir Mraissa) in the
Cap Bon region of Pronconsularis proper; Utica and Hippo Diarrhytus
(Bizerte) to the north of Carthage; and Thabraca (Tabarka) and Hippo on
the coastline between Numidia and Proconsularis.

Within the interior of Proconsularis and stretching to the Saharan
boundaries (*limes*) of Roman Africa, thirty dioceses can be counted. They
were particularly concentrated in the southern suburbs of Carthage in
the Oued Miliane valley and the neighboring region. Seven churches, located in close proximity one to another, have been located based on scant
archaeological evidence. A larger number and more dispersed group of
churches existed in the lower valley of Bagradas (Oued Medjerda), which
is noted for its tributaries, and on the plateaus of Byzacena. Some of these
dioceses included Thuburbo Minus (Tebourba), Membressa (Medjez el-
Bab), Vaga (Beja), Mactaris (Makthar), Ammaedara (Haidra), Thugga
(Dougga), Thibaris (Thibar), Assuras (Zanfour), Sicca Veneria (El Kef),

Sufetula (Sbeitla), and Capsa (Gafsa), located in the direction of the Sahara.

In Numidia, aside from the church at Rusicade (Skikda), located on the coast and west of Hippo, fourteen of the twenty dioceses established in the interior towns and cities have been located. They include: Cirta (Constantine), Milevus (Mila), and Cuicul (Djemila) in the north-central areas of the province; Lambaesis, Thamugadi (Timgad), Theveste, and Bagai (a later stronghold of Donatism) toward the south and crossing the northern range of the Aures; Mascula (Khenchela), twelve kilometers south of Thamugadi; Thubunae (Tobna), located in the Hodna depression; and finally Ad Badias (Badis), located south of the Aures and east of Biskra, a military outpost on the edge of the Sahara.

Concerning Mauretania Caesarea, the introduction to the *acta* of the September, 256 council of Carthage refers to the gathering of "the majority of bishops from the provinces of Africa, Numidia, and Mauretania" who were accompanied by some of their clergy. A review of the list of bishops present seems to show that the final province had no episcopal representative, indicating that little can be known about church expansion in the western half of North Africa. However, epigraphic inscriptions reveal the presence of Christian communities in the region from the third century. These include: Ruscuru (Dellys, Taksebt, along the coast of Kabylie), Tipasa, Caesarea, and Cartennae (Tenes), situated along the coast moving from east to west; Sitifis, Auzia (Sour el-Ghozlane located twenty-five kilometers southeast of Algiers), and Oppidum Novum (Ain Defla on the Oued Chelif), all located in the interior of the province; Castellum Tingitanum (El Asnam, Chlef), situated in the west; and Atlava (Ouled Mimoun, thirty kilometers east of Tlemcen), located in the far western end of the province. Cyprian also corresponded with two Mauretanian bishops, Quintus and Jubaianus, though their exact locations are unknown. It is also likely that Tipasa and Caesarea had bishops by the third century. The Mauretanian bishops' absence at the church council in 256 could be explained by the fact that they disagreed with the views of their African colleagues, or that that they did not want to get involved in the conflict with Rome over the heretical baptism issue. Cyprian's letters to the Mauretanian bishops seem to offer credibility to this view.

Was the multiplication of dioceses in the second half of the third century a good reflection of Christianity's growth in North Africa at this time? This correlation is probably not the best indication of church expansion. For example, if we relied on the number of bishops present at the plenary councils to chart the church's progress, this would actually represent a decline in the church. The last plenary council was convened by Cyprian in September of 256 and included eighty-seven bishops from Proconsularis and Numidia; yet, twenty years earlier, Donatus, Cyprian's predecessor, hosted a gathering of ninety bishops. We could further argue that the council of seventy bishops led by Agrippinus in 220 was more significant than the four councils overseen by Cyprian between 252 and 256, which often only included the bishops of Proconsularis.

Though the number of bishops present at the African councils does not represent the general growth of the church, the council of September, 256, which saw at least eighty-six dioceses represented, was actually a better indication of Romanization in Africa, showing the development of urbanization in the provinces as well as the evolving official relationship between the cities and neighboring towns and colonies. For instance, the seven churches in the Oued Miliane valley seem to have been established according to the legal boundaries of the cities in the region—not so much because of the church's great needs there. Also, Thimida Regia (located thirty kilometers southeast of Carthage) and Uthina—situated very close by—both had bishops: the first was a town and the second was a colony. Located sixty kilometers southwest of modern Tunis in the Medjerda basin, the colony of Abitina (Chouhoud al-Batin) and the neighboring town of Membressa also had bishops. The northwestern town of Taccabor (Toukabeur) also had a bishop. Dispersed within the modern Tunisian interior, which extended to the countryside and sparsely populated areas, the cities of Ammaedara, Theveste, Sufetula, and Thelepte (located farther south) were colonies with their own bishops.

While these examples pertain to Proconsularis, the same argument can be made for Numidia. Four churches—Thamugadi, Lambaesis, Lamasba (Merouna), and Tubunae (Tobna)—were established on the northern side of the Aures Mountains and were connected by an important road. The first two localities were colonies, while the latter two were towns. While not every town or colony had a bishop, it should be noted that in the second half of the third century—the period of our present inquiry—the church's organizational structures were still in development.

THE BISHOP OF CARTHAGE, PRIMATE OF AFRICA

The forty years of peace from 259 to 303 allowed the church to expand its work and to develop its infrastructure. From the mid-third century, Carthage established itself as the African church's leading city. In fact, in the Greek text of the *Acts of the Scillitan Martyrs*, Carthage is referred to as the "metropolis." The bishop or primate of Carthage was also the African primate, and his authority extended to all of the provinces. Specifically, his authority stretched from the border of Libya (Cyrene) and Tripolitania in the east (Tripolitania was in reality a narrow coastal strip that included three churches) to the border of Mauretania Tingitane in the west, an area that was developing ties with Spain.

The bishops of Mauretania Caesarea seem to have had a more distant working relationship with the bishop of Carthage than their other African colleagues, which, as noted, probably explains their absence at the plenary council of Carthage in the fall of 256. On one hand, the sea route between Caesarea and Ostia (Rome) that already facilitated commercial contact between the two cities may have also facilitated ecclesiastical connections. On the other hand, the apparent gap between Carthage and Mauretania may have resulted from differing views on church discipline, which explains why the Mauretanian bishops hesitated to side with their African colleagues and baptize those joining the church from heretical backgrounds. Even after the Vandal invasion, the Mauretanian bishops appealed to Rome instead of Carthage in resolving their problems. On August 10, 446, Leo the Great, asserting his authority, wrote the following letter to the bishop of Mauretania Caesarea: "Rome provides solutions for the issues addressed to Rome—solutions serving as prescriptions for ongoing practice." After affirming the primacy of Rome, he also recognized Carthage's important role in Africa: "Indeed, after the Roman bishop, the leading bishop and metropolitan bishop for all of Africa is the bishop of Carthage." Nevertheless, Pope Leo reminded his correspondent that the bishop of Carthage received his authority from the Roman bishop: "Even throughout Africa, the Roman bishop does not lose his rightful place of authority, which he received from the Holy Roman apostolic church."[1]

As Cyprian noted,[2] the Numidian bishops were tempted to rally around the leadership of Bishop Januarius of Lambaesis, which had be-

---

1. Leo the Great *Letters* 89 [English translation my own].
2. Cf. Cyprian *Letters* 62, 70.

come the political capital of the province in 198 under Septemius Severus. However, the office of primate of Numidia did not develop before the beginning of the fourth century. This was first realized in March 305, at the end of persecution and prior to the Donatist controversy, when Numidian bishops gathered under the authority of Bishop Secundus of Tigisis for a council in the provincial capital of Cirta (modern Ain el-Bordj, located some sixty kilometers southeast of Constantine). Secundus was called the "bishop holding the first chair"—the senior ranking bishop. Indeed, the Numidian primate would always be the bishop with the most seniority, and his jurisdiction extended beyond the typical civil boundaries and included the dioceses of Hippo, Tagaste (Souk Ahras), and Calama (Guelma).

Though the position of Numidian primate was officially established at the beginning of the fourth century, ecclesiastical organization within the African provinces had been in place for some time. Though the limits of the present study do not allow for an elaborate discussion on the provincial primates, it should simply be noted that Byzacena did not have a bishop functioning even informally in the role of primate until 345–348. It was not until the council of Carthage of 397 that an official primate from Byzacena was recognized. Like his Numidian counterpart, he received this distinction because of his seniority as bishop. The only time a primate from Mauretania Sitifien was identified was at the council of Hippo in 393, and it was not until 407 that the primate of Mauretania Caesarea was recognized.

ECCLESIASTICAL HIERARCHY AND THE LIFE OF THE CHURCHES

Referring to the essence of the church, Cyprian began by describing the relationship between the bishop and his clergy and the laity. Cyprian used the terms *clerus* (clergy) and *plebs* (the people) in a technical manner not only to describe the two major components of the body of believers, but also to distinguish their functions within the church: "The church has been established upon the bishop, the clergy and all of those who remain faithful."[3] While this notion of church was not entirely new and could be found in Tertullian's writings, every analytical study on the African

---

3. Cyprian *Letter* 33.1.

church structure eventually points to Cyprian, whose writings serve as the sole source of understanding the third-century African church.

The laity, who made up the vast majority of Christians, were not divided into different categories according to function; rather, they remained a homogenous group. However, circumstances, such as the periods of persecution, have led us to distinguish the confessors and martyrs from those who fell into apostasy. Also, for purely religious reasons, a distinction should be made between baptized believers and those who were still catechumens. Finally, the rights and obligations of certain members of the community were recognized by church leadership due to their place in society: mothers, who were pillars of the church from the outset; virgins, who participated in church life though most probably lived with their parents; and widows, those worthy of respect and admiration. Cyprian wrote to his clergy: "I urge that you be scrupulous in your care for the widows, the sick, and the poor."[4]

These believers were not to be reduced to a subordinate role serving their pastors, nor were they assigned the thankless task of doing manual labor for the community. Rather, they should benefit from a clergy completely free to minister because of the offerings given to the church. Cyprian wrote:

> Those who are advanced in the church of God by clerical appointment are not to be distracted in any way from their sacred duties; they are not to become entangled in the anxieties and worries of this world but rather, receiving as they do in the gifts and donations of their brethren the tenth portion, as it were, of the fruits of the earth, they are not to withdraw from the altar and sacrifices but day and night are to be dedicated to heavenly and spiritual concerns.[5]

According to Cyprian, it was impossible to arrive at a consensus on church issues without the active participation of the laity. He also did not neglect considering the strong opinions of some of his clergy: "It has been a resolve of mine, right from the beginning of my episcopate, to do nothing on my own private judgment without your [the clergy's] counsel and the consent of the people."[6] Though the active role of the laity was

---

4. Cyprian *Letter* 7.2.

5. Cyprian *Letter* 1.1.2.

6. Cyprian *Letter* 14.4.

apparent in their participation in the liturgical assembly, it was observed even more in their influence on the direction of the church. Apart from displaying a general initiative which included proposing ideas to church leaders about improving the church, they also gave their opinions on all decisions affecting the church: the means of reintegrating apostates or dismissed clergy into fellowship; and the ordination and promotion of deacons, priests, and bishops. In a letter to the clergy and laity, Cyprian added: "Dearest brethren, it is our custom when we make appointments to clerical office to consult you beforehand."[7]

By the mid-third century, a complete ecclesiastical hierarchy, with its differing clerical orders, was established in the African church—at least at Carthage. The clerical offices included exorcists, acolytes, readers (*lectores*), sub-deacons, deacons, priests, and bishops. A church leader could advance in the clerical ranks through promotion, which was the case of the Carthaginian priest Cornelius who arrived at the office of priest after serving faithfully in each of the lower orders.[8]

It is impossible to describe accurately the functions of each ministerial rank. We know, for example, that exorcists, acolytes, and sub-deacons all served the Carthage church by delivering the bishop's letters to other clergy. Though they may have also distributed money to the needy, their functions in general are difficult to determine. On the other hand, readers (*lectores*), set apart following an exam before the bishop and his counsel, were charged with important tasks such as: assisting the priests during the instruction of catechumens and reading the Scriptures from a raised pulpit in front of the congregation during the liturgical assembly. Deacons served at the altar during the Eucharist and, in the absence of a priest, could perform priestly functions. However, their tasks were generally administrative—overseeing the daily workings and organization of the diocese—and social, especially in caring for the poor. Though Tertullian assigned no great importance to priests, Cyprian entrusted them with the responsibility of teaching. Assisting and representing the bishop, they presided over the altar and administered the sacraments.

At the highest point of the ecclesiastical hierarchy was the bishop, the leader of the flock and representative of Christ. In order for a priest to be promoted to bishop, the needs of the church community had to

---

7. Cyprian *Letter* 38.1.
8. cf. Cyprian *Letter* 55.8.2.

warrant the promotion, and then a number of conditions also needed to be satisfied. First, the college of priests—sometimes a council of priests— was consulted to judge and evaluate the professional aptitude and moral life of the candidate. Next, the congregation expressed its opinion and approved the chosen candidate. Following the official election, the new bishop was consecrated through the laying on of hands by a group of consecrating bishops. Thus, an episcopal appointment was apparently finalized on multiple levels: affirmation of the candidate by the majority of his colleagues in the priesthood; agreement from the majority of lay people invited to participate in the process; and the candidate's assimilation by the consecrating bishops.

Episcopal authority was exercised in two main areas—discipline and administration. From the point of view of discipline, the bishop possessed authority to govern the church and preside over worship meetings. As pastor, he dictated an expectation of conduct and held the believers to this standard. At times this included applying measures of discipline against believers who had been baptized under his authority, or against clergy who, based on their ordination, had been entrusted with a ministry. Specifically, the bishop could temporarily exclude an offender from worship, definitively excommunicate those guilty of serious sins, or dismiss a member of his clergy. As a church administrator, the bishop oversaw financial receipts, expenses, and the church treasury. It was the primate's responsibility to represent his province's churches, to insure the necessary unity and cooperation between the African bishops, and to encourage unity between the African church and the bishop of Rome and church leaders from other countries.

As a result of Cyprian's leadership and example, the church at Carthage upheld its doctrinal convictions and asserted its rules for church discipline in a spiritual reform that earned the community an important place within the communion of saints. Despite being undermined at times by moral failure and weak faith, the church was fortunate to have had structured leadership. As a result, the church at Carthage found itself on equal footing with its Roman counterpart.

A parallel between the Roman and Carthaginian clergy is difficult to establish. In a letter to his Antiochene colleague in 251, Cornelius of Rome indicated that the clerical community under his charge numbered around 254 persons, though a list of names was not provided.[9] The list included members of the higher clerical ranks in Rome—forty-six presbyters, seven deacons, and seven sub-deacons. Though a similar, exhaustive list concerning Cyprian's clergy does not exist, the names of the Carthaginian clergy mentioned in his correspondence included fifteen presbyters, four deacons, and seven sub-deacons.

While these numbers should not be taken as an instant or official count of the Carthaginian clergy for a specific period, they nevertheless give an account of the clergy and their ranks in light of the specific events in the life of the church from 250 to 257. While this period was relatively brief and these clerical posts were eventually vacated and later filled by others, this clerical count, mentioned in passing in Cyprian's letters, is still significant for showing the importance of the church hierarchy in Carthage.

Regarding the higher clerical orders, the four deacons mentioned by Cyprian are slightly more than half the number of Cornelius' deacons in Rome, while both churches had seven sub-deacons. The group of fifteen presbyters listed in Cyprian's correspondence was also one-third of the size of its Roman counterpart; however, it should be noted that when Cornelius wrote his letter in 251, five of Cyprian's presbyters who had joined Felicissimus' African schism had also been excommunicated.

In summary, a comparison of these clerical statistics, established under different circumstances and resulting in unequal values, may only result in vague hypotheses on the importance of the Carthaginian clergy. In the very least, the significant number of deacons and sub-deacons mentioned in Cyprian's letters help to make an argument that the number of clergy in Carthage and Rome in the mid-third century was roughly the same. Moreover, the 1500 widows and needy also mentioned by Cornelius—the number regularly cared for and fed by the church—were among at least 12,000 active members in the Roman church, not counting catechumens. Though based on conjecture, it can be plausibly argued that the church at Carthage had just as many believers as the Roman church, especially taking into consideration the number of clergy, the hundreds of confessors, and the thousands of *lapsi* who received certificates of reconciliation. As noted, Carthage, with its population of 150,000, was the second largest city in the western Roman world after

9. Cf. Eusebius of Caesarea *History of the Church* 6.43.11.

Rome. However, fluctuations in the Christian population should also be noted. These resulted from the *lapsi* who did not return to the church after the Decian and Valerian persecutions; the large number of victims who died in the plague of 252 and 253; and the new converts who were added to the church.

A final point should be raised concerning how the two dioceses apparently adopted a parallel organizational structure. Since the time of Pope Fabian (236–250), the Roman diocese had been divided into seven regions or "diaconates"—undoubtedly each one was assigned to two neighboring administrative districts of Rome, which totaled fourteen in the capital. Each region was led by a deacon who was assisted in the work by a sub-deacon. The Carthage church also seems to have organized itself in similar administrative regions, which was quite apparent in Cyprian's letter mentioning the confessor Numidicus' work during the Decian persecution. In the absence of the bishop, this priest served among the superintendents (*vicarii*)—those entrusted to lead the church, to discern the material needs of the community, and to survey the church for potential candidates for the priesthood.[10]

THE CULT OF THE DEAD AND THE CULT OF MARTYRS

For a long time, Christian burial practices continued to be influenced by African pagan practices. Such customs were apparently dictated by African society, and Christians were not willing to abandon them. With certain actions and traditions embedded in the deepest part of their beings, parents and loved ones of the deceased desired to express their human pain and sadness as their ancestors had done. The Christians' new faith did not contradict these traditions, and all Christian efforts to reform burial practices came as a shock, especially as many of their deceased loved ones were themselves not Christians.

Tertullian made reference to the practice of traditional funeral washing, in which the body was cleansed, embalmed, and clothed, and covered with incense offerings and perfume. In African society, as alluded to by Cyprian, the mourning period for the family of the deceased was characterized by strong displays of emotion. He wrote that the lapsed were less distressed over the state of their own souls than the death of a

10. Cf. Cyprian *Letters* 40.1.1; 41.1.2.

loved one. He added: "If you had lost any dear one of your friends by the death incident to mortality, you would groan grievously, and weep with disordered countenance, with changed dress, with neglected hair, with clouded face, with dejected appearance, you would show the signs of grief."[11] As the plague was ravaging Carthage, Cyprian reminded his readers in another work that such mourning was completely pagan: "He who is to attain to the throne of Christ, to the glory of the heavenly kingdoms, ought not to mourn nor lament, but rather, in accordance with the Lord's promise, in accordance with his faith in the truth, to rejoice in this his departure and translation."[12] According to Cyprian, these quasi-pagan funeral practices were actually worse than those of the pagans. Christian conformity to pagan burial traditions was ultimately an indicator of conformity to pagan beliefs.

Christian funeral processions—complete with candles and torches—that led the deceased to the place of burial, hardly differed from such processions in the greater African society. Christian cemeteries existed in Africa since Tertullian's day. As noted, they were previously the private property of Christians who had donated them to the church. This is evident, for example, in a third-century commemorative inscription recovered from the sight of an ancient cemetery west of Caesarea in Mauretania: "A lover of the Word gave the *area* for the graves and he built the *cella* entirely at his own expense; to the holy church, he left this monument. Greetings my brothers from a simple and pure heart. I, Evelpius, greet you in the name of the Holy Spirit." At the end of the text, the following was written in a different style of lettering: "The church of the brethren restored this monument of the illustrious Antonius Severianus." The eroded *titulus* was restored and the additional notation reveals the identity of the generous donor—simply referred to as "a lover of the Word"—who gave the land and the chapel. Evelpius was undoubtedly the city's bishop and had taken possession of the chapel and cemetery in the name of the church.

Among the traditional practices, a portrait or image of the deceased was kept in the home, a practice borrowed from the pagan family cult that honored the Panates (lesser deities) and Manes (souls of deceased family members). Another custom taken from paganism was the funeral

11. Cyprian *On the Lapsed* 30.
12. Cyprian *On the Mortality* 22.

banquet—a Christian practice that appeared quite early and continued as the African church developed. Comparing them to pagan sacrifices, Tertullian condemned these traditions as idolatrous, though he never spoke of them as immoral.

Celebrations commemorating the deceased took place on the third and the ninth day after the individual's passing. They were further remembered each year on their birthdays. Imitating the pagan practice, family members, clients, friends, and household workers gathered around the tomb, covered with a slab of stone (*mensa*), to adorn it with flowers and to be united in thought with the deceased. In the western necropolis at Tipasa, where a funerary enclosure labeled "of the martyrs" can be found (others are found around St. Salsa Church, which is located on a hill advancing to the east of the city), a large number of funerary boxes covered with such *mensae* have been discovered—the oldest of which dates back to the third century. Some tombs were visited regularly, and conversations there—like those in a typical family gathering—continued well into the evening. These visits were sometimes followed by friends and family gathering around tables for a funerary love feast—a simple meal in which the deceased was symbolically included and food or a wine offering was poured into the tomb. These practices continued to develop in the following century, becoming more excessive and scandalous to the point that Augustine strongly denounced them. In Numidia, north of Setif and near ancient Satafis—a prosperous village famous for its olive oil production—a late third-century inscription was found in which the children in a family recounted their visit to the tomb of their mother, who was certainly pagan. The inscription creates a vivid context for understanding funerary practices:

> In memory of Aelia Secundula. For our mother Secundula, we have all given her an elegant tomb. It also pleased us to place above her tomb a stone table so that everyone could sit around and speak about her. With dishes prepared, glasses filled, and cushions laid out, we long to be healed of the bitter wound that eats away at our hearts. Amid such conversation, the pleasant evenings are spent worshipping our mother. She nourished us. Silent and sober, as she always was, today lying down, she sleeps, she is no more. She lived seventy-two years. Provincial year 260. Completed by Statulinia Julia.[13]

13. As the province was founded ("year one") by Caligula in AD 40, this inscription

Though the cult of martyrs developed to such proportions and levels of abuse in the fourth and fifth centuries that it needed to be regulated, it actually developed slowly in Africa. Tertullian had already taught that martyrs immediately entered into heaven and waited for the final judgment. As for other Christians, aided by the prayers of the living, they were transported to "Abraham's bosom"—a period of rest and comfort as they waited for the last day and the resurrection of the body. In his typical exaltation of martyrs, Tertullian made a distinction between those who died for their faith and otherwise normal believers who had simply passed away.

The fact remains that, in the third century, there was a close relationship between the cult of the dead and the cult of martyrs, which were nearly identical. In fact, at least in earlier times, deceased Christians were not remembered or honored any differently than pagans. During the Decian persecution, Cyprian, in a letter to church leaders regarding confessors imprisoned for their faith, made this request: "Accordingly, you should keep note of the days on which they depart this life; we will then be able to include the celebration of their memories in our commemoration of the martyrs."[14] Thus, just as the church had done for believers who had died, the Eucharistic sacrifice was offered for the martyrs—an atoning sacrifice to give them rest in their souls. Later, Augustine, while naming the names of martyrs during the mass, clarified—"we remember them not by praying for them, but more so that they would pray for us"— because praying for the martyrs would actually be an insult. According to Cyprian, however, the honors offered to the dead were the same whether the person was a martyr or an average believer: "if the bodies of the martyrs or of the other are left unburied, severe danger threatens those whose duty it is to do this work."[15] Despite these observations, it should be noted that by the mid-third century there was no specific example of a martyr cult.

In fact, the only difference between the cult of the dead and the cult of martyrs was that the former was practiced more by the family, while the latter involved the entire church community. Though in its essence the cult of martyrs hardly possessed any unique features, church celebra-

---

dates to AD 299. [English translation my own.]

14. Cyprian *Letter* 12.2.

15. Cyprian *Letter* 8.3.

tions taking place on the anniversary of the martyrs were nevertheless enveloped in a triumphal spirit. This term *triumphus*—used in Rome to refer to the procession of a victorious general or the emperor's route from the *Campus Martius* toward the Capitol—was used in the *Acta Cypriani* in reference to the procession of believers accompanying Cyprian's remains from the place of his execution to his tomb.

THE GREAT PERSECUTION

Following a long crisis that shook the Roman Empire to its foundations, Diocletian was named Augustus by the eastern army in November of 284. In order to share the burden of restoring Rome, Diocletian named Maximian his co-emperor in 286. In the spring of 293, in the face of mounting difficulties, he further enlisted two *caesares* as lieutenants and future successors—Galerius to serve under him in the East, and Constantius under Maximian in the West. Hence, the "Tetrarchy" was established in which four emperors divided up the empire along territorial lines. This political system was reinforced by a clear religious base: the Tetrarchy claimed that they were assuming the earthly place of the traditional deities. Jupiter was manifested in Diocletian and Galerius, while Hercules was represented by Maximian and Constantius. Moreover, Roman religious traditions were vigorously reinstated in an atmosphere of extreme patriotism.

The Christians certainly presented an obstacle in the implementation of this great restoration project. Fourth-century Christian historiographers Lactantius and Eusebius of Caesarea attributed to the pagan fanatic Galerius the inception of these anti-Christian politics that would crash down on the church beginning in 303. In fact, from the final years of the third century, there were already Christian martyrs despite the fact that no official edict had been handed down. This happened on account of decisions made by the head of the Tetrarchy himself or through the simple application of military rules. For instance, between 295 and 299 at Tingi (Tangier), the centurion Marcellus threw off his badges, and at Theveste, a recruit named Maximilianus, the son of a military veteran, refused to enlist in the army. They claimed to be servants of Christ and did not want to make sacrifices to the emperors. The rebellious were condemned for refusing to serve in the military and they were subsequently decapitated; it was necessary for the government to make examples of such dissenters.

Faithful to their convictions, these Christian soldiers and officers were led to abstain from participating in any event that celebrated any official pagan belief. Also, in the tradition of Tertullian, they invoked their faith as a basis for refusing to follow certain orders, which created an intolerable situation for the military authorities. The authorities could have at least understood and accepted the anti-military or "conscientious objector" position of these soldiers as Africa had already been deeply troubled by tribal revolts—the Quinquegentanei and Bavares in Mauretania Caesarea and in the Numidian high plains. Despite these disciplinary measures by the military, it cannot be concluded that such sanctions were signaling an imminent persecution.

From February 303, to February 304, Diocletian and his colleagues in the Tetrarchy issued four successive edicts that shaped the "great persecution"—undoubtedly, the most ruthless and lengthy persecution in the empire's history and one that would have dire consequences for the African church. The fiercest repression occurred in the regions controlled by Maximian (including Africa) and Galerius. Initially in Proconsularis and Numidia (we have no accurate information on the repercussions in the Mauretanias), the governors and civil magistrates were content to conduct searches in order to set fire to church buildings, liturgical objects, and holy books. Basilicas were often confiscated and, at times, even destroyed.

Many bishops and priests, later referred to by the infamous title *traditores* ("traitors"), yielded to the demands of the civil magistrates who presided over the investigations. At times, however, some clergy who eventually complied did show at least a semblance of resistance. Some church leaders resorted to clever strategies to protect their Holy Scriptures. For instance, Bishop Mensurius of Carthage hid the Scriptures away from the basilica and placed heretical books in their place to be confiscated by the authorities. Having learned of this deception, the proconsul Annullius, depicted by some apocryphal *acta* as the most severe of the persecutors, chose not to pursue the matter. However, this maneuvering by Mensurius would later be considered a punishable act of cowardice by the Donatists and some ardent confessors. Not feeling the call to martyrdom, Bishop Donatus of Calama was clever enough to convince the imperial agents to accept books on medicine. Yet investigations and searches were not always carried out by such ignorant or compliant magistrates. This is clear from the minutes of an interrogation recorded May 19, 303, under Munatius Felix, the civil magistrate of Cirta. After seizing gold and silver chalices and other valuables from the church, Felix demanded that other objects also be handed over. A jewelry box and silver lamp, which had been concealed in the church library, were then surrendered. "You will be put to death if you do not find them," the official clerk inventorying the items had warned. When Felix was told by church leaders that the Scriptures were in the possession of the readers (*lectores*), the magistrate ordered two sub-deacons to tell him the readers' names. They responded, "We are not traitors, put us to death instead" and then were immediately arrested. Though they had surrendered some liturgical objects, they could not bring themselves to compromise the identity of their brothers. Another interesting aspect of this report is that many of the other items confiscated were articles of clothing set aside for the poor in the community: "Eighty-two tunics for women, sixteen tunics for men, thirteen pair of men's shoes, forty-seven pair of women's shoes, and nineteen farmer's coats."

Some local authorities were inclined to show mercy to the Christians, which at times resulted in a measure of cooperation between the government and church. For example, at Carthage, Cirta, and Calama, police agents were hardly zealous about entering a church building to confiscate Christian Scriptures. Perhaps the greatest example of cooperation between the church and civil authorities occurred at Abthugni (Henchir el-Souar located southeast of Carthage). Having observed that, following the first edict of Feburary 303, churches in neighboring towns had been destroyed and church properties desecrated, the small town's *duumvir* (Roman official) Alfius Caecilianus was content to carry out a basic investigation. The local church was simply closed, the episcopal chair removed, and some documents were taken; however, none of the other anticipated actions were carried out and Christians were not threatened with the death penalty. It seems that there was evidence of some sort of agreement between Caecilianus—an artisan who worked alongside his laborers—and Bishop Felix, who maintained a friendly relationship with the *duumvir*. Forewarned by the pagan *duumvir* to leave town on the day of the investigation and interrogations, Felix avoided the risk of becoming a *traditor* through his absence that day. It should be added that in this modest and peaceful village, none of the measures dictated by the edict and that targeted individuals—such as burning incense offerings in honor of the gods or emperors—were applied. Thus, the local authorities—simple, honest, and peaceable men not given to fanaticism—avoided giving the clergy or their flock the alternative forced on other African Christians: deny their faith or become a "hero."

At the beginning of 304, after the last edict was delivered, persecution took a new turn—surely due to Galerius' influence—and governors were given free rein to show their severity toward the church. Such governors included Valerius Florus in southern Numidia, whose actions were mentioned later in the works of Optatus of Milevus and Augustine. In a renewal of the measures prescribed by Decius, the edict called for a universal sacrifice throughout the empire; those refusing to comply were faced with the death penalty or a sentence to hard labor in the mines.

Despite the weaknesses of its clergy, the African church had no lack of martyrs. From the *Acts of Saturninus*, later used by the Donatists, we learn about a group of forty-nine martyrs—thirty-one men and eighteen women—from Abitina in Proconsularis. The martyrs largely had Romanized African names, except for a handful that had Punic or Libyan names. While most of them probably came from modest backgrounds, they were joined by one *senator*—a *decurion* or military officer from Carthage. Though the local bishop Fundanus had handed over Scriptures to be burned in the forum by the civil magistrates, the Christians continued to meet secretly on Sundays in a private home. Worship was led by a presbyter named Saturninus before the group was arrested by magistrates and their security force. Legal proceedings began, and the group was transferred to Carthage where on February 12, 304, they appeared before the tribunal of the proconsul Anullinus and were officially accused of continuing secret meetings despite the dictates of the imperial decree. An extended period of interrogation followed, especially for Saturninus who refused to hand over the Scriptures. His answer to the proconsul was "I have them [the Scriptures] in my heart." Afterward, all of the accused were thrown into prison, stretched out on racks, and pierced with hot iron nails. The *Acts of Saturninus* do not indicate whether the group was executed or, as a later Donatist document appended to an official Roman document indicated, if they were left in jail to die of hunger.

As it was in Cyprian's day, the number of apostates, among the clergy and church members alike, was quite considerable, even without the threat of systematic violence. For instance, in December, 304,

Anullinus was, according to the *acta*, applying Diocletian's fourth edict and attempting to convince a certain Crispina at Theveste to sacrifice to the gods by telling him: "As you know, everyone in Africa has done it." The proconsul was certainly exaggerating to some extent in his clever maneuvering, which alternated between intimidation and persuasion, in order to influence a good number of Christians to deny their faith. Yet his tactics failed as Crispina, who was later beheaded, refused to sacrifice. In Proconsularis, primarily at Carthage, and in Numidia, including Theveste and Milevus, Christians were found to be so committed to their faith that they did pay with their own lives. Referring to the Numidian church, which was particularly persecuted, Augustine, who often cited the example of Crispina, wrote: "Many, arrested because of their refusal to sacrifice, suffered all sorts of evil, underwent cruel torture and were put to death: these should be rightly honored as martyrs."

Taking into consideration all of the evidence about this period of bloody persecution, it should be noted that it actually occurred over a relatively brief period in Africa. Beginning in May 303, it came to an end during the spring of 305 through the application of an "act of toleration," well before any official edict was given. The actual return to "peace" was not sanctioned until 307 during the reign of Emperor Maxentius. At this point, the African church would experience a more serious crisis from which it would never fully recover—a crisis that came as a sequel of sorts to the period of persecution and would forever divide the church.

ADDITIONAL RESOURCES

Delehaye, *Les Origines du culte des martyrs.*
Duva, "Densité et répartition des évêchés dans les provinces africaines au temps de Cyprien."
Février, "Aux origines du christianisme en Maurétanie Césarienne."
Saxer, *Vie liturgique et quotidienne à Carthage vers le milieu du IIIe siècle.*

The Donatist Schism and the Division of African Christianity

THE ORIGINS OF DONATISM

Among the myriad issues raised in Roman African studies, the Donatist crisis is by far the subject that has elicited the largest amount of scholarly work. Theses and dissertations—new and old, and often arriving at contradictory conclusions—continue to be published despite the inability to reach a firm conclusion on this movement that surged in Africa over the course of the fourth century prior to its disappearance two centuries later. Though the Donatists were initially deposed at a council presided over by the pope in Rome in 313, they were still being condemned in 596, when another pope, Gregory the Great, called upon imperial officials to carry out legislation against the schismatic African group. In light of the uniqueness of the period, the multiple implications of a schism that rose up against the *catholica*, and the resolute African context in which the schism was born and developed, it becomes increasingly difficult to reduce Donatism to a few simple components or to a mere moment in history.

The surviving literary evidence concerning the movement is, of course, important; however, we possess relatively few works written by Donatist authors. The majority of the evidence comes from Augustine and his colleague, Bishop Optatus of Milevus. Both men were ardent defenders of the Catholic church in the schism; thus their writings are decidedly anti-Donatist. While historical documentation can be received through a critical reading of such texts, it should be noted that Optatus was writing around 365, some forty years following the developments he addressed. Similarly, Augustine's treatises and letters were written a century—perhaps three full generations—after the movement's birth. Aside from this literary evidence, relatively rich but also clearly biased, other historical evidence pertaining to the Donatists can be drawn from canons from the period's African church councils; official imperial documents, including the *Theodosian Code*; the minutes of court proceedings involving the Donatists; and a significant amount of archaeological material.

The crisis was ignited under circumstances similar to those already observed in the schisms following the Decian persecution, in which Novatus and Felicissimas advocated an uncompromising and rigorist position toward the *lapsi*. The latter, as noted, were apostates who submitted to the imperial edict to sacrifice and, once persecution had ended, requested to be reconciled with the church. At this stage, however, the church at Carthage was no longer under the capable leadership of a bishop and primate like Cyprian, who could uphold unity and discipline within the church.

Though dissenting movements, indeed a source of aggravation for the church at Carthage, probably developed within the period of the "great persecution," the Donatist schism itself did not flower until 307—though some scholars have suggested 312. This developed after "peace" was accorded by Maxentius, who had come to power in the fall of 306 and whose power was recognized in Africa in the months immediately following. Other events also radically changed the church's place in the Roman Empire, beginning in Africa. For instance, from 308 to 310, Africa became detached from Rome when the usurper Domitius Alexander came to power. Thus, in the midst of an already complicated context, another crisis developed with an apparent pretext—an ecclesiastical quarrel between opposing clergy regarding the integrity of the church—that was in reality an indication of deeper problems. Indeed, during the fourth and fifth centuries, African Christianity was characterized by intense turmoil, and social and cultural problems were often expressed, even violently, through religious forms. This was the case despite the fact that Donatism, a catalyst for social tensions in Africa, never attained the status of an official entity.

The "Protocal of Cirta," the minutes of a gathering of bishops that probably convened in the spring of 307 and included the episcopal election of Silvanus, offers some interesting insights. The council was presided over by Secundus of Tigisis, the Numidian primate, who seemed to be committed to a serious and rigorous spiritual life. Yet there were several bishops taking part in this election, including Silvanus, who had been accused of being *traditores* during persecution. This group also included a certain Purpurius of Limata, who had not only diverted money intended for the poor for his own gain, but had also murdered two of his nephews. Thus, this episcopal consecration took place in the midst of much social upheaval. Elected under pressure from the crowds, the new bishop was carried in triumphal procession by peasants from the surrounding areas, and valets from the circus, while flanked by prostitutes. Cirta's clergy and believers—desiring to confer this position on a fellow citizen and man of integrity, free from all suspicion of compromise—were unable to make their voices heard. Hence, it seems quite clear that in the Numidian capital, socio-economic issues prevailed over ecclesiastical disputes and church order.

Around 305, after the death of Mensurius, the Carthaginian primate whose values have already been the subject of criticism, his former deacon Caecilianus, an unlikely candidate for uniting the clergy and the people, was named as his successor. Thus, following the council of Cirta in 307—the same year that Maxentius issued an *indulgentia* granting peace to the church in Africa—the provincial bishops came to Carthage and, without waiting for their Numidian colleagues to arrive, consecrated Caecilianus as bishop. This was immediately problematic because, traditionally, the bishop of Carthage was ordained by his counterpart—the primate or leading bishop of Numidia. A second problem arose because one of the consecrating bishops, Felix of Abthugni in Byzacena, was under suspicion for his good relationships with local authorities and had been accused of apostasy during persecution—a charge for which he was later exonerated. When Secundus of Tigisis arrived in Carthage with seventy Numidian bishops, he declared Caecilianus' election to be null and void. Though the latter refused to abdicate his new position, the Numidians, with strong local support in Carthage, ordained Majorinus as bishop and primate. As a result of another conflict between church leaders ambitious to occupy or control the position formerly held with such integrity by Cyprian, another episcopal schism shattered the unity of African Christianity. From this point on, two rival altars were erected and two parallel church hierarchies began to oppose on another. An opposing communion that rivaled the official *catholica* was birthed, complete with a considerable number of clergy and a large membership, as well as its own councils, tradition of martyrs, and basilicas.

Majorinus, who had already appealed to Rome in order to present his case before the emperor, died before this could become a reality. In

313, he was replaced as the rival bishop of Carthage by Donatus of Casae Nigrae (perhaps given this name because of his episcopal position), who was known as Donatus the Great, the initiator of the schism. A prophet and teacher; an honest and energetic organizer, who was fierce in battle against his enemies, hard on himself, and ambitious and arrogant; a mentor to men; a shrewd diplomat, who won over his allies and attracted followers to his church; a speaker and writer, Donatus ably gave leadership to the schism for more than thirty years before being expelled from Africa in 347. He probably died in Gaul in 355, where he was exiled with other schismatic leaders.

THE DONATIST SCHISM AND POLITICAL AUTHORITY IN THE ERA OF CONSTANTINE

The schismatics made their appeal to the secular authority—Constantine, the new emperor of the western empire, who continued Maxentius' religious policies. From the beginning of his reign, he was benevolent toward the Catholic church, ordering all church property confiscated by the proconsul to be returned. Also, Constantine promised Caecilianus, whom he regarded as the rightful primate of Carthage, that Catholic clergy in Proconsularis, Numidia, and Mauretania Caesarea would receive a government subsidy.

Beginning in 313, the emperor brought together a special commission at Rome, under the pope's authority, to settle the African controversy. Ruling in favor of Caecilianus, the commission's verdict was also confirmed the following year at the council of Arles. Rejecting the decision, the losing schismatics retaliated by accusing Bishop Militiades of Rome of being a *traditor*. They thus presented themselves as the rightful heirs of Tertullian and Cyprian, rejecting a church that conspired with political authorities. Nevertheless, they appealed once more to the court of the emperor, who was becoming worried and irritated by the Donatist problem, which was tearing at the fabric of African Christianity. The schismatics were emerging as a social and political opposition to the central government. Constantine could not conceive of the church as anything but a faithful servant devoted to the political unity of the empire. Hence, as a divisive religious movement that opposed the official church's hierarchy, the Donatist schism was necessarily regarded as a political entity by the government. As public uprisings broke out here and there, the separatists were blamed, and repressive measures followed—though they were largely limited to Carthage. Hoping that his actions would bring closure to the matter, in November 316, Constantine again favored Caecilianus and ordered that all of the Donatist churches be confiscated. After such an order, those who refused to comply effectively became outlaws. The results of such rigorous political actions only worsened an already bad situation. The more the government intervened in the African controversy, which it simply understood as two opposing ideas about church discipline, the more the Donatists denounced the alliance between the state and the official Catholic church.

As persecution against the Donatists heightened, and the secular authorities brutally intervened in an area where they had no rightful authority, the state succeeded in fortifying the undying resistance of the "rebels." With the enthusiasm of new converts, the Donatists began to believe that, as their Christian faith was being attacked and suppressed as that of the martyrs had been under the pagan emperors, their only sufficient refuge from the authorities was a "spiritual" church—a pure movement that embodied the African religious spirit and had nothing to do with the interests of Rome, the pope, or the emperor. As the Donatists were expelled from their basilicas in Proconsularis and Numidia, the soldiers tasked with carrying out the imperial order against the schismatics did so with a great deal of violence. While claiming that their martyrs and leaders were constantly being taken before the tribunals, the Donatists could not hide the fact that among their clergy and even bishops there were many who compromised their faith in the face of persecuting authorities—a trend already quite apparent since Silvanus' election in 307.

Desiring to put an end to a consuming ordeal, and because of his failure to bring about religious unity—a necessity for political tranquility in the African provinces—Constantine issued an edict of toleration on May 5, 321. This decision was also imperative because the emperor needed to shore up support on the eve of the campaign that he was about to launch against his rival Licinius. As a result, exiled clergy were allowed to return to Africa, and the Donatists were granted religious freedom and the right to assemble in worship—given that the public order was not disturbed. Catholic church leaders were asked to deal with their Donatist counterparts with moderation and patience, despite the fact that the schismatics, aware of their newly empowered status, continued to act in a reckless manner.

Initiated by this edict favoring the Donatist church, the resulting period of peace allowed for the movement's consolidation and expansion. During a church council that took place between 336 and 340, 270 bishops met over a period of seventy-five days. Even at Rome, there was a Donatist community with its own bishop, nurtured by the schism in Carthage. Because the schismatics in the empire's capital did not have a basilica, they met in the catacombs of a certain hill. They were called *montenses* ("mountaineers"), which was also a pejorative reference to the group's uncultured ways. A meager presence in Rome notwithstanding, the Donatist schism was purely an African phenomenon. Indeed, the movement never took root outside of Africa and was never recognized by churches in the East or West.

From the first quarter of the fourth century, Donatism established itself between Tripolitania and Mauretania Caesarea, and particularly flourished in Numidia—the movement's cradle and the source of its most significant leaders. The Roman government's official policy was to avoid all confrontation with the Donatists. For instance, when they forcefully took over the Catholic basilica in Cirta in 330, the emperor chose not to expel the Donatists; rather, he built another church for the Catholics at his own expense. When Gregory, the most powerful prefect over the tribunal, attempted to take action against the Donatists in 336, he was insulted by Donatus. Yet according to Optatus, the prefect responded with "the patience befitting a bishop." Donatus, who played a decisive role in the schism's origins, was the uncontested leader of a church whose members regarded themselves as the only true Christians. As Monceaux has argued, Donatus should be remembered for his "ingenious organizational ability and his spiritual leadership."[1] When Caecilianus died, Donatus appealed to the Emperor Constans seeking recognition as the legitimate bishop of Carthage.

Quite occupied with re-establishing church unity, an area where his father had failed, Constans was zealous about orthodoxy and had already imposed his will in the eastern church over the Arian heresy. Thus, Constans could not ignore the Donatists, whose success posed a real danger to the Catholic church and to unity in the empire. In an effort to keep the Donatists from strengthening themselves through provoking social disorder, the emperor sent two imperial legates, Paulus and Macarius, to Africa in the spring of 347. Officially, their mission was to investigate

---

1. Cf. Monceaux, *Histoire littéraire de l'Afrique chrétienne*, 5.113.

the African religious situation; however, in reality, they were attempting to force a union with the Catholic church by bribing the most stubborn Donatist leaders. Upon arriving in Carthage, Paulus and Macarius attended the liturgical assembly led by Bishop Gratus, Caecilianus' successor. Convinced early on that the matter had already been decided in favor of the Catholics, Donatus denounced the wicked scheme. With his customary zeal, he challenged the state's right to interfere with church matters and affirmed, in the spirit of Tertullian, a separation of church and state: "What has the emperor to do with the church?"[2] While Catholic leaders received the legates as laborers in the cause of holy unity, Donatus instructed his clergy to ignore them and refuse them any hospitality—a response that could be observed throughout Africa. In Numidia, the charged mob was led to believe that the men had come to restore paganism. Failing in their mission, Paulus and Macarius wanted to resort to force but were met with very strong resistance, especially among the churches in Numidia.

The Donatist churches outnumbered their Catholic counterparts in Mauretania Sitifien and Numidia, a point raised by Augustine several times. For instance, in a letter dated between 400 and 405, well before the Donatist suppression following the council of Carthage of 411, Augustine referred to the schismatics as the "dominant party in Numidia."[3] More specifically, it was in the region of Cirta, with its high plains, austere culture, barley fields, and olive trees, that the movement got its start. Writing to the wealthy landowner Pammachius, Augustine spoke of "that part of the world where the fury of the Donatists arose, that is, in the midst of Numidia."[4] There were thirteen Numidian cities where the Donatist bishop had no Catholic counterpart, and the schismatics also had their fortified cities—Thamugadi and Vaga. During perilous times, the Donatist bishops met for councils in Vaga.

In the midst of a violent reaction set off by Paulus and Macarius' tactics, another rebellious Donatist faction arose. Though their origins were quite different, the Circumcellions would further aggravate the schism between the Catholic and Donatist churches.

---

2. Optatus *Against the Donatist Parmenianus* 3.3 [unless otherwise noted, all English translation of *Against the Donatist Parmenianus* are from http://www.tertullian.org/fathers/index.htm#Against_the_Donatists].

3. Augustine *Letter* 19.51 [English translation my own].

4. Augustine *Letter* 58.1.

THE CIRCUMCELLION PHENOMENON

The Circumcellions are first mentioned sometime between 340 and 345 when Count Taurinus, commander and chief of the Roman African army, intervened at the request of Donatist bishops to provide protection and subdue these "fanatics," whom the Donatist leadership could not control. Acknowledging their lack of authority over their own flocks, the bishops wrote: "The individuals in this region cannot be won over to the church through reason." Axido and Fasir, whose names indicate that they were indigenous to the region, were the ringleaders or the "chief saints" of this group.

The African count sent his troops through the crowds on market days and carried out a veritable massacre against the "bandits," an outcome that surely pleased the bishops. Despite the Donatist clergy's ban against the massacred victim's tombs being placed in the churches, the Donatist faithful prepared the graves, and the crowds venerated them as martyrs. This action seemingly combined religious faith with the battle for social justice. A general revolt by a significantly indebted peasant class, crushed by economic conditions that conversely favored the *latifundia* (agricultural estate) owners, peasant uprisings had developed independently and initially opposed the local ruling parties. The Circumcellions, on the other hand, were to forge their identity in the context of the oppressed Donatist church. It is very likely that these opposition efforts evolved, and that developing ideals captured the imagination of a new group of "fanatics," especially those seeking to imitate Axido and Fasir. Thus, the battle for social and economic justice of earlier days eventually gave way to a type of religious fanaticism. The acclamation *Deo laudes* ("God be praised") became a war cry as well as a liturgical expression that began to appear quite often on their epitaphs. They also referred to themselves as *agonistae* ("God's warriors").

Augustine, who waged a fierce polemic against Donatism and its leaders between 400 and 420, grew up in the Numidian province and was well qualified to understand the origins of the movement. However, as he was a part of the camp opposing Donatism, his testimony, like that of Optatus, must be accepted with caution—especially as he sought to establish a connection between the Circumcellions and Donatists in order to encourage imperial suppression of the Donatists. In his treatise *Against Gaudentius*, written against the Donatist bishop of Thamugadi, he related these past events:

Who is not aware of these people, who never tire of committing horrible crimes, who avoid useful work, who cruelly kill others and have despicably killed themselves. They primarily live in the countryside, yet they refuse to work the land. To find food, they wander from barn to barn, which has earned them the name Circumcellion. They are the most shameful group in the entire world, and very close to the African heresy.[5]

By making such claims, Augustine's primary goal was to show the origins and nature of this group (*circum cellas*, "those who wander from barn to barn"). In another work, Augustine made the same argument: "We call them Circumcellions because they wander around storerooms."[6] Because of scant and biased sources, numerous theories have been proposed—some of which are complementary—to try to place the Circumcellions in a certain category:

- Moral—Bands recruited from the lower classes, composed of the poverty-stricken, portrayed in a pejorative manner.

- Social—Evident from Honorius' law in 412, they were administratively classified as a conglomerate of free agricultural workers.

- Professional—As seasonal or day laborers moving from farm to farm, they hired themselves out during the harvest or to pick olives. Wheat and olives, at times cultivated in a hybrid manner, constituted most of the agricultural wealth in the countryside.

- Religious.

Some hypotheses have suggested that the name Circumcellion refers to wandering monks who frequented the chapels (*cellae*) of Donatist martyrs. According to Augustine, these pilgrimages were celebrations that turned into drunken orgies with groups of women calling themselves "religious Donatists."[7]

Though the Circumcellions' religious tendencies should not be underestimated, especially during a period of significant Christian expansion in Africa, this group has often been identified simply as a monastic order or sect, characterized by an uncompromising and simplistic atti-

---

5. Augustine *Against Gaudentius* 1.28.32 [unless otherwise noted, all English translation of *Against Gaudentius* are my own].

6. Augustine *Ennarations on Psalms* 137.3 [English translation my own].

7. Cf. Augustine *Against the Letter of Parmenianus* 2.6.19.

tude. While we should not forget that the movement originated in the context of peasant groups fighting for economic and social justice, the assertion that these were organized professional unions should not be taken seriously. Jobless seasonal workers or small farmers dispossessed of their land, they were reduced to wandering and pilfering, which explains why we find them in the marketplaces. These daily workers provided much needed labor in the major agricultural centers during the busiest times in the year (i.e., harvest); hence they often organized themselves into working groups. As the African economy developed, and a certain class profited from the political situation, these disinherited ones, feeling oppressed and watching their precarious situation get worse, aspired toward a "social revolution." Their aim was to put an end to the landowners' exploitation and liberate those miserably in debt, crushed at times from the demands of merciless creditors.

We noted that Augustine stigmatized the Circumcellions for killing themselves. He alluded to a series of recurring suicides in which these "stubborn ones," deeply traumatized by the vigorous crusade carried out by Constans' legates, believed that through their actions they could attain the rank of martyr. This epidemic of absurd behavior developed initially in the early years of the repression, and certainly by 347. These fanatics set themselves on fire and were burned at the stake, while others, at times in groups, hurled themselves from cliffs. Augustine wrote to Gaudentius: "We see gigantic rocks, mountains with gaping chasms, made famous by your voluntary martyrs. The herds on the bluffs have swallowed them up."[8] Numerous epitaphs, discovered at the foot of certain cliffs in central Numidia, were perhaps memorials to these "saints." Augustine added, "Killing themselves by jumping from rocky cliffs, into water, or into fire, was a daily game for these fanatics." Augustine also cited cases of suicide–volunteers, essentially inviting violence against their person: in a chance meeting with a magistrate along the road, some lobbied for a death sentence and appointment with an executioner; others, though unarmed, attacked the governor's escort in order to get themselves killed; some threatened travelers along the road in an effort to provoke violence; finally, others disrupted pagan ceremonies, not for the purpose of knocking statues of Roman gods, but to provoke a massacre at the hands of pagans.[9]

8. Augustine *Against Gaudentius* 1.28.32.

9. Cf. Augustine *Letter* 185.12.

For when men of this sort were, before the attainment of unity, wandering about in every place, and in their insanity called Axido and Fasir "captains of the saints," no man could rest secure in his possessions. Written acknowledgments of indebtedness had lost their value. At that time no creditor was free to press his claim, and all were terrified by the letters of these fellows, who boasted that they were "captains of the saints." If there was any delay in obeying their commands, of a sudden a host of madmen flew to the place. A reign of terror was established. Creditors were hemmed in with perils, so that they who had a right to be supplicated on account of that which was due to them, were driven, through fear of death, to be themselves the humble suppliants. Very soon everyone lost what was owing to him—even to very large amounts, and held himself to have gained something in escaping from the violence of these men. Even journeys could not be made with perfect safety, for masters were often thrown out of their own chariots and forced to run, in servile fashion, in front of their own slaves, seated in their lord's place. By the judgment and command of these outlaws, the condition of masters and slaves was completely reversed.[10]

Optatus' position was faithfully transmitted by Augustine, who shared the same concern for protecting the public order against these self-appointed agents of justice. Augustine also made special mention of the debt-repayment issue. In a letter to the African Count Boniface in 417, in which he lumped together the Donatists and the Circumcellions to justify repressing the anarchists, the bishop of Hippo exhorted the general to do his civic duty by ensuring a healthy public order against these insurgents:

What master was not forced to fear his slave if his slave sought refuge under the protection of the Donatists? Who dared even to threaten a rioter or the instigator of a riot? Who was able to demand a reckoning from a slave who consumed his provisions or from a debtor who asked the Donatists for help and defense? Out of a fear of clubs and fires and imminent death the records of the worst slaves were destroyed so that they might go free. Lists of what they had extorted from creditors were handed over to debtors. Whoever ignored their harsh language was forced by harsher blows to do what they ordered. The homes of the innocent who had offended them were either razed to the ground or destroyed

10. Optatus *Against the Donatist Parmenianus* 3.4.

by fires. Some heads of families, men nobly born and well educated, were carried off barely alive after their attacks and chained
to a mill stone; they were forced by beatings to make it turn, as if
they were mere animals.[11]

COLLUSION BETWEEN THE CIRCUMCELLIONS
AND THE DONATISTS

While Donatist history certainly intersects with that of the Circumcellions,
the relationship between the schism and the seditious movement is complex and ambiguous, revealing more of a tactical connection than an ideological one. If the Donatist schism constituted a split along religious lines,
and thus a break with Rome, the seat of the church, the Circumcellion
group presented itself as a movement or union directed by social and
even political concerns, and thus opposing Rome, the seat of the empire.
To assimilate the two movements would mean mixing the religious with
the political—without transforming religion into a single movement of
protest with a socio-political agenda aimed at revolution.

In 347, during the imperial legates' mission, an alliance was apparently reached between the two dissenting parties—against the church that
was protected by the state, or against the order established by the Roman
government. The Donatists, therefore, acquired protection from the Circumcellions, which they had opposed just few years before. According
to Augustine, the Circumcellions would remain the Donatists' precious
allies and become their "armed branch."[12] It remains to be understood
why such an alliance was effective and served the cause of the schismatic
church, which could not be stamped as a church for the poor. As the edict
of 412 testified, the Donatist communion had attracted members from
every level of society.

A number of contradictions are apparent in this "union of circum-
stance." Indeed, Donatism's sociology, like its geography, was made up
of every class in African society: simple agricultural workers certainly
mobilized by the Circumcellions; large landowners, some of whom were
senators; average people from the villages; and city-dwelling aristocrats.
At the same time, it should be noted that not all members of the Catholic
church were from privileged backgrounds. Finally, it is not inconceiv-

11. Augustine *Letter* 185.4.
12. Cf. Augustine *Enchiridion* 17.

able that some Circumcellions were actually members of the Catholic church.

It would be overly simplistic, as it has often been done, to describe the general controversy as a conflict between city-dwelling, Romanized Catholics, and rural, Punic, or Libyan speaking Donatists. First, we cannot responsibly argue that the countryside was primarily occupied by the Donatists. Second, it should not be forgotten that the schism began at Carthage over the election of a bishop, and not in Numidia. These Donatist leaders were often Roman by birth or by culture, and Latin was the liturgical and theological language of the church. Third, a connection between Numidia and the rural countryside cannot be plausibly made. Recent archaeological research allows for a more nuanced understanding of the province. For instance, from the fourth century on, the population in the high Numidian plains, which were bastions for Donatism, was densely distributed and quite unlike the dispersions in rural areas. Further, the people were concentrated in strongly urbanized regions and in clusters of towns, as observed elsewhere in Africa. While Numidia did strategically provide protection from a repressive army and became the key reinforcement zone and sanctuary for a dissident church fighting for survival, one century after its birth, there were Donatist strongholds in Mauretania Caesarea and Proconsularis, in the region's interior as well as in the coastal cities.

Finally, despite the official attitude of opposition to political power preached by the schism's protagonists, we should not forget that at the beginning of the schism the Donatists were the first to take their case before Constantine. Also, as noted, they requested the intervention of soldiers from Taurinus against the Circumcellions. Later, they did not hesitate to make their appeals to Julian, the restorer of paganism. Also, in 395, amid the schism with Maximianus that divided their own church, the Donatists appealed to the proconsul's court to restrain these fighting brothers and to recuperate their confiscated basilicas. It is also clear that the Donatists benefited from the local Roman government (i.e., the Carthaginian Proconsul Seranus cooperated very much with the schismatics) and the imperial army. Ironically, the schismatics never ceased to criticize their Catholic counterparts when the latter benefited from such connections. Thus, it cannot be argued that the Donatist church even kept itself pure and free from compromise with the state.

It is evident that the movement benefited greatly from the Circumcellions. However, Donatism's growth and development should be attributed to its own dynamic nature, its organization, and the fervor of its members, who did not always share the opportunistic views of their bishops. It was only with caution that the bishops accepted the support of such a rebellious entity, whose motivations often seemed ambiguous and suspect, and quite foreign to the bishops' ideas and plans for the church.

The Circumcellions were a significant source of aggravation to the Donatist movement because of its revolt against the more privileged classes, whose greatest support came from the Donatists. Hence, this "church of the poor" represented a seed of discord within the Donatist–Circumcellion collusion and threatened to destroy the party. Also, through their disturbances, the Circumcellions discredited the Donatists in the eyes of their Catholic adversaries, those valuing the public order. However, the governing authorities seemed less provoked by the Circumcellions' actions. Thus, they resembled Tertullian and his early third-century supporters, who were regarded as "troublemakers" by the church hierarchy and remained under the suspicion of the *catholica*. As a result, actual meetings between the Donatists and "terrorists" only took place occasionally. Finally, the schismatic bishops, whose subordinate clergy in the villages and countryside were maintaining sympathetic ties with the Circumcellions, had no power to stop such questionable conniving. Ironically, these connections actually provided the most benefit to the bishops.

Sources like Optatus' account allow us to identify several phases in the movement, though every stage was marked by violence. After an initial revolutionary period following Axido and Fasir's initiative, agricultural workers, poor peasants crushed by their debts, and slaves all became organized. Also, as elements of the Circumcellion movement became too much for the Donatist bishops to handle, the bishops actually decided to employ the Circumcellions in defending their churches during the disastrous imperial mission of Paulus and Macarius. Finally, following the bloody repressions in which they were the victims, the Circumcellions provided a contingency of "fanatics," who, having failed in all of their goals of instituting a more just society for the oppressed and defending a church condemned by the imperial authorities, resigned themselves to a foolish plan of suicide where they would at least earn a martyr's crown. As noted, during Augustine's day this group was made up of a class of citizens from the lower echelon of society. Confined to the rural areas where there was a significant Donatist following, the majority represented little more than a poor and frustrated element of Christianity, always ready for violence but led by unclear ideals for social revolution. The number of "suicide" martyrs among them was quite high, and most of this violent activity was directed at the Catholic church or at ex-Donatist clergy. This activity was indeed a source of worry and burden for the Donatist bishops.

An initial example of solidarity between the Catholic church and the state occurred in the middle of 347, during the imperial legates' failed mission. As a result, the emperor issued an edict of "union" ordering a fusion of the two churches, and for the schismatics to hand over their basilicas to the Catholics. A political resistance movement was organized and a veritable religious war ensued that would ravage the Donatist churches.

Though the pagan writer Macrobius wrote a *Passion* about Maximianus and Isaac, who were martyred at Carthage, the most violent persecution took place in Numidia. When their escort was attacked near Vaga by bands of robbers who frequented the region, the imperial legates decided to make an example out of them. The Donatist bishop responded by gathering a group of Circumcellions to defend his threatened city. Having taken refuge in the church, the rebels and bishop alike were besieged by Count Sylvester's troops and put to death. Accused of conspiring with the rebels, the city's Donatist population was also massacred. Thus, the "artisans of peace" earned a reputation for inflicting torture, and their criminal acts would only encourage solidarity between all of the victims, the Circumcellions, and the Donatists.

Following a provincial church council in 347, the Donatist bishops decided to bring a grievance against Macarius, who maintained his headquarters in nearby Vegesela (Ksar el-Kelb) in the heart of Numidia, a cradle of Donatism. Written by a schismatic church leader for the purpose of commemorating the life and death of a Donatist bishop, the *Passion of Marculus,* one of the most significant pieces of Donatist literature, recounted this dramatic episode. Furious at their remarks, Macarius had the members of the delegation whipped, and Bishop Marculus, the leader of the group, was executed five months later at Nova Petra. From this point on, November 29 became an important day of commemoration in the Donatist liturgy, and many pilgrims began coming to honor the place where Marculus was martyred.

The period following 347—the *tempora Macariana* ("times of Macarius")—until 362 was even more difficult for the schismatic church. As Donatist basilicas were being confiscated and their leaders exiled, the schismatics began to refer to their Catholic counterparts as the "party of Macarius" or the "Macarians." Though they were allowed to meet to honor their dead, the members' enthusiasm had been crushed. There were, however, two bishops, both residing outside of Africa, who labored for their church's future: Pontius, Donatus' companion in exile, and Macrobius, a bishop in Rome.

For some fifteen years the Donatist movement was silenced, and Constans' edict of "union" was imposed by force. A great number of schismatics, including some bishops, went over to the Catholic church. Catholic church councils met in an attempt to sort out the spiritual status of clergy and laity who had come into the official church. Though their baptisms were declared valid, all attempts to honor the Donatist martyrs were forbidden. In 353, when Constantius II became *caesar* in the western empire, the "peace" that resulted from the edict of union was maintained. However, this would radically change when Julian became emperor.

FROM JULIAN'S EDICT OF TOLERATION TO THE GREAT AFRICAN REVOLTS

From the beginning of 362, three Donatist bishops, including Pontius, sent a petition to the new emperor demanding freedom of conscience, the right to worship, and the ability to promote their church. They further asked for their church to be restored and its basilicas returned, along with any confiscated property. Without delay, Julian decided "that everything should be restored to the way it was previously." This act of toleration, similar to what had already been granted to the Arians, generally reflected Julian's religious policies. Julian seemed especially willing to favor the Donatists—a movement that he despised as much as he despised the Catholics—because such toleration only intensified the mutual dislike and opposition of the two churches. Thus, the exiled bishops returned to their churches, and Parmenianus, a non-African, was set apart as Donatus' successor and began to lead the Donatist community at Carthage.

As the new imperial rescripts were enacted, the Donatists recovered their churches, properties, and liturgical buildings. The returned basilicas were then purified with "atoning" ceremonies: the walls and floors were washed with salt water, and the altars were carefully scoured to remove any trace of impurities from the hands of *traditores*. They declared that the sacraments offered by the Catholic clergy were null and void, and the eucharistic offering was thrown to the dogs. Legal cases were brought against the rebellious, and the judges ruled according to the new legal provisions. In other cases, the Donatist restoration was accompanied by atrocities. Optatus wrote:

> You came raging; you came full of wrath, rending the members of the church; subtle in your deceits; savage in your slaughters, provoking the children of peace to war. A large number you banished from their homes. Approaching with a hired band, you rushed upon the basilicas. Many of your party throughout numerous districts (which it would be too long to mention by their names) worked massacres so bloody, that the judges of the time sent a report to the emperor concerning deeds of such atrocity.[13]

Nothing remained of the illusory peace imposed by Constans, and, once again, Rome's policies resulted in great failure.

The liaison between the Donatists and the Circumcellions was becoming quite apparent. The latter, at the request of the bishops, were the primary agents of criminal violence and destruction and had little regard for the humiliation endured by the Catholic clergy or the consecrated virgins. These outlaws of yesterday endeavored to make known to their Catholic rivals the difficulties they suffered following the edict of 347. As Donatism was in the midst of reorganizing itself, an active propaganda campaign was revived, and the bishops convened several councils. These improvements were only temporary and would not have a future. In fact, Julian's reign was too brief for these new measures to have an enduring impact on the African religious landscape.

The emperors who came to power after Julian generally returned to politics that favored the Catholic church. Valentinian I, otherwise known for his neutrality on religious issues, decreed that bishops who required re-baptism—essentially the Donatist practice toward those coming from the Catholic church—were unfit for the priesthood. This was a classic

---

13. Optatus *Against the Donatist Parmenianus* 2.17.

case of the state interfering in a religious matter. Later, Emperor Gratian decided to confiscate the Donatist church buildings. With his edict from Thessalonica (February 28, 380), Theodosius declared Catholicism the official religion of the state. Those not professing Catholic beliefs were to be regarded as foreigners in the empire and were deprived of the essential civil rights of a Roman citizen. In all, no less than nine edicts were handed down by the government against the Donatists during this period. One law, issued June 15, 392—referred to by Augustine in his polemical work against Crispinus of Calama—slapped a crushing ten-sterling fine on all heretical bishops and clergy. Those unable to pay were flogged and sent into exile. In Africa, however, where the local and provincial administration was still in the hands of pagan functionaries who often showed significant benevolence toward those undermining the official religion, this legislation was hardly applied. It was in this context that the Donatists developed a good relationship with Nicomachus Flavian, an aristocratic Roman who embodied the pagan reaction to Catholicism and who served in 376 and 377 as the vicar of Roman Africa—the leader of all of the governors with the exception of the proconsul. Augustine labeled Flavian a defender of the Donatist party.[14] Hence, this period was characterized by decades of fluctuation between toleration and repression.

While the new legislation resulting from Theodosius' edict of 380 primarily targeted heretics, those guilty of "public crimes," the Donatists were not immune from prosecution. In fact, Augustine considered the distinction between heresy and schism to be fallacious. In his mind, when they seceded from the church following Caecilianus' episcopal election, the Donatists fell into the heresy of schism.[15] A decree from the very Catholic Emperor Honorius on February 12, 405, referred to Donatism as a sect that cannot be classified as a heresy; rather, he preferred the term "schismatic." Here, Honorius was probably making reference to Donatist attempts to get around Theodosius' anti-heretical legislation.

Throughout this difficult period, the Donatist church was under the leadership of Parmenianus. His episcopate lasting until 390, he became one of Donatism's best representatives and was even recognized by his adversaries as a man of integrity and moderation. As the Donatist church was experiencing significant growth, Optatus wrote his great

14. Cf. Augustine *Letter* 87.8.
15. Cf. Augustine *On Heresies* 69.

polemical and apologetic work in which he retraced the history of the schism and its excessive tendencies. In an effort to invite state intervention against the schismatics, he also highlighted their collusion with the state's enemies. In fact, during the final decades of the fourth century, the Donatist bishops would align themselves with insurgent groups that posed much more danger to the empire than did the peasant uprisings of the Circumcellions.

The Catholic bishop of Milevus elaborated at length on the relationships that developed between the Donatist leaders and two Romanized African brothers from a "feudal" family—an inadequate term at best to present the African context in this period. One after the other, Firmus and Gildo succeeded in provoking and leading some powerful uprisings in Africa. Beginning in the mountainous region of Kabylia, their revolts spread to the vast regions of Mauretania Caesarea and Numidia in the last third of the fourth century. These events certainly testified to significant socio-economic changes leading toward a certain sense of nationalism among the Africans. Though we should be careful about reading modern notions of independence into this fourth-century development, attitudes of autonomy and the desire to constitute an independent state can be observed.

The first uprising, led by Firmus, undoubtedly erupted in 370 and continued for three years with varying levels of success and failure. In order to end this war that threatened the empire's stability in the African provinces—Rome's "bread basket" and a key to its economy—Theodosius ordered his soldiers to carry out a systematic plan of terror and collective retaliation that ultimately drove Firmus to commit suicide. This chief of the Moorish confederations failed in his attempt to bring together a kingdom of Mauretanian peoples, and his family's tragic fate followed. Gildo, who had previously opposed his brother's rebellion, largely collaborated over a period of twelve years with the Roman state to the point of being named "count of Africa, the master of the cavalry and infantry." In 396, however, he began to pursue the same dream of African autonomy that had driven his brother. In order to crush the ambitious African, Rome conscripted his brother Mascezel, who promptly put an end to Gildo's hopeless adventure. After Mascezel's successful service to the empire, he was not allowed the opportunity to mimic the exploits of his two brothers. Kept busy following the orders of Stilicho, the leader of Honorius' militia, Mascezel faded from any place of prominence.

Firmus, whose father Nubel was probably a Christian, easily won a large following, particularly in the regions where the Donatists were strongly rooted. This included the city of Rusicade, which joined the rebellious faction at the instigation of its Donatist bishop. The schismatics' decision to align favorably with the rebels explained their lack regard for Romanus, the count of Africa. Characterized by the Latin historian Ammianus Marcellinus as a dishonest cynic, Romanus was a corrupt functionary who, according to the Donatists, was their most fierce persecutor. Beginning in 395, the Donatists and Circumcellions joined Gildo's revolt, which revealed their opposition to the government. In the purges that followed, all who involved themselves in the uprising were severely chastised. This was the case of the Donatist Optatus, the bishop of Thamugadi, who died in prison and then was later honored as a martyr. In his anti-Donatist treatises, Augustine referred to Optatus as "Gildo's servant" and "the Gildonian," while characterizing him as a mercenary, revolutionary leader, and counselor to the rebel chief.

The African peoples' tendency toward revolt cannot fully be understood without adding that Catholics probably also took part in the uprisings. There is no evidence to suggest that Firmus—a Christian like his brother Mascezel—was a Donatist. Gildo, on the other hand, remained a pagan. The question should then be posed: did the position of Augustine and the other bishops—offered thirty years later and appealing to the imperial authorities to quell the Donatists—accurately represent the spirit of African Christianity in Mauretania Caesarea during the period of the great uprisings?

SCHISMS WITHIN THE GREAT SCHISM

Beginning with the bloodily suppressed insurrections, the third- and fourth-century Donatist and Catholic church movements developed as political and military aims influenced religious history. The Donatist movement suffered even more difficulties—legal proceedings and physical beatings—at the hands of the imperial authorities due to its association with the revolts of Firmus and Gildo. During the same period, Parmenianus powerlessly tended to internal conflicts and division, often the result of personal quarrels, within his own church. Indeed, a series of schisms of varying levels of magnitude developed throughout the provinces, at times led by capable theologians such as the layman Tyconius.

A free-spirited and deeply religious man who desired reconciliation between Christians, Tyconius argued for some doctrinal points that were distinctly Catholic. In particular, he opposed the need to re-baptize those entering Donatist communions from Catholic ones, while rejecting the Donatist-alleged "monopoly" on spiritual truth. Despite being excommunicated by his bishops, he apparently remained committed to the Donatist church.

During this same period, around 370, another schism affected the Donatist movement in Mauretania Caesarea. Condemning his colleagues for doctrinal stubbornness and leniency toward church members who were guilty of violence, Bishop Rogatus of Cartennae broke with the movement. Hunted down and sometimes massacred by armed bands of Firmus' rebels (*Firmiani* as they called themselves) who were often employed by Parmenianus' followers, this small group advocated a moderate Donatism and a return to the tradition of Donatus the Great. They lived in the region of Caesarea and included around a dozen bishops by the beginning of the fifth century. During the group's brief presence, they defended themselves against the "official" Donatists by joining forces with another group—the "Maximianists"—who had just carried out their own schism against the church.

In fact, after succeeding Parmenianus in 391–392 as the Donatist bishop of Carthage, Primianus, a vulgar and violent man who represented the most extreme elements of Numidian Donatism, quickly brought dissension within his own circles. A council of some 100 bishops met at Cabarussa in Byzacena on June 26, 393, and replaced Primianus with the deacon Maximianus. The latter was a relative of Donatus, was more conservative, claimed to follow in the tradition of Cyprian, and best represented the opinions of Donatists in Proconsularis and Byzacena. The ensuing battle between the followers of Primianus and Maximianus became just as fierce as the fighting between the Donatists and Catholics. Indeed, Primianus and the 310 bishops at the council of Vaga in 394 met to support their rightful leader, to bring condemnation against the usurper Maximianus, and even to bring these schismatics to justice by confiscating their basilicas. They won their case. As the "Maximianists" were merely a sect—though quite active until the beginning of the fifth century—their bishops, regarded as neither Catholic nor Donatist, were not admitted to the council of Carthage in 411. Thus, the Donatist church found itself divided into three factions of varying prominence: the followers of Primianus, the largest group with especially large numbers in Numidia; the party of Maximianus, located in the eastern provinces; and Rogatus' followers, in Mauretania.

These divisions provided Augustine with a new argument for attacking the Donatist principles for baptism—that Catholics entering the sect must be baptized because their previous baptism, received outside of the true church, was of no value. The bishop of Hippo made a point to show the inconsistency of the self-proclaimed "cardinal Donatists" on this matter. Thanks to imperial legislation, Primianus' party emerged victorious over the "Maximianists" and immediately reintegrated the latter into their communion without re-baptizing them. Hence, these heretics of yesterday were now admitted to fellowship on the basis of a baptism conferred outside of the true Donatist church.

Despite these schisms within the schism (others could also be cited), the Donatist church, liberated by Julian's act of toleration, attained a level of power and stood up to its enemies. In some cities, the Donatist bishop had no opposing Catholic bishop. In other towns and cities, including those situated along the coast far from the Donatist centers in Numidia or the high plains, the schismatics outnumbered the Catholics.

Thus, when Augustine arrived at Hippo in 391, the Donatists were the majority of the Christian population in that city. According to Augustine, some Catholics were joining the Donatists in order to win lawsuits.[16] Otherwise, relationships between the Catholics and Donatists, when they were not completely severed, were quite awful. The Donatist bishop of Hippo went so far as to forbid the city's bakers from baking bread for Catholics. Such discord even existed within families: "A husband and wife agree to share the same bed, but they are in disagreement over the altar of Christ. . . . Parents and children share the same home, yet they do not share the same house of God." As the Catholic bishop gathered his flock for worship, he was forced to endure the noisy commotion from the neighboring basilica where the schismatics celebrated their martyrs' feast days. At Fussala, a Punic-speaking town located forty miles from Hippo, the entire population was Donatist and the first Catholic clergy attempting to serve there were attacked. Augustine set apart Antoninus, a Punic-speaking cleric, to lead the church at Fussala; however, Antoninus would later be removed because of corruption. In the same diocese, the village of Thiava was also entirely Donatist.

16. Cf. Augustine *Sermon* 46.7.15.

A number of rich landowners became Donatists and all of their workers, whether they liked it or not, were obliged to join the sect. The colonists, tenant farmers, and cultivators on the large Roman agricultural estates (*latifundia*) were also required to accept the religion of their master. Thus, using his own means, the Donatist Bishop Crispinus of Calama acquired a farm within the diocese of Hippo and forced the eighty Catholic farmers working the land to receive the second, schismatic baptism. According to Augustine, they were "forced into the water despite their displeasure and groaning."[17]

Again, despite its own internal schisms, social problems, significant uprisings against the Roman state that certainly weakened the movement, and despite imperial legislation against the Donatists (though poorly applied), the sect continued to find strength in Africa. During this period, the Catholic church was largely under the leadership of mediocre bishops, and the *catholica* had essentially lost the vitality of just a short time ago, when it faced persecution. It is significant to note that the church, which had been anchored in a solid conciliar tradition since the days of Cyprian, did not meet for a council for forty years in the latter half of the fourth century. Perhaps on account of toleration or weakness, Bishop Genethlius of Carthage, who probably acquiesced to the deteriorated state of the church, made no mention at all of Donatism while presiding over the council of Carthage in 390. Genethlius enjoyed a kind and peaceful rapport with the schismatics, which included allowing an imperial decree against them to remain dormant. With the exception of Optatus' polemic against the Donatists, which he waged on his own initiative, there was no official Catholic reaction to the schism during this period.

The Catholic church's recovery was put on hold until Aurelius was elected bishop of Carthage in 391–392. A man with significant leadership abilities, Aurelius restored discipline to the church by renewing the practice of regular church councils—no less than twenty-six meetings took place under his leadership. At the same time, Augustine, Aurelius' personal friend, was ordained a priest in Hippo in 391, and began his own battle with these "heretics." Indeed, the bishop of Hippo's work would deliver the decisive blow against the Donatists. Prior to the end of the fourth century, no specific legislation had targeted African Donatism—the edicts of Valentinian and Gratien had only addressed Donatism in

---

17. Augustine *Letter* 66.1 [English translation my own].

Italy. Yet the revolts of Firmus and Gildo had certainly directed Rome's attention across the Mediterranean to the Donatists in Africa.

Disappointed by imperial measures that failed to bring results, some Catholic bishops held out hope that a solution could be reached through meaningful discourse between the leaders of the two churches. From 395, Augustine had the opportunity to meet with Fortunius, the aging bishop of Thubursicu Numidarum (Khamissa, south of Tebessa), an encounter that Augustine considered fraternal and promising. However, his "ecumenical" hopes turned out to be an illusion as the Donatists were unwavering. Petilianus, a former lawyer who became the bishop of Cirta, described these offers to meet as "waging war through kisses."[18] Primianus, the Donatist bishop of Carthage, responded with contempt: "It would be an unworthy act for the sons of martyrs to come together with the offspring of *traditores*. With the letters of emperors, they come against us, we, who possess only the Gospel. The true church is that one that endures persecution, not the one that persecutes."[19]

THE COUNCILS OF CARTHAGE AND THE POLITICS OF HONORIUS

The conciliatory approach ended in a fiasco. In 404, Maximianus of Vaga—the former Donatist bishop who maintained his position when he crossed over to the Catholic church—was ministering in a rural church when he was attacked at the altar and seriously injured. He was then thrown from the top of a tour, and left for dead. After recovering, he quickly traveled to Ravenna to show his injuries to the emperor and ask for protection. He was apparently joined at the royal court by other victims of Donatist violence.[20]

In an exasperated state, the Catholic bishops met for a council at Carthage in June 404. Contrary to Augustine, who continually called for dialogue with the schismatics, there were many Catholic bishops hoping for a forceful solution—not unlike that of Macarius—that would bring peace. In light of the differing opinions present at the council, two del-

---

18. Augustine *In Answer to the Letters of Petilianus* 2.17.38 [English translation my own].

19. Augustine *After the Conference Against the Donatists* 2.31.53 [unless otherwise noted, all English translations of *After the Conference Against the Donatists* are my own].

20. Cf. Augustine *Letter* 185.27–28.

egates were dispatched to Italy to request that the *Theodosian Code* would at least be reinstated, and that the Catholic church also receive police protection. However, alarmed by the increasingly deteriorating situation in Africa—with Maximianus as the key witness—Honorius made a swift and extreme judgment even before the African delegation arrived.

Between February 12 and March 5, 405, the emperor, well-advised by his powerful counselor Stilicho, issued an edict of "unity" that was delivered in three decrees. The measures were quite severe and even surpassed the demands made by the council of Carthage. Because of their practice of re-baptizing Catholics, which indicated a divergent sacramental theology, a text was issued denouncing the Donatists as heretics, and they found themselves subject to the existing anti-heretical legislation. Though Donatist followers were not forced to return to the Catholic church, their movement was effectively outlawed, making unity with the Catholic church the only alternative. The Donatists were ordered to surrender their basilicas to the Catholics, and they were forced to suspend their meetings. Failure to comply with the last provision was punishable by the confiscation of homes, property, or meeting places. Finally, Donatist clergy, who persisted in the heresy, were exiled indefinitely.

Though these measures were promptly applied in Carthage, where unity was apparently realized, the story was quite different in the provinces, where the emperor repeatedly intervened to assure that the legislation was being carried out. The main resistance came from local authorities, often Donatist or pagan magistrates, who showed little zeal to apply the edict. The grammarian Cresconius, a Donatist layman, remarked that it was unthinkable that a Christian would advocate persecution; rather, he should work strongly to oppose it. In the areas where the Donatists had large followings, the violence only intensified, and the Catholic clergy were often the victims of ill-treatment. Augustine himself barely escaped an attempted Circumcellion ambush only because his guide made a wrong turn in the road. When Maximinus, the Donatist bishop of Siniti near Hippo, joined the Catholic church, the schismatics, fearing that the church members would follow the example of their pastor, sent a messenger to the village proclaiming that "if anyone is in communion with Maximinus, his house will be burned."[21]

The Catholics responded by addressing their petitions to the royal court, and they were heard. For example, in November 408, several edicts

21. Augustine *Letter* 105.4.

were issued, including one that prohibited non-Catholics from working as civil servants or in the imperial palace—a stringent sanction among many that targeted the Donatists. Augustine responded by writing to the Proconsul Donatus, who brutally enforced the laws even to the point of applying the death penalty, and begged the official to refrain from such punishment that eliminated the possibility of repentance.

In most cases, across the provinces in both urban and rural areas, the Catholic bishops easily acquired the Donatist basilicas. In order for ex-Donatists to enter their former places of worship, they were required to adopt a more amenable approach to worship. Aware of the Donatist devotion to the cult of martyrs, Bishop Evodius of Uzalis (El-Alia, near Bizerte), who also took an interest in the miraculous, desired to accommodate the new members of his flock. Hence, he acquired some relics of St. Stephen from the East and had them placed in the church. In a short period of time, Uzalis became famous for the "miracles" performed by the saint.

The new measures enacted by the emperor progressively moved certain Donatist bishops toward being open to the idea of meeting with their Catholic counterparts. Though the Donatists were able to retain their basilicas and positions of leadership in the countryside, especially with the support of the Circumcellions, the opposite was true in the cities where the magistrates were present and upholding the imperial laws. In the context of such religious coercion, many Donatists converted out of necessity, though their resentment was often apparent.

Some citizens who previously supported the schism for the advantages they gained with local authorities developed—out of expedience or prudence—a respect for the Catholic bishops who enjoyed the support of the emperors. On the other hand, as a result of Theodosius' religious policies beginning in 381, which targeted the Manicheans and then all heretical groups (the first explicit mention of Donatism was in a law delivered by Honorius February 22, 407), the laws affected individuals and forbade them to will inheritances, to settle affairs, to sell things, or to draw up a contract.[22] Also, they were denied the services of the local government and were not allowed a proper defense in court. Many Donatists in the ruling and upper classes lost their land, which left them quite concerned about maintaining their place in society. This perhaps allows us to under-

---

22. Cf. *Theodosian Code* 16.5.

stand the motivation of Celerinus, a senator who probably became the proconsul of Africa in 429. Originally a Donatist, he owned a great deal of land in the region of Hippo where all of the settlers were Donatists, yet he later became a disciple of Augustine and a member of the Catholic church.

Though this firm political approach toward the schismatics was re-affirmed through various decrees and laws until 409, in 410, the government's policy was essentially reversed. Communicated through an edict delivered to the African count in Carthage, the text prescribed that "from this point on, one should not embrace Christianity unless compelled to do so by his own free will." From June 14, the Catholic bishops, already gathered for a council, began to protest the government's action and sent a delegation to Ravenna to demand that the edict be repealed. On the other hand, the Donatists, after many agonizing years, benefited from this brief, bright interval in which their freedom to assemble and worship was restored. For instance, Macrobius, the Donatist bishop of Hippo, who had previously escaped imperial persecution and taken refuge in some remote Punic-speaking villages, returned to Hippo and took control of his basilica. Augustine, with much discomfort, observed his counterpart return to the city, escorted by a rowdy band of Circumcellions, whose language he could not understand.

Honorius' rationale for publishing the new edict probably had nothing to do with his preferred religious policies for the empire. A better explanation comes with closer examination of the developing drama in Italy, which was under the threat of Alaric and the Visigoths. Alaric, who had already convinced the senate to declare Attalus the new emperor, sacked Rome. In the panic-stricken atmosphere, Honorius believed it necessary to gather together all of the empire's forces, Christians and non-Christians alike. Having already delegated much responsibility to the Germans, some of whom were pagans, Honorius also needed to curb his overzealous support of the Catholic church by renouncing religious intolerance. However, on August 24, 410, the Vandals besieged Rome and the following day Honorius issued a decree reversing his position on toleration, and all of the previous measures against the Donatists were reinstated. Following Alaric's invasion, things were never the same, and the stakes changed completely. As Rome was besieged and burned over a period of time, the resulting famine was devastating. Without grain imported from Africa, Alaric's position in Rome was unsustainable, which made it necessary for him to take control of the African territories. In order to oppose this plan, Honorius needed to count on the Africans' loyalty, which he managed to win. On one hand, it was imperative that he respond to the *latifundia* owners and their appeals for decreased taxes. On the other hand, he needed to satisfy the Catholic bishops, who demanded that unity finally be realized. This was, of course, contrary to repeated official announcements mixed with an edict of toleration that allowed the Donatists leaders to regain their positions. All of this struck a blow to the official church.

THE COUNCIL OF CARTHAGE OF JUNE 411

The Catholic council of June 14, 410, requested that the emperor put into effect the previous legislation rendering Donatism illegal, while also issuing a call for unity with the Catholic church. That is, the bishops demanded that the emperor intervene and use his authority to organize and convene a conference, force the Donatists to participate, and send an imperial commissioner to preside and judge between the two parties. In this way, an enduring and mutually beneficial unity could be achieved between the rival churches. Appealing to the secular authorities for help in solving ecclesiastical disputes was, of course, not a new practice in this era of "Christian emperors." The emperors had taken an active role in addressing the Arian controversy, and, in the origins of this schism, the Donatists were the first to address their case to Constantine, asking him to judge between themselves and Caecilinaus at Carthage.

Honorius willingly agreed to the Catholic bishops' request. Evidently biased in a case that he already considered decided in the Catholics' favor, Honorius issued a rescript on October 14, 410, naming Flavius Marcellinus as his commissioner in the matter. Marcellinus, a young senator, tribune and imperial notary, was a civil servant with a scrupulous conscience and was a member of the Catholic community at Rome. The conference was called a *collatio*, a confrontation, and it lasted four months. Arriving in Carthage at the end of 410, the commissioner issued an edict on January 19, 411, summoning all of the African bishops to appear by June 1. For those Donatists fearing the Catholic official's partiality, an added assurance was communicated—no matter the outcome of the controversy, those responding to the June invitation would be allowed to return to their homes without fear and could keep their basilicas. In a show of favor, the local authorities were ordered to restore, at least for the duration of the conference, the Donatist places of worship that were previously confiscated by earlier edicts. Finally, Marcellinus ordered the magistrates, under the threat of sanctions, to suspend all legal proceedings against the Donatists until a definite judgment could be reached.

Perhaps reassured by these actions or fearing an impending judgment in absentia, not to mention being pressured by Primianus to come and proclaim to the imperial emissary the true Christianity, which only they could defend, the schismatics took advantage of this opportunity to show the emperor's representative their church's greatness despite the persecution it suffered. Hence, beginning May 18, 284 Donatist bishops from every province made their presence known in the streets of Carthage, arriving in a solemn procession. "Neither age nor the rigors of a long journey" dissuaded them—including some distinguished old men—from making the trip. On the opening day of the conference, 286 Catholic bishops also appeared, while another twenty were detained due to illness.

The conference, which took place in the public baths of Gargilius, met for three days—June 1, 3, and 8. During these days, the Donatists refused to "sit down with the unrighteous" and, in the presence of the imperial commissioner, they remained standing "like Christ before Pilate." Not at liberty to sit down in front of the bishops, the layman Marcellinus also remained standing. This adversarial attitude characterized well the atmosphere of a meeting that was far from being "ecumenical."

While the minutes of the first two sessions of the council have survived in their entirety, we have only a portion of the *acta* from the decisive third session. In the course of the meeting, both parties were represented by seven delegates, while secretaries for both delegations recorded the debates. Though a detailed history of the conference is beyond the scope of the present work, it should be noted that the first session focused on verifying the list of delegates appointed by each church, and confirming the identities of those present. Initiating numerous administrative squabbles from the outset, the Donatists proved to be quite combative. Petilianus of Cirta, who initiated the first skirmishes, was the principal spokesperson for the schismatics. In the second session, further tactics for obstructing the meeting could also be observed. In an effort to stall the proceedings and have more time to prepare their attacks, the

Donatists demanded a five-day recess so they could receive a copy of the first meeting's minutes.

At daybreak on June 8, the conference reconvened to address the question: who are the true Catholics? Petilianus issued the challenge to his opposing "Donatist accusers" to establish the identity of those who represented the true church. Through addressing the origins of the schism, the debate took a decisively different turn. Augustine, who emerged as the official spokesperson for the Catholic bishops during the conference, showed that Caecilianus' episcopal election had been perfectly in order, and that the accusation that he had been consecrated by a *traditor* had been refuted by every piece of documentary evidence. Hence, the evidence possessed by both parties showed that the schism had no basis. Finally, the bishop of Hippo asserted that the Catholics believe in one church, spread out all over the world, and that African Christians have fellowship with this universal church.

Nothing further was required by Marcellinus, who adjourned the final session in order to write up his decision. Afterward, he gathered together each party's delegates to pronounce his judgment: "proclaiming that the Catholics have confounded the Donatists based on all of the documentary evidence provided."[23] Finally, on June 26, in an effort to inform the public about the debates, the imperial commissioner had the minutes of the conference posted, along with an edict of unity in favor of the Catholics.

As promised, the Donatist bishops were allowed to return home without being disturbed. The edict communicated the parameters and possibilities for the schismatic bishops. If they joined the Catholic church, then they could retain their basilicas and episcopal positions. This did raise a problem of jurisdiction that would need to be worked out with Catholic bishops in the same areas. On the other hand, those bishops who refused to go over to the Catholic church became subject to the existing anti-heretical legislation. Referencing the 405 edict, Donatists were ordered to surrender their basilicas to the Catholics, including those that they were temporarily allowed to use before the conclusion of the conference. They were further subject to the law of August 25, 410, which made heretical meetings (i.e., Manichean, Donatist) an offense punishable by

---

23. Augustine *Brief Meeting with the Donatists* 3.25.43 [English translation my own].

death. Finally, landowners and magistrates were held responsible for any Donatist or Circumcellion activities that took place on their land or within their jurisdiction.

THE TRIUMPH OF THE STATE CHURCH

Through a new edict of "unity" issued January 30, 412, Honorius added to the measures passed by Marcellinus. Vigorously reinstating the older edicts of coercion, he penalized obstinate Donatists by imposing financial sanctions, which included the confiscation of property. Renegade clergy, continuing to lead Donatist worship services, were banished from Africa. Over the next fifteen years, Honorious or his successor Valentian III would pass eight more laws renewing this edict or increasing its severity (March 21, 413; June 17 and August 30, 414; August 25 and November 6, 415; July 6 and August 6, 425; and May 30, 428). In fact, this relentless legislation did not come to an end until the eve of the Vandal invasion in Africa. Augustine also continued his battle against the "defeated" schism. A couple of months after the *collatio* of 411, he published a *Brief Meeting with the Donatists*. Afterward, he wrote a longer work addressed to the Donatist laity, reminding them of the main issues discussed in the conference, while also warning them of their pastor's tactics and untrue assertion that "in spite of their defeat, they spread where they can and as they have the opportunity."[24]

The bishop of Hippo had written his other key anti-Donatist treatises between 400 and 406: *Against the Letter of Parmenianus, On Baptism, Against the Letters of Petilianus,* and *Against Cresconius the Grammarian.* Along with these, he wrote some fifty letters and preached 100 sermons against the schism. In 420, Augustine wrote his last polemical work, *Against Gaudentius*—the Donatist bishop of Thamugadi and delegate at the *collatio* at Carthage in 411, who was also Optatus' famous successor.

Honorius' edicts, despite their severity, fell far short of resolving the Donatist controversy. Initially, these measures succeeded in exasperating the "defeated," and the violence only intensified. In light of the steady stream of imperial edicts during this period and the constant reminder to provincial authorities to enforce them, it seems that in areas where

24. Augustine *Reconsiderations* 2.66 [unless otherwise noted, all English translations of *Reconsiderations* are my own].

the schism was dominant, the local authorities largely ignored the measures.

In the region of Hippo, the Donatist Bishop Macrobius attempted to re-open the churches located on Celerinus' land, gathering Donatist followers for meetings there.[25] Around 416, at Mutugenna, a rural village not far from Hippo where rebaptisms continued despite the imperial legislation, two priests were brought to the city to give an account for the activities. One of the two, a certain Donatus, refusing to comply with the summons, threw himself from the side of the mountain on which he was travelling, and seriously injured himself. Later, Donatus would commit suicide by throwing himself into a well. Faithfully continuing a long-established tradition that the sect glorified, the fiercest Donatist followers were seduced by the temptation of martyrdom—by means of weapons, jumping from cliffs, through drowning, or by setting themselves on fire.

Augustine sarcastically referred to these martyrdoms, which he regarded as pure folly, and remarked how the practice was actually becoming less common: "Who is not aware of these individuals, who just a short time ago, subjected themselves to various types of death? Now, in comparison, there are relatively few who burn themselves in the fires they have started."[26] In a letter to Count Boniface, the African commander in chief who was quite shocked by such behavior, Augustine reassured him that these were old practices that predated the earliest legislation given by the emperors, and that these deaths should not be cause for such alarm. Rather, these actions should be regarded as a manic shift in the context of otherwise excessive behavior.[27] Gaudentius, who refused to appear before Dulcitius, the tribune ordered to enforce the edicts, threatened to burn himself alive inside his basilica where he was barricaded with his flock. Responding to a civil servant who had asked for Augustine's counsel, the bishop of Hippo made the following comments about heretics committing suicide: "it is undoubtedly better that some of them perish in their own fires rather than all of them burn in the everlasting fires of hell as a punishment for their sacrilegious schism."[28] Though the Donatists were still in the majority in Africa, the Catholics also failed to treat their rivals

25. Cf. Augustine *Letter* 139.2.

26. Augustine *Against Gaudentius* 1.29.93.

27. Cf. Augustine *Letter* 185.3.12.

28. Augustine *Letter* 204.2.

with Christian gentleness. During the conference of 411, one bishop from Proconsularis announced rather frankly: "In our town, whoever declares himself to be a Donatist will be stoned."

Rebel violence—especially that of the Circumcellions—was generally aimed at the Catholics. To make his case for government intervention during this period, Augustine did not hesitate to remind Boniface of the perilous times: attacks at night, looting, homes being raided, and churches being destroyed and burned. In a letter written around 411, he denounced the torture and the "sufferings of the servants of God."[29] In another letter, dated around 417, Augustine mentioned bishops and priests who had suffered atrocities: Rogatus of Assuras (Zenfour), a former heretic who had his hands and tongue cut off; some who had their eyes put out; and others who were put to death.[30]

It was also during this period that the devout imperial commissioner Marcellinus was decapitated at Carthage on September 13, 413. His death was ordered by Count Maurinus, who had falsely accused Marcellinus of taking part in Heraclianus' attempted rebellion in Africa. In reality, he was arrested and executed at the instigation of those who opposed his judgment at the end of the 411 conference. Marcellinus was one of Augustine's dearest friends, and the bishop of Hippo had dedicated *The City of God* to this official whom he regarded as a "beloved son." Augustine attempted to pursue the matter in Carthage and even sent a delegation to Ravenna; both efforts were in vain. Regardless of its apparent position of privilege, in reality, the African church had little clout before the imperial authorities.

Despite these dramas and defeats during a turbulent period in Africa, and despite a "small minority that remained obstinate," the edict of unity in 412 generally yielded positive results for the Catholic church. For instance, the Donatist community in Caesarea united with the Catholic church, while others, according to Augustine, were converted without ever leaving the church. In Numidia, despite the significant amount of Donatist resistance, the majority joined the Catholic church. The Catholic bishops were ordered to commit themselves zealously to the work of bringing the Donatists into the church. Those negligent in the task risked being denounced by their colleagues and could be turned over

29. Augustine *Letter* 133.1.
30. Cf. Augustine *Letter* 185.30.

to the imperial commissioners dispatched to the provinces. They were then given six months to repent or face excommunication. According to Augustine, religious coercion had its advantages. Between 400 and 403, the bishop of Hippo, in his treatise to Petilianus, wrote: "a rod is also a form of grace."[31] Elsewhere, he added:

> And I would say this against those who were only wrapped in the fog of heretical error—for which sacrilege they would pay the penalties they fully deserve—and have not dared to injure anyone out of any violent madness. But what should I say against these whose pernicious perversity is either repressed by a fear of fines or is taught by exile how the church is spread everywhere.[32]

The Donatists could travel abroad and, in every place, find the church—that which they so strongly opposed without truly understanding it.

According to Augustine, *disciplina* was largely a means of teaching—"an education through restraint." Quite evident from the Donatist migrations to the Catholic church following the decrees of 408, the motivations for "conversion" were not always very pure or disinterested. These rehabilitated schismatics seemed moved by the desire to find shelter under the government's laws, to return to a peaceful public life, and the freedom to conduct business without the fear of having property or belongings confiscated. On the contrary, the poor could no longer count on the security and the alms provided by the Donatist church. As the schismatic churches were deprived of their material resources, the poor had no choice but to appeal to the *catholica*. Thus, the destitute had the possibility of benefiting from Donatist resources transferred to the Catholic church, and also the means already at the disposal of the official church.[33] The laws of 408 actually proved to be a providential means of bringing the misled flocks to the true faith, including the worst fanatics who joined the church and repented of their previous ways. Augustine wrote to the Donatist bishop of Cartennae: "Oh, if I could show you how many sincere Catholics we now have from the Circumcellions! They condemn their former life and wretched error."[34]

---

31. Augustine *In Answer to the Letter of Petilianus* 3.1, 5 [English translation my own].

32. Augustine *Letter* 89.2.

33. Cf. Augustine *Letter* 185.8.36.

34. Augustine *Letter* 93.2.

Collective conversions also occurred, reminiscent of an earlier time when, under the orders of Donatist landowners and farmers, the Donatist communions were swelling. For instance, from the time that the *Theodosian Code* was reinstated, the Senator Pammachius enrolled the Donatist settlers working his lands in central Numidia in the Catholic church. In a letter sent with a delegation of bishops visiting Pope Anastasius, Augustine thanked the senator for his praise-worthy initiative. He added that the settlers were willing, "with the greatest diligence," to follow their master's orders. Augustine encouraged his illustrious correspondent not only to circulate his letter among Roman Christians who owned land in Africa, but also to send them to Africa and follow Pammachius' example. When the bishop of Hippo exhorted Celerinus, the richest landowner in his diocese, to come to the true church, he knew that Celerinus' conversion would also instigate that of his workers.[35] On the other hand, fearing the zealous Donatist threats toward the *traditores,* many peasant workers on the *latifundia* did not budge that easily. For example, workers on Festus' land in the region of Hippo balked at every invitation to the Catholic church. Augustine counseled the landowner to persuade the workers by sending someone that they knew to appeal to them. He instructed Festus to meet discretely with the individual before sending him out to the land to speak with the tenants.[36] According to the edict of 412, slaves refusing to follow their master's example were ordered to be whipped until they relented.

While integrating the Donatist faithful into the Catholic church posed some difficulties—often due to the challenges of converting of a staunchly Donatist population, which at times included threats to block conversion efforts—assimilating the Donatist clergy was even more arduous. Apart from ultra-conservative leaders like Petilianus of Cirta, a certain number of Donatist leaders united with the Catholic church out of fear of the law, while others, following the lead of their flocks, converted in order to retain their position. Finally, others personally took the initiative to join the Catholic church, and then endeavored to lead their congregations there. Donatist "deserters" were threatened with being put on public display, or worse, being put to death.

---

35. Cf. Augustine *Letters* 56–57.
36. Cf. Augustine *Letter* 89.8.

This raised a second, related issue: could Donatist clergy seeking reconciliation with the Catholic church continue in their priestly role? Since the council of 251, in accordance with the rigorous discipline in the African church in Cyprian's day, clergy performing penance after being involved in schism were forever stripped of their sacerdotal functions. A council met in Rome in 386 and effectively reconciled some Donatist clergy through the imposition of hands, a public form of penance that removed the clergy's *ipso facto* (excommunicated status). In light of the ongoing crisis of recruiting Catholic clergy, the church was led to pursue some positive alternatives for integrating converted Donatist clergy into church ministry. Before the conference of 411, Donatist clergy were promised that if they joined the *catholica*, they could maintain their priestly status. In 412, Augustine wrote to two former Donatist priests, Saturninus and Euphrates, exhorting them: "With faithfulness and joy, carry out the ecclesiastical duties that accompany your clerical office."[37] Though Augustine believed that a reconciliation ceremony was necessary, including the imposition of hands by Catholic clergy, he found no reason to exclude ex-Donatist clergy from serving the Catholic church. In 401, the African bishops, aware of what it would take to bring peace to the church, had already gone over this issue of church discipline and decided that converted schismatic clergy could remain in leadership of their converted flocks. The edict of 412, however, could not force the Donatist clergy to convert, on a conscience level, to the Catholic church. According to the decree, if they discontinued their worship assemblies and activities, they would be free from hard labor, yet they would lose their position of authority. Refusing this degradation, the majority of bishops were compelled to flee into the non-Romanized countryside and remote areas where they were beyond reach of imperial control and repression. A council of thirty Donatist bishops actually met at Cirta in 418. Their business included setting apart some bishops and deciding who would be pardoned and readmitted into the ranks of the Donatist clergy—even those who had spent time among the *traditores*. The latter were allowed to continue as Donatist priests if they had not accepted a similar appointment with the Catholics or preached a sermon in a Catholic meeting.

Another problem, which provoked serious tension, including some maneuvering and intrigue, was finding the best way to integrate Donatist

---

37. Augustine *Letter* 142.4 [English translation my own].

churches and their bishops into existing Catholic dioceses. It is not certain whether this issue of jurisdiction was settled prior to the Vandal invasion in Africa. Initially, a three-year deadline was established to put into effect the necessary reorganization. However, in most cases, none of the parties involved could be satisfied, and the effort resulted in little more than temporary solutions and shaky compromises as one diocese overlapped with another. Selflessness was indeed a rare quality among the bishops during this process, as we can only imagine the diverse personalities that emerged among the approximately 600 Donatist-Catholic dioceses in the African provinces.

In cities without a Catholic diocese, the converted Donatist bishop continued to lead his flock and assumed this role for the Catholic church. Hence, Donatist conversions also resulted in the removal of local "parishes." On the other hand, when the congregations of Catholic and converted Donatist bishops overlapped—though this did not always happen because the territories were so large—several solutions were proposed. Augustine recommended that, when there were two bishops in the same diocese, they sit together in the liturgical assembly and rotate meetings between the two basilicas, with each bishop presiding over the liturgy in his particular basilica. This solution was hardly practical as rival bishops, accustomed only to rude confrontation, had little warmth or sympathy for one another. For the most part, the churches reached an agreement that they would divide the diocese into two equal portions. A temporary solution, the diocese would be unified again upon the death of one of the pastors. Despite these adopted measures, countless conflicts, which weighed heavily on an atmosphere of "church unity," arose.

Truthfully, the African *catholica*, torn apart by the great schism, never again recovered perfect unity. The last known Donatist epitaph was discovered at Ala Miliaria (Beniane, south of Mascara) on the southern border of western Mauretania Caesarea. It commemorated the construction of a church in honor of a saint named Robba, sister of the Donatist Bishop Honoratus, who died in the "grip of the *traditores*" in 434 during the Vandal occupation.[38] Aside from this evidence, documentation from this period is rare, and it is often difficult to identify inscriptions recovered from Numidia prior to the sixth century. The Donatist movement apparently continued underground and included a few abrupt surges

38. Cf. Diehl, *Inscriptiones latinae christianae veteres*, 2052.

that plagued Catholic leadership until the Byzantine conquest of Africa. It seems that Donatism regained some momentum in southern Numidia during the papacy of Gregory I. From 590 to 596, the pope appealed to the secular authorities to put down the sect, and even convened a church council to address the issue. He also wrote to the bishop of Bruttium in southern Italy, warning him that Manicheans and Donatists from Africa might be attempting to infiltrate his church. In 722, Gregory II alerted his clergy about the danger of the "rebaptized." Though certainly a baseless concern, Gregory's fears are indicative of the great fear that had overcome the church as a result of the African schism.

ASPECTS OF DONATIST RELIGIOUS THOUGHT

Donatism arose as a movement of protest led by men, leaders and followers alike, who were absolutely convinced of and deeply motivated by the justice of their cause. At the same time, it was a movement focused on a very anachronistic goal. That is, the Donatist position on the relationship between the church and state was quite appropriate to the period of the pagan emperors who were persecuting the church. It comes as no surprise that the schismatic movement came to fruition during the last period of persecution—a period from which the Donatists claimed their origins. Like Tertullian before them, the Donatists were not completely hostile to the state; they simply wanted nothing to do with it. In their regard, political power was quite useless "because it is only in the church that the commandments of the Law can be taught to God's people."[39] It was the church that provided the only source of power, which was embodied in the bishop, the shepherd of his people. Though the Donatists could not ignore the imperial authorities, who never ceased to put pressure on them, and though the schismatics at times appealed to the state, their concerns were always dismissed—except in the notable case of the Emperor Julian. Writing to the Catholics in order to remind them of Paulus and Macarius' mission, Petilianus of Cirta wrote: "But what have you to do with the kings of this world, in whom Christianity has never found anything save envy towards her?"[40]

39. Augustine *Against Cresconius* 1.10.13 [English translation my own].

40. Augustine *In Answer to the Letter of Petilianus* 2.92.202 [unless otherwise noted, all English translations of *Against the Letter of Petilianus* are from *NPNF* 1.4].

Despite the assertions of some, we are unable to make a clear connection between Donatism and a national resistance movement against the Roman state. Though the schismatics had an intermittent relationship with the Circumcellions, and had well-known ties to Berber leaders like Firmus and Gildo, the argument for an overarching fourth-century resistance movement comprised of the Donatists and these other elements is quite fallacious. It should be noted that Donatism never declared itself the ideological or social spokesperson for the poor and the oppressed. When the Donatist leaders spoke of poverty and presented their movement as the "church of the poor," this claim signified that they did not enjoy the same privileged status with the state that the Catholics did. When they opposed the Catholic church, they also refused every form of compromise with the state and the world. In their minds, the Roman world was not the key to establishing a Christian world.

The Donatists were anachronistic in that they refused to integrate into the political and social world of their day. With that, they stubbornly sought to maintain a status quo that was already outdated. Regarding themselves as the rightful heirs of the African church's glorious past, especially Cyprian's legacy, they fought zealously to preserve this heritage. For instance, their ecclesiastical organization was just as it had been before Diocletian's persecution, they retained the old African Latin Bible (though the Catholics had adopted Jerome's Vulgate), and their liturgical calendar had not developed to include seasons like Epiphany.

The Donatist faithful continued to call themselves "the church of the pure," in contrast to the Catholic communion of *traditores*. In a long letter to Vicentius, his former fellow disciple who became the schismatic bishop of Cartennae, Augustine reminded him that, in their second council, the Donatist bishops had voted to readmit into communion—without rebaptism—"the *traditores* guilty of grave sin, as though they were innocent (*integri*)."[41] Yet, shortly afterwards, the Donatists abandoned this position, completely contradicting their sacramental theology. They condemned Tyconius, who, along with Vitellius Afer, was their best theologian, because of his contrary ecclesiology. Opposing the Donatist view that unless the church ("the bride of Christ") was completely pure, it was rendered completely impure, the wise exegete argued that the church was composed of the good and the wicked—straw mixed together with seed.

41. Augustine *Letter* 93.10.43.

The Donatists endeavored to identify with Cyprian, often abusing his teaching that "there is no salvation outside of the church." The third-century bishop of Carthage held that baptism received in a heretical context was of no value, and that the apostolic church was the only means of conferring salvation to men. Thus, the Donatists taught that purification and sanctification could only be found in the so-called Lord's flock, which is why they re-baptized Catholics coming into their communion. Petilianus of Cirta described the latter in this way: "Those who have polluted their souls with a guilty laver, under the name of baptism, reproach us with baptizing twice, than whose obscenity, indeed, any kind of filth is more cleanly, seeing that through a perversion of cleanliness they have come to be made fouler by their washing."[42] In short, receiving baptism from a bishop outside of the Donatist church was like entrusting one's soul to a dead person.

In order for the sacrament to be valid in the Donatist church, it was not imperative that the minister personally be morally above reproach; rather, it was the holiness of his faith and his right standing with the church that mattered most. Thus, he needed to be in full communion with the church, in whose name he administered the sacraments. Hence, it was an unpardonable sin for one to separate from the communion of saints through heresy, schism, or being a *traditor*—sins of an ecclesiastical nature. Therefore, those who committed such sins were rendered incapable of offering what they did not possess. According to the Donatist bishops, there was a straight line between the church, baptism, the forgiveness of sins, and salvation.

Despite being viewed by the Catholics ("Caecilianus' offspring") as an unfortunate flock and lost in the "party of Donatus," the schismatics were supremely confident of their church's eventual triumph. Because all Catholics, following Caecilianus, had fallen into apostasy, and because Christianity had only flourished in Africa, "the most obstinate Donatist puritans argued that 'only Africa had a fragrant aroma, everywhere else has a stench.'" They claimed that Simon of Cyrene, who helped Jesus carry the cross on the way to Calvary, was himself an African. Naturally, stemming from their uncompromising sectarian spirit, they cared little for the great number of believers in the world who were not part of their fortressed communion. As one Donatist bishop related, they were like

---

42. Augustine *Against the Letters of Petilianus* 2, 4, 51–55, 117–125.

Noah's ark—tightly shut up to keep the saving waters of baptism from escaping, while also keeping the soiled waters from the outside from entering. In fact, they needed to keep a careful eye on the Catholic church, which, supported by the earthly powers, "took delight in biting in order to draw blood, and fattening itself on the flesh and blood of the saints."[43] We should note that, quite unlike some of the strongest Catholic Christians who pursued a religious and ascetic life in a monastic context, the Donatists thoroughly rejected monasticism, which cut fraternal ties—the "enclosed garden and sealed fountain" united around the bishops.

The Donatists regarded themselves as the true Catholics, and during the conference of 411 their leaders referred to themselves as bishops of the "true *catholica* and of authentic Christianity." Not employing "catholicity" as an expression of universal faith, they used it to mean a pure body of believers in full communion with their bishop; that is, in the tradition of Cyprian, the bishop was a mediator, a source of holiness, and a guardian of the pure faith in his church. In short, the Donatists desired to monopolize the Christian faith. Augustine wrote indignantly: "and the frogs cry from the marsh, we alone are Christians."[44]

A church of saints and the pure; the bride of Christ; the great brotherhood gathered in the ark of salvation; a perfectly sealed vessel, and with believers united by an *esprit de corps* and a common hope, the Donatists also laid claim to a final title—"the church of the martyrs." Reflecting on its historical roots, African Christianity exalted itself through the blood of its martyrs. Cyprian, whose authority was supremely venerated, desired to be an example of a martyred bishop. He wrote: "the appointed leader in the church should bring glory upon all his people by making his confession in their midst."[45] Hence, part of being God's suffering people included martyrdom. Continuing Tertullian's thought—"the blood of the martyrs is seed for the Christians"[46]—Petilianus wrote: "Therefore I say, He ordained that we should undergo death for the faith, which each man should do for the communion of the church. For Christianity makes progress by the deaths of its followers."[47] In the Numidian countryside,

43. Optatus *Against the Donatist Parmenianus* 2.4 [English translation my own].

44. Augustine *Expositions on the Psalms* 95 (96).11 [unless otherwise noted, all English translations from *Expositions on the Psalms* are from *NPNF* 1.8].

45. Cyprian *Letter* 81.1.1.

46. Tertullian *Apology* 50.16 [English translation my own].

47. Augustine *Against the Letter of Petilianus* 2.89.196.

Donatist chapels were erected on sites where martyrs were believed to have fallen. Their bodies or relics placed under the altars, a cult of martyrs developed that included feasts being celebrated in the vicinity of the tombs. Despite difficulties with dating due to insufficient data, it is probable that these chapels were built and frequented by Donatist believers between 380 and 450.

The Donatists were apparently not alone in their devotion to a cult of saints or martyrs. Quite aware of the development, Augustine wrote to the clergy and believers in Hippo: "Is not Africa filled with the bodies of holy martyrs?"[48] Among these martyrs, it is quite difficult to distinguish whether they were Donatist or Catholic. Though the majority of fourth- and fifth-century martyrs' epitaphs in Numidia are commonly believed to be Donatist, a martyr's church affiliation cannot be conclusively determined based on a simple inscription. Sometimes, such decisions were made because the martyr's name was of Punic origin and was not included in the list of martyrs or church calendar at Carthage. The number of Donatist martyrs recorded was especially high in 347, during the somber *tempora Macariana* when Bishop Marculus was killed, and also between 405 and 412, the period of Honorius' edicts. This list does not, however, include the Circumcellions, who died between 340 and 347.

This hardening conflict that divided African Christianity was further expressed in the opposition between the church of the martyrs and the *traditores*—a faceoff between good and evil. As noted, this glorified, mystical, and somewhat pathological regard for martyrdom, which idealized a testimony given in blood, drove some fanatics to commit suicide. Advocating the apocalyptic tradition championed by Tertullian, one aspect of this theology certainly characterized the Donatists—suffering persecution at the hands of the wicked. In fact, for the Donatists, this was an indisputable sign of their election by Christ, who had declared blessed those who suffer persecution and who do not retaliate. Donatism articulated its most compelling apologetic by being a martyr church.

Schisms and heresies significantly characterized the Christian adventure in Africa, which begs the question—was African Christianity, with its long history and deep roots, represented better by such heterodox movements than by official Catholic orthodoxy? Among all of these movements, Donatism, with its specific religious aims, seems to

48. Augustine *Letter* 78.3.

have been the most "African." It was the only group that was birthed and died on the same soil, where it blossomed and flourished for more than three centuries. Moreover, it is likely that because of its strong influence, which wore down the Catholic church's resistance, Donatism indirectly encouraged other heresies to take root in Africa—a strongly religious context marked by excessive pagan beliefs and practices that predated the Phoenician arrival in Carthage.

ADDITIONAL RESOURCES

Barnes, "Beginnings of Donatistism."

Brisson, *Autonomisme et Christianisme dans l'Afrique romaine de Septime Sévère à l'invasion vandale.*

Congar, "Introduction générale."

Crepsin, *Ministère et Sainteté.*

Duval, *Loca sanctorum Africae.*

Duval, *Auprès des saints, corps, et âmes.*

Février, "Martyrs, polémique, et politique en Afrique (IVe–Ve siècles)."

Février, "Toujours le donatisme, à quand l'Afrique."

Février, "Religion et domination dans l'Afrique romaine."

Frend, *Donatist Church.*

Frend, "Circumcellions and Monks."

Kriegbaum, "Kirche der Traditoren oder Kirche der Märtyrer? Die Vorgeschichte der Donatismus."

Lancel, *Actes de la Conférence de Carthage de 411.*

Lancel, "Les Débuts du donatisme: la date du 'Protocole de Cirta' et de l'élection épiscopale de Silvanus."

Maier, *Le Dossier du donatisme.*

Mandouze, "Le donatisme représente-t-il la résistance à Rome de l'Afrique tradive?"

Mandouze, "Les donatistes entre ville et campagne."

Marrou, "Survivances païennes dans les rites funéraires des donatistes."

Tengström, *Donatisten un Katholiken.*

CHRISTIANITY IN A PAGAN SOCIETY

Already quite large in Cyprian's day, the African *catholica* continued to grow after the peace of Constantine, and the church became quite an enterprise, complete with all of the associated ambiguities. While the entire African population included six million inhabitants in the first half of the fifth century, the Christian population—including Catholic and Donatist churches—never surpassed one-third of the total population, and probably numbered around two million.

Let us first consider the role of paganism at this time. Despite the religious policies carried out by the emperors following Constantine, and Theodosius' edict of February 18, 380, which made Christianity the official religion of the state, the traditional Roman cult always had its followers. For example in 382, while still a student at Carthage, Augustine attended a ceremony in honor of Caelestis, the mother of heaven:

> I myself, when I was a young man, used sometimes to go to the sacrilegious entertainments and spectacles; I saw the priests raving in religious excitement, and heard the choristers; I took pleasure in the shameful games which were celebrated in honor of gods and goddesses, of the virgin Caelestis . . . and on the holy day consecrated to her purification, there were sung before her couch productions so obscene and filthy for the ear—I do not say of the mother of the gods, but of the mother of any senator or honest man . . . before her shrine, in which her image is set, and amidst a vast crowd gathering from all quarters, and standing closely packed together, we were intensely interested spectators of the games which were going on, and saw, as we pleased to turn the eye, on this side a grand display of harlots, on the other the

virgin goddess; we saw this virgin worshipped with prayer and with obscene rites.[1]

To avoid the mistake of overemphasizing paganism in Augustine's day, it should be noted that a vibrant paganism had already existed before then and was just as present in the influential administrative spheres as it was among the indigenous population. It was thriving in intellectual circles where, since the reign of Julian, the traditional religion experienced a veritable revival. Noted previously, Ba'al Hammon, the great Punic god of the sky and the harvest, continued to be revered in Roman Africa as Saturn. Wearing a Roman toga to preserve his prestigious identity, he was a regular object of worship in the Libyo-Berber ceremonies.

At Hippo and throughout the rest of Africa, the Christian magistrates were always a significant minority. Though the bishop was among the important civic leaders, his authority carried little weight. For example, as previously noted, despite his entreaties before the proconsul, Augustine was unable to secure a pardon for his friend Marcellinus. Some believed that the intervention of a well-placed pagan at the local or provincial level was actually more effective than that of a Catholic bishop. For example, around 400, Felix and Quintus, *decuriones* from Hippo, began their appeal to the proconsul by first turning to Symmachus—the leader of the pagan opposition and former African proconsul (373–374). As prefect of Milan and member of the ruling council, he had also gotten involved in the conflict with Bishop Ambrose over the re-establishment of the pagan Altar of Victory in Milan.

A large number of high-ranking officials in the African provinces—vicars, proconsuls, governors, and legates—did not conceal their sympathies with paganism and, in opposition to imperial legislation, favored the traditional religion. Indeed, it would be difficult to imagine such devoted pagans dealing severely with their fellow co-religionists. In 372, Symmachus dedicated two statues to the Victory in the Capitol at Carthage. Other Roman officials persisted in building temples or erecting statutes to the traditional deities while serving the "Christian" empire. It was not until Honorius' edict of November 15, 407, that the order was given to destroy pagan altars, remove statues, and turn over the pagan

---

1. Augustine *City of God* 2.4, 26 [unless otherwise noted, all English translations of *City of God* are taken from *NPNF* 1.2].

temples for public use. Though Honorius probably threatened the magistrates who had failed to apply the anti-pagan legislation, the laws still remained largely unenforced.

With significant numbers of people in Carthage and Hippo becoming Christians, and a vibrant pagan presence, Augustine's account of the religious landscape is rather ambiguous. In one sermon, he declared that in Hippo, Christians could be counted in every household—though he fails to distinguish between Donatists and Catholics. He added that in every place, the Christians were outnumbering the pagans and that there were households without a single pagan adherent.[2] However, in another sermon, he deplored the pagan presence that filled his city, saying "So if the Roman gods have disappeared from Rome, why do they still remain here?"[3]

Paganism, indigenous or imported, enjoyed a remarkably strong presence in Africa in late antiquity, a fact that archaeology has continued to confirm. The traditional cults profoundly impacted the African worldview and even influenced some Christian practices. There were many faces to paganism, and, at times, it was expressed through popular ceremonies in which the crudeness bordered on the absurd. This was true of the processions devoted to Caelestis, the former Carthaginian deity Tanit, as well as the actions of her priests:

> Concerning the effeminates consecrated to the same great mother, in defiance of all the modesty which belongs to men and women, Varro has not wished to say anything, nor do I remember to have read anywhere aught concerning them. These effeminates, no later than yesterday, were going through the streets and places of Carthage with anointed hair, whitened faces, relaxed bodies, and feminine gait, exacting from the people the means of maintaining their ignominious lives.[4]

While still a young student, Augustine moved to Madauros, a town forty kilometers from Tagaste, to continue his studies. There, he observed firsthand the pagan feasts, perhaps in honor of the eastern goddess Ma,

---

2. Cf. Augustine *Sermon* 302.19.

3. Augustine *Sermon* 24.6.

4. Augustine *City of God* 7.26.

in which the *decuriones* and other civic leaders worked themselves into frenzies while flooding the city's streets.[5]

In a second account from Madauros, another face of late fourth-century paganism is presented. In this intellectual center, which was proud of its learned citizens and its most famous scholar Apuleius, the gods reigned in the forum, and statues of Jupiter, Juno, Venus, and Vesta were kept on display. A certain Maximus, a grammar teacher in the important Roman-African town, wrote to Augustine around 390, expressing his great delight that the provincial capitals were returning to their pagan heritage: "We see and approve that the forum of our city is inhabited by a crowd of salutary deities . . . For we worship our gods with pious prayers openly in the daylight before the eyes and ears of all mortals."[6] The grammarian continued by making the ironic connection between the Christian cult of martyrs and the indigenous pagan ones, including Migginus, Sanae, Lucitas, and the "chief martyr" Namphano. Popular among the Donatists and Catholics, the practice of the cult of martyrs was seen by pagans as a form of worshipping the dead, which prompted the adherents of Manes to mock the Christians.

In response to what he regarded as idolatrous notions, Maximus opposed a paganism that adapted to new religious ideas. Thus, rejecting all mythological forms, he proposed a more philosophically oriented paganism, and a refined and spiritual theology:

> In fact, who is so demented, so mentally incapacitated as to deny that it is most certain that there is one highest God, without beginning, without natural offspring, the great and magnificent father, as it were? With many names we call upon his powers spread through the created world, since we are all ignorant of his proper name. After all, "god" is a name common to all religions.[7]

Supported by imperial policies that favored their religion, the Catholics at times experienced conflict with the pagan population. This was the case at Sufes (Henchir Sbiba), a wealthy city in Byzacena where there was constant devotion to the Roman deities. In 399, following Theodosius' edicts banning the pagan cult, the Christians, desiring to impose the law by force, tore down the statue of Hercules, the city's patron

---

5. Cf. Augustine *Letter* 17.4.

6. Augustine *Letter* 16.

7. Augustine *Letter* 16.

god. These actions incited the fury of the local pagan population, and, in an ensuing riot, some sixty Christians were killed. The fanatical populace, given over to carnage and murder, was actually led by the *decuriones*. Among the latter were some that, through their participation in the massacre, hoped to attain a leading role in the *curia*. The Christians were then condemned for destroying public property and ordered to pay for a new statue. Undoubtedly apprised of the situation by the city's bishop, Augustine responded indignantly to the local authorities:

> The most notorious crime and unexpected cruelty of your savagery has rocked the earth and struck at the sky so that blood shines and murder is decried in your streets and temples. Among you the laws of Rome have been buried, and the fear of righteous courts has been spurned. There is certainly no respect for the emperors . . . if you say that it was your Hercules, we have collected coins one by one and have bought your god for you from the artist. Restore, then, the lives that your bloody hand has torn away.[8]

Despite such local crises, the relationships between the Christians and pagans were still better than those between the Donatists and Catholics. Augustine was also aware that some pagans demonstrated a high level of virtue and commitment. He acknowledged that some of these were involved in feeding and clothing the poor and were actually good examples for his flock. He added that such individuals could not be won to the church through discussion; rather, Christians needed to reach out in friendship and exemplify upright character. Augustine added: "Why, asks the pagan, would you persuade me to become a Christian? A Christian robbed me; but I have never done that. A Christian made a false pledge to me; I would never do that."[9]

In light of Maximus' spiritual claims, his paganism, which was based on some attractive philosophical teachings, was a source of irritation for the African Christians, who were often accused of gross materialism. Despite this, there was never a movement of conversion from Christianity to paganism in this period, except in the rare cases of those desiring to oppose the government's official religious policies. However, another problem developed that threatened to undermine the African

8. Augustine *Letter* 50.

9. Augustine *Expositions on the Psalms* 25.14 [English translation my own].

churches—an effective proselytizing work by the Judaizers, which required the attention of the African pastors.

THE PROSELYTIZING JUDAIZERS

We have previously discussed the role of the Diaspora in the origins of the African church, and the importance of the African Jewish settlements, which from the second century stretched from the coastal cities to the edges of the desert. In his *History of the Berbers,* Ibn Khaldoun referred to the seventh-century North African context at the beginning of the Arab invasions: "Some of the Berbers professed Judaism, the religion they received from their powerful neighbors—the Israelites of Syria." This account asserts that there was a significant Jewish expansion into Africa, which perhaps pre-dated the origins of the Diaspora. While the majority of the Berber Jews were of Syrian descent, others were native Maghrebins who converted to Judaism during the Roman period. This Judaizing probably occurred on a tribe-by-tribe basis and certainly happened progressively over time. North African Judaism—like Christianity and Islam, the latter arriving in the seventh century—probably also included some elements of local pagan rituals such as magic and divination.

In a story that may be legend or history, we are told that the celebrated figure Kahina—the "prophetess" and powerful queen—practiced Judaism with the members of her tribe in the Aures Mountains. She was the soul of the fierce Berber resistance that opposed the eighth-century Arab invasions. Following victories by the Arab armies led by Hassan Ibn No'man, who had taken Carthage from the last Byzantine prince, Kahina's demise signaled an end to all resistance against the Arab invaders. That aside, Judaism was a significant force in the ancient Berber way of life.

The controversies between Tertullian and Jewish leaders have also been noted. Such skirmishes were rare by the beginning of the fourth century as imperial laws prohibited Jewish proselytizing, and, indeed, African Christianity was never significantly affected by a Judaizing movement. This was especially true in the urban centers where Catholic orthodoxy was particularly affirmed—as opposed to the less Romanized regions that were more open to sects. Despite this general tendency, Augustine observed some Judaizing infiltration into the Christian community.

Although there is sufficient reason to believe that African Christianity initially developed alongside the Diaspora, from Tertullian's day onward, there was a complete break between the Synagogue and church. Further clashes resulted in the two communities becoming separate, opposing entities. While Cyprian had no personal contact with the Jews, and the Jewish-Christian conflicts were much less intense in his day, he likened the Jewish practices to those of heretics. When Augustine became bishop of Hippo, a rather antagonistic relationship had developed between the two religions, mostly on account of sharp doctrinal disagreements. Though Augustine was hardly innovative in the confrontation, his writings allow us to understand the extent of the Jewish presence in Africa during his day. He was especially aware of some of the strategies of the Judaizers; however, it is unclear whether the Catholics themselves were also engaged in evangelism in Jewish areas.

In a letter to Bishop Aselicus of Tusuros (Tozeur), located on the banks of the Triton Lake (Chott el-Djerid in southern Tunisia), Augustine spoke of a certain Aptus, who "was teaching Christians to become Jews." Calling himself a Jew and an Israelite, Aptus made an effort to restore a rigid adherence to the Jewish dietary laws and other practices dictated by the Law. Asked for his opinion on the matter, Augustine remarked that though a Christian could claim the title *Iudaeus* or *Israelita*, this "label" should be understood in a spiritual sense; yet, he wrote, to avoid confusion it was preferable to avoid such terms. Finally, he remarked that a Christian should absolutely avoid returning to the ritual practices and dietary laws of the Old Testament.[10]

The Tusuros affair was not the only evidence for a Judaizing movement within African Christianity. In fact, some rather open proselytizing activities can also be cited. These included those of the "healer" of Uzalis, whose tactics included having his clients wear a girdle.[11] Again, such activities, on the whole rare, did not pose a threat to the church.

Some attention should be given to the activities of the Celicoles sect. These "worshippers of the heavens" were active in Numidia where their heresy developed. During a trip to Cirta in 395, Augustine made a detour through Thuburiscu (forty kilometers south of Tagaste) in order to meet with the city's Donatist bishop, but also to meet with the leader of the Celicoles. The latter had developed quite a following and subjected his disciples to a new baptism. Did this baptism include circumcision, simi-

10. Cf. Augustine *Letter* 196.
11. Cf. Augustine *City of God* 22.8.21.

lar to the Judaizing practice in the early church at Jerusalem? Augustine's brief mention of the Celicoles fails to give any further clarification. Nevertheless, the group seems to have resembled the "Samaritans," who were also present in Africa. In fact, due to their perceived similarities, "Jews, Celicoles, and Samaritans" were grouped together under the same religious category by the *Theodosian Code*.[12] In a law dated April 1, 409, Honorius directly targeted the Celicoles, accusing them of "criminal superstition." The law further stated "that it was urgent to protect the true religion against these innovative heretics who forced Christians to adopt the odious Jewish name, and forced Christian faith and practices to be sullied through Jewish perversity and unbelief." These descriptions reveal some aspects of the Judaizing sect, which took root in Numidia and was based some 100 kilometers from Hippo.

Overall, Augustine gives little attention to these factions, which were actually not indigenous to Africa. On the other hand, the Manicheans made much of the Judaizers. They also made reference to the "Nazarenes" or Symmachians, who, professing Christianity, were circumcised, observed the Sabbath, and abstained from eating pork while following the remaining dietary restrictions prescribed in Deuteronomy and Leviticus.[13] In the eyes of the Manicheans, the Judaizers were good *semichristiani* ("half-Christians")—a description that they also used for the Catholics. Indeed, the Judaizers provided the Manicheans with "ammunition" in their anti-Catholic propaganda campaign. That is, if the Judaizers were faithfully applying the Mosaic Law in obedience to their Scriptures, then Catholic Christians, who also accepted the Old Testament as authoritative, should do likewise.

MANICHEANISM: THE "PESTILENT HERESY"

Much more than the sporadic efforts of Jewish proselytizers or Judeo-Christian movements, the Manichean communities, long established in North Africa, constituted a permanent threat to the Catholic church. This earned the Manicheans the title *pestilentissima haeresis* ("the most pestilent heresy")—a heresy par excellence.

12. Cf. *Theodosian Code* 16.8.19.
13. Cf. Augustine *Against Faustus* 19.4, 17.

Out of all the great religious movements birthed in antiquity, Manicheanism and its doctrines have probably suffered the most distortion due to a historical and literary tradition that was quite hostile to the sect. Throughout their history, beginning with the martyrdom of Mani himself, the Manicheans had the unenviable privilege of being a religious movement that suffered unceasing and merciless persecution.

Born in the third century in the heart of Persia, a context strongly influenced by Gnostic and Judeo-Christian movements, the church founded by the heretic Mani (216–277) spread both to the East and West, claiming followers from China to Spain. Along this corridor of expansion, North Africa—more precisely what is now modern Tunisia and Algeria—became a choice location and bastion where the sect proved to be quite active. It was certainly the region where Manicheanism became the most well-known.

Manicheanism's historical emergence in the African provinces resembles that of Christianity. That is, the sect abruptly appeared on the African shores in the midst of persecution, quickly developed a following, and organized itself into communities. The first legislation against the "superstition originating from Persia" was handed down March 31, 302. Issued by Diocletian, the edict was addressed to Julianus, the proconsul of Carthage who asked the emperor for direction in handling the Manicheans, who had developed quite a presence in his province. Hence, within twenty years of Mani's death, every region of the empire, including Africa and Egypt, had been touched by proselytizing Manichean missionaries. The emperor called for a range of punishments. The most obstinate members of the sect were ordered to be decapitated or have their belongings confiscated. The Manichean leaders were burned alive along with their heretical scriptures. While Diocletian had enacted the death penalty in the name of Roman paganism, Theodosius imposed his own capital punishment against the sect in 382 because of the threat they posed to the official state church.

Manicheanism presented itself as authentic Christianity in its most developed form. Though Christ occupied an eminent place in Manichean thought, he was largely a "spiritual savior" who, in the docetic tradition, did not actually take on human flesh. The Manichean teachers also maintained that Mani was the Paraclete—the one Jesus promised would "guide men into all truth" (cf. John 16:3). They viewed the African church—Catholics and Donatists together—as heretical and guilty of corrupting the original doctrine. The Manicheans further rejected the Old Testament Scriptures, regarded the Law as a demonized perversion, and accused the prophets of being criminal and corrupt. Regarding the New Testament, they only accepted what they deemed authentic and interpreted the texts according to their own exegetical principles. The sect affirmed the existence of an ultimate evil, the source of sin and death, which afflicted human beings. Humans were thus exiled to the lesser, material world, while preserving the memory of an original lost paradise.

As Julianus' detailed report revealed, the Manichean missionaries were successful in making converts across different social classes, including members of the ruling class and the Roman administration—the latter being expressly mentioned in Diocletian's rescript. The proconsul's report also indicated that Manichean teaching had been propagated in the African provinces for some time, dating back to the last decades of the third century. The records, however, do not reveal the exact content of what was preached by Mani's "apostles" in Africa or in other areas. It is also impossible to determine an "apostolic" origin for Manicheanism in Africa, though it is sometimes attributed to a certain Adimantus or Addas, who spread Manicheanism in Egypt between 244 and 268 and whose writings were particularly well-known among the African communities.

Though a thorough survey of Mani's teachings is beyond the scope of the present work, Mani's seven major works, which made up the Manichean canon, included some complex and grandiose themes, as well as a dogmatic mythology. Mani's major argument was that a divine drama was being played out in the cosmic universe and in the heart of each person—a combat between eternal and antithetical first principles, between good and evil, and between light and darkness. Fundamentally dualistic, the propositions of this "seal of the prophets" aim to recount a history in which anthropology is merely one aspect of the cosmos, and in which man's destiny is simply a part of the universe's great adventure, from beginning to end. Escaping from scientific speculation and intelligence, such understanding—synonymous with salvation—will ultimately lead one into the light of knowledge (gnosis).

The Manicheans organized their communities around the model of a church body where all members were actively united. Like many minority movements, the atmosphere seemed to be marked by warmth and fraternity. Adherents were grouped into two levels. The first group included the elect, the religious who subjected themselves to a rigorous asceticism, detaching themselves completely from the world in order to be devoted to the teaching and expansion of the church. The very structured Manichean leadership was chosen from this group. The second group was made up of the hearers—members of the laity whose moral code was much more relaxed, yet who were expected to serve and show devotion to the Manichean clergy. Their meetings and corporate celebrations, which occurred respectively on a weekly and annual basis, were communal gatherings open to men and women, and people from all social classes. Manichean converts came from Christian and pagan backgrounds, sometimes included entire families, and included urban and rural dwellers.

Claiming to be a religion of knowledge and light, Manicheanism attracted intellectuals, especially those dissatisfied with the *catholica*. In Carthage, this included students, professors, those working in banking and finance, and those trained in the liberal arts. In the name of free thought, Manichean leaders sarcastically lashed out at the narrow-minded practices of the Catholic congregations and denounced the dogmas imposed on these pitiful ones by leaders who were more ignorant than authoritative. Manichean missionaries also knew how to make their appeal in simple and common-sense terms, without neglecting the caustic spirit so valued by the enlightened sect. In this sense, Apuleius embodied the movement well. Hence, throughout the towns and villages, the Manicheans penetrated the world of artisans and merchants and also claimed farmers and laborers among their numbers.

Indeed, the Manichean movement did not limit its activity to the port cities of Carthage and Hippo in Proconsularis, and Caearea and Tipasa in Mauretania Caesarea. Historical records indicate that, due to missionary efforts along key commercial routes between the coastal cities and towns in the African interior, the Manicheans were present in Tagaste, Malliana (Khemis-Miliana), Milevus (hometown to the famous Donatist leader Faustus), from the high plains around Constantine to the back of the Aures, and at Vegesela (Ksar el-Kelb, located 100 kilometers south of Theveste). This latter region was probably well populated in the Roman period based on the archaeological remains of urban areas like Ubaza Castellum, which was represented by both a Catholic and a Donatist bishop at the council of Carthage in 411. In light of this evidence alone, it seems that Manicheanism was probably well established and active in the North African interior. The heretical presence was known from the capital of Proconsularis to that of Mauretania Caesarea—a distance measuring 700 kilometers from east to west—and from the port of Hippo to the Aures and the mountains of Nemencha—200 kilometers from north to south.

Manicheanism's spread in African society and in the African provinces is perhaps as remarkable as the sect's history itself, a development that can be traced over two centuries and included a long series of persecutions. In fact, during the period of the "Christian emperors" alone, the *Theodosian Code* (from the reign of Valentinian I in 372 to Valetinian III in 445) includes twenty-one anti-Manichean edicts. Though the final two edicts were issued after Rome had fallen under Vandal control, they also conformed to the previous laws that outlawed Manicheanism. However, as in the case of the anti-Donatist legislation, the edicts against the Manicheans were hardly enforced. Firmly established on the African shores, Manicheanism's "indigenous" nature allowed it to be overlooked during official investigations, despite appeals made by the imperial authorities and bishops requesting information on the sect from the general public. We do know, however, that police raids took place. At Carthage, for instance, charges were brought against some Manicheans and, after periods of interrogation, "confessions" were obtained. It would be impossible to speak of the Catholic church's anti-Manichean campaign, supported by the Roman state's "inquisition," without highlighting the decisive role played by the former Manichean hearer who went on to become the bishop of Hippo.

Augustine (cf. chapter 9), spent around ten years of his youth as a Manichean adherent—from 372 to 382, or from age nineteen to twenty-nine. This period, of course, followed the "wilder" period of his earlier youth. Having broken with his co-religionists and friends, he immediately began to wage a ruthless battle against the Manicheans, writing some thirty works of varying levels of importance. These writings supported his public battle against the sect and its leaders, which had gained strength in Hippo and in the surrounding region.

Beginning in 387 on the day after his baptism, his anti-Manichean polemic continued until 430, the year of his death and the collapse of Roman power in Africa. Augustine seemed much more passionate about uprooting the heresy than he ever was about promoting it—something that he acknowledged on several occasions.[14] In the midst of such intense fighting, Augustine seems to offer a *pro domo* type defense, especially as he confronted theological enemies like the Pelagians, who accused him of continuing to be a Manichean. Augustine desired to show that he was completely cleansed of this unfortunate past, forever healed from his former "leprosy."

Augustine's battle with the Manicheans was long—though varying in intensity at different points—and the victories were uncertain. This was partly due to the fact that the bishop of Hippo always had the luxury of sending stubborn Manichean opponents before his city's tribunal. His anti-Manichean works were in no way a peaceful treatment of the heresy or a systematic study of Manichean doctrine. Rather, they were combative works in which Augustine clearly took a strong stand. Thus, the Catholic polemicist presented the "hollow" Manichean arguments in order to shed light on the heresy's obscure claims, which opposed the Christian faith. We can never appreciate Augustine enough for the amount of his literary output, which included treatises, booklets, sermons, letters, and polemical works—both written and oral.

The works recording the Manichean leaders' arguments are particularly valuable—*Against Fortunatus, Against Adimantus, Against Faustus, Against Felix,* and *Against Secundinus.* These debates furnish a first-hand understanding of Manichean teaching by leaders authorized to speak for the sect—invaluable primary source material. In the African context, the key Manichean leaders included the "bishop" Faustus, the "priest" Fortunatus, and Felix—a member of the "elect" who was regarded as an important teacher. As the imperial edicts against the Manicheans were applied, all of their writings were destroyed, except for some fragments of a Latin manuscript discovered in a cave near Theveste. Without Augustine's polemical works, we would know nothing about Manicheanism in North Africa. Aside from some Coptic and Persian texts and fragments found in Egypt and Central Asia at the beginning of the twentieth century, Augustine's account of Mani's religion is unrivaled as the most coherent and complete work that we possess toward understanding the history and doctrine of the sect. Portraying an active and even "human" Manicheanism, Augustine's writings ultimately provide invaluable insight into early North Africa.

14. Cf. *On the Gift of Perseverance* 20.53; *On the Two Souls* 9.11.

Following the Arian Vandals' conquest of Africa, persecution against the Manicheans continued. The sect was subjected to a new wave of cruelty, which was reminiscent of Diocletian's actions, carried out in the name of paganism, and those of Theodosius, executed in support of the Catholic church. Previously, in an effort to etch out a *modus vivendi* with the Catholics and their Roman protectors, King Huneric wanted to offer a token of his good will. As a result he launched a bloody persecution against the Manicheans—regarded as heretics by Catholics and Arians alike. This was ironic because the Catholics and Arians also regarded one another as heretics. Victor de Vita, a Catholic bishop in Byzacena who lived during Huneric's rule, wrote that the Catholics viewed the Vandal king as "worthy of praise." They were obviously unaware that the tyrant would soon turn against them. To "cleanse this diseased part" of African society, Huneric upheld the existing Roman legislation against heresy. Thus, large numbers of Manicheans were sent into exile in Europe, while multitudes (*multi*), according to Victor, were sent to the slaughter and executed in Africa.

After this savage yet "effective" persecution, the final stage of two centuries of repression, Africa was cleansed from this plague, at least in appearance. However, police investigations, exiles, and burnings at the stake could not completely uproot a religion that had become so profoundly anchored in African society. With the "bastion" destroyed, the survivors were sent into exile toward Italy and Sicily, where they were granted refuge. Also, they were sent to Spain, where Priscillianism had "blazed a trail" and was recovering some aspects of Manichean thought.

Manicheanism continued to exist and enjoyed a long and glorious history. In the second half of the eighth century, in an effort to put an end to a schism within the sect in its native region of Persia, the Manicheans looked to an African for leadership. Arriving at Ctesiphon, Abu Hillal al-Dayhuri assumed the title of supreme master for the "church of light."

Augustine's major role in opposing Donatism and Manicheanism has been noted. He also occupied a prominent place in the fight against Pelagianism. Unlike Donatism and Manicheanism, Pelagianism never became a popular movement. Effectively a battle between opponents in theological and monastic circles, the new heresy hardly affected the African church. It will become clear in this final battle, the longest and most arduous of Augustine's career, that the bishop of Hippo, an African, will play a more important role than the bishop of Rome and serve as the primary spokesperson for Christianity and the global church.

ADDITIONAL RESOURCES

Blumkenkrantz, *Die Judenpredigt Augustins.*
Decret, *L'Afrique manichéene.*
Monceaux, "Les colonies juives dans l'Afrique romaine."
Simon, "Le judaïsme berbère dans l'Afrique romain."

9 Augustine of Hippo and the Glory of the "Great Church"

In his letter to Augustine around 390, Maximus of Madauros arrogantly boasted about the Roman gods whose statues adorned the center of his city. The rather unknown pagan rhetor also considered it his spiritual duty to point out how ironic it was that the Christian martyrs in his province had "barbaric" names (*odiosa nomina*), though, in fact, they were of Punic or Libyan origin. In his sharp reply, the future bishop of Hippo, who had not yet been ordained a priest at the time of writing, communicated a proud African spirit that was always alive in the hearts of his countrymen and that would stay with Augustine throughout his life: "Have you forgotten that you are an African, writing to Africans, and that both of us live in Africa!"[1] In fact, it seems that Augustine had an almost "earthy" connection with his native land, which his travels to Rome, Milan, and Cassiciacum only reinforced. For instance, Augustine and his companions complained at their inability to carry out their nightly "philosophical dialogues" in a spiritually deprived Italian context. He wrote: "There was no light in Italy; even for the rich, this is a necessity."[2] On the other hand, in the rich African atmosphere, one's "lamp could remain lit" throughout the night.

Without a doubt, this African was the most illustrious representative of Christianity in antiquity. Augustine was responsible for providing the African church, despite all of its shortcomings and challenges, with the most prominent place in the ecclesiastical world of his day. Without him, the European churches would not have been what been what they were from the fifth century onward, and the global church would not be

---

1. Augustine *Letter* 17.4 [English translation my own].
2. Augustine *On Order* 1.3.6 [English translation my own].

what it is today. We are hard pressed to find another example of a man who demonstrated such a level of intelligence and heart-felt friendship, especially toward his allies. His severity toward his theological opponents has been noted. Augustine also had an incredible capacity for work and maintained an almost sovereign authority in the church. In short, he left his mark on the Christian churches, which, after sixteen centuries, all lay claim to his legacy.

Augustine was born November 13, 354, in Tagaste (Souk Ahras), an ancient Numidian city that was a two-day journey south on foot from the important port city of Hippo. Along the uneven mountain ranges of the eastern Tell, the picturesque village developed in the center of a fertile region where vineyards, wheat, and olive trees grew. Augustine always retained fond memories of a happy childhood in Tagaste. Many years later, evoking memories of his youth, Augustine found pleasure in recounting his escapades of running through the countryside and chasing birds out of their nests, while also basking in the extraordinary African sun. He wrote: "Light is the queen of colors and bathes everything we see, and wherever I am in the daytime it flows all around me, and caresses me."[3] Also during these years at Tagaste, he tells of going with some friends late one night to steal pears from a neighbor's garden: "I would not have done it alone . . . since my pleasure did not lie in pears, it must have been in the crime as committed in the company of others who shared in the sin . . . the theft gave us a thrill, and we laughed to think we were outwitting people."[4]

Augustine was quite studious, and the poetry of Virgil, an "earth lover" like himself, fascinated him. He pursued his education in Tagaste until the age of sixteen and afterward continued it at nearby Madauros. Augustine apparently received little encouragement in his spiritual life at this stage. His mother Monica, who was eventually canonized by the church, certainly gave him some sort of religious instruction at home; however, he did not hide how much her constant concern weighed upon him. His father Patricius, who owned a modest amount of land and served as a functionary in the Roman administration, was a tepid pagan before being baptized as a Christian shortly before his death. His dream was that Augustine would have a career in rhetoric or in law. In short,

3. Augustine *Confessions* 10.34.51 [unless otherwise noted, all English translations of *Confessions* are taken from *WSA* 1.1].

4. Augustine *Confessions* 2.8.16; 2.9.17.

Augustine's family served as a good representative of the African family during this period.

At the age of seventeen, the young Augustine, who had shown intellectual promise, left to continue his studies at Carthage. *Carthago Veneris*, the city of Venus, was also regarded as Africa's metropolis. Between his university studies and initial career as a professor of rhetoric, Augustine spent nearly a dozen years in Carthage. He wrote: "So I arrived at Carthage, where the din of scandalous love-affairs raged cauldron-like around me. I was not yet in love, but I was enamored with the idea of love . . . loving and being loved were sweet to me, the more so if I could also enjoy a lover's body."[5] Augustine, of course, recounts how these "confessions" were lived out. Giovanni Papini writes that Augustine was "a sex maniac during these years" and, from his sixteenth year until his baptism, the young man "could not live without a woman in his bed—to the point that Augustine felt sorry for Ambrose in his celibacy."

In reality, coming from the small Numidian province, Augustine was dazzled by the cosmopolitan metropolis. Yet, also lost in the big city, he wanted to escape from his solitude. In fact, it was a young African woman who helped him to move out of his "state of wandering" by providing him with the stability that he had previously searched for in vain through "diverse and dark love affairs." Indeed, at this time, he settled down with this companion, a woman of modest social standing, and remained with her for the next sixteen years. He added: "At this time too I lived with a girl . . . she was the only girl I had, and I was sexually faithful to her."[6] Not long after, Augustine and the unnamed woman had a son, Adeodatus, who brought Augustine much joy.

THE MANICHEAN HEARER OR THE "LONG, ERRONEOUS PATH"

At Carthage around 372–373, Augustine's story became even more interesting as he began a ten-year journey as a member of the Manichean sect. In the previous chapter, we saw that this religion of Babylonian origin experienced a rather surprising fate, despite the persecutions it endured, particularly in Africa. We know that Augustine committed himself to the new faith with all of the passion that characterized all of his undertakings.

---

5. Augustine *Confessions* 3.1.1.

6. Augustine *Confessions* 4.2.2.

While arguing later against Manicheanism's false teachings, he admitted that the sect appealed to him as grandiose, exalted, and well-founded, and that it fascinated "the soul of a youth impassioned for truth . . . and full of scorn for old wives' tales."[7] Catholic bishops, perched on episcopal chairs in their basilicas, only propagated such wives' tales. Among the Manicheans, Augustine's great need for intimacy and friendship was met. He was probably also proud to be a part of a rebel church that suffered persecution from the imperial authorities. As a layman, he participated in Manichean meetings and liturgical assemblies, while diligently helping to provide for the material needs of the Manichean elect. A fervent missionary, he castigated his Catholic adversaries, routing them in public debate.[8]

Over time, Augustine's great hopes were snuffed out by repeated disappointments and disillusionment in a sect that he would later call "an erroneous path."[9] For instance, Augustine related his meaningless encounter at the end of 382 with the Manichean bishop Faustus, whom Augustine hoped would offer answers to some of his deepest theological questions. As his religious convictions faded, he became absorbed with the concerns of life and career, and managed to secure the chair of rhetoric at the university at Carthage. He also sought to cultivate relationships with influential people in hopes of obtaining a position in the higher echelons of the Roman administration. Indeed, the leading magistrates in the empire got their start in government as rhetors and lawyers. Having won a poetry contest, Augustine received his prize from Vindicianus, a doctor with a great reputation at the imperial court, with whom Augustine eventually became friends. He also developed a friendship with the senator Flaccianus, who later became the proconsul of Carthage. Thus, with his eyes completely fixed on the *cursus honorum* ("political ladder"), Augustine's passion as a Manichean hearer was soon extinguished.

In 383, Augustine decided to move to Rome where he hoped to find calmer students—a contrast to his undisciplined pupils at Carthage who regularly disappeared without paying their fees. Though having parted ways with the Manichean sect where he had spent the previous ten years, he managed to benefit from recommendations made by fellow African

---

7. Augustine *On the Advantage of Believing* 1.2 [English translation my own].

8. Cf. Augustine *On the Gift of Perseverance* 20.53.

9. Cf. Augustine *Confessions* 4.1.1.

Manicheans in his transition to Italy. At Rome, he was welcomed into the home of a Manichean hearer, who lodged him during a period of prolonged illness. He was also acquainted with the Manichean elect and maintained a more "friendly association with Manichees than with others not of the heresy."[10]

In the fall of 384, the thirty-year old Augustine was appointed as the official rhetor of Milan, an imperial post in Valentinian II's court. No longer a Manichean, Augustine again benefited from their intervention as they recommended him for the position to Symmachus, the city's prefect. Settling in Milan, the location of the imperial residence and capital of the western half of the Roman Empire, Augustine split his time in his new role teaching courses in rhetoric and attending to the requests of high ranking dignitaries in the Roman administration. He wrote: "Consider what a fine thing it is for a person to win a reputation. What prize could be more desirable? We have plenty of influential friends: without setting our sights unduly high, one may expect at least a governorship to come one's way."[11] On January 1, 385, the new rhetor gave his first official oration. However, despite all of his hopes to receive an important administrative appointment quickly, he did not last two years in this position.

In the spring of 385, Monica came to join her son in Milan, and she had her own ideas for his future. The ambitious mother decided that it was time to put her son's household in order. Monica arranged a marriage for Augustine with a young girl from a good family; however, they needed to wait another two years before she reached a marriageable age. Having become "unacceptable" for Augustine, the provincial "upstart," it was necessary for Adeodatus' mother to return to Africa alone. Though Augustine generally refers to her quite discretely in *Confessions*, he cannot help but write: "So deeply was she engrafted into my heart that it was left torn and wounded and trailing blood."[12] However, this trail of blood quickly dried up because, waiting for his fiancé to reach the acceptable age, Augustine wasted no time in taking another concubine. It was at this point that Augustine took a step in an entirely different direction, and he chose a new way of life that he would follow for this rest of his life.

---

10. Augustine *Confessions* 5.10.19.

11. Augustine *Confessions* 6.11.19.

12. Augustine *Confessions* 6.15.25.

FROM CASSICIACUM TO HIPPO

Seated in his garden in Milan in August of 386, and after reading a page from the Apostle Paul, Augustine felt the call to a new life: "Let us walk properly as in the daytime, not in orgies and drunkenness, not in sexual immorality and sensuality, not in quarreling and jealousy" (Rom 13:13). After resigning from his position in the imperial court, he retired to a peaceful country estate at Cassiciacum, north of Milan, where he gathered together a small circle of friends. His *Dialogues* from Cassiciacum documented his journey "on the path to truth." On Easter eve in April of 387, Augustine, then thirty-two years old, was baptized along with his fifteen-year-old son and long-time friend and countryman Alypius. They were baptized by Bishop Ambrose, who had played a decisive role in Augustine's conversion. For Augustine, this step of faith also marked his new commitment to a "perfect life," in which he repudiated his former way of life and renounced all desire for marriage. Attracted to the rigors of monasticism, which he discovered during his stay in Italy, Augustine was in the process of being drawn to what he regarded as the highest calling.

With nothing keeping him in Milan, Augustine set out for Africa in the fall of 387. While his mother died at Ostia during the trip, Adeodatus, his dearly beloved son, died shortly after their return to Tagaste. Both deaths were harsh blows to Augustine and deeply affected him. Renouncing his worldly possessions, he retired to a location not far from Tagaste and attempted to recreate the atmosphere of Cassiciacum. He was joined by a group of like-minded friends who referred to themselves as "servants of God."

After spending three years establishing the community at Tagaste, Augustine became quite well known at Hippo. While passing through the city and attending the worship assembly, he was presented to the congregation for ordination by the aging Bishop Valerius, who was in great need of help in his ministry. Initially ordained as a priest, he became Valerius' co-bishop in the spring of 395. He wrote: "I came to this city to see a friend . . . I was seized, made a priest and from there was made a bishop."[13]

While repeated references have been made to Augustine's sermons and polemical works, space will not allow for a detailed treatment of his

---

13. Augustine *Letter* 21.1 [English translation my own].

significant corpus of writings—ninety-three catalogued works of various genres, some of considerable length, in 252 books. Like the majority of writers in this period, he employed a secretary. In fact, he did not write his own letters (a total of 236, of which twenty-nine were discovered and edited in 1981), sermons, treatises, or even his longest works. Rather, while walking around, he dictated them to a clerk or copyist, reviewed the texts, and then edited them on the spot. The perspective of Possidius, Augustine's friend and biographer, should be noted. After observing that "so many are the works he dictated and published . . . that even a student would hardly have the energy to read and become acquainted with them," Possidius added, "I believe, however, that they profited even more . . . especially if they were familiar with his manner of life among his fellow beings."[14]

"THE BURDEN OF THE EPISCOPATE"

Augustine described the weight of his responsibilities and tasks as bishop—a career that he had not chosen yet had accepted—as the *sarcina episcopatus* ("burden of the episcopate"). Previously a very active trading post, the port city of Hippo Regius ("the royal port") was the ancient capital of the Numidian kings. Made up of a cosmopolitan population that included sailors and merchants from the four corners of the Mediterranean, it was the second leading city in Africa after Carthage. Augustine decided to carry out his new duties as bishop in a monastic setting, continuing to live out the call to communal living that had characterized his life in Cassiciacum and Tagaste. He lived with the priests and clergy, those who had also accepted this mode of living, in a clerical monastery within the bishop's house next to the basilica at Hippo. In 424, the clergy at Hippo included six deacons (seven by 427) and three priests serving around the bishop. Each member of the clerical monastery abandoned his worldly possessions and, in order to avoid the temptation of accumulating wealth in the monastery, inheritances and legacies were refused. Possidius wrote:

---

14. Possidius *Life of Augustine* 18.9; 31.9 [unless otherwise noted, all English translations of *Life of Augustine* are from Possidius, *Life of Saint Augustine*, translated by Matthew O'Connell.].

His clothing and shoes, and even his bedding, were simple and appropriate, being neither overly fastidious nor slovenly. It is in these externals that people usually go in either for arrogant display or for self abasement. . . . His meals were frugal and economical; at times, however, in addition to herbs and vegetables, they include meat for the sake of guests or sick brethren. Moreover, they always included wine. . . . Only the spoons were of silver; the vessels in which the food was brought to the table were of earthenware, wood, or marble. . . . He practiced hospitality at all times. Even at table, he found more delight in reading and conversation than in eating and drinking. To prevent one plague that afflicts social intercourse, he had these words inscribed on the table: "Let those who like to slander the lives of the absent know that their own are not worthy at this table." . . . On one occasion, when some fellow bishops, close friends of his, had forgotten the inscription and disobeyed its warning, he rebuked them so sternly, being so upset as to say that either the verses must be erased from the table or he would get up from the table in the middle of the meal and retire to his room."[15]

These clergy were not monks and were not disposed to such an *otium*—the peace and complete inner-leisure that was necessary for a life of spiritual retreat or meditation. This monastic ideal was marked by a demanding pastoral emphasis that required the commitment of each member of the clergy.

Outside of the city, the diocese of Hippo comprised a vast rural area that extended some forty kilometers into the interior of the province, an area largely un-Romanized that included the previously mentioned *castellum* of Fussala. While the diocese's urban dwellers spoke Latin, those living in the countryside continued to communicate in Punic.

The primary duties of the minister included preaching the Scriptures and instructing catechumens who were preparing for baptism. At Hippo, however, it was also necessary for the pastor to take the necessary steps to protect his flock from the unsound teaching of the Manichean and Donatist movements. Such efforts to protect the church—including debates, interventions, and measures to root out these dangerous heretical movements from Africa—have been adequately discussed. It should simply be noted that despite Augustine's passionate debates—characterized by faith, confidence, and radiant vigor—the two sides were not equal

15. Possidius *Life of Augustine* 22.

because the official church was assured victory on account of its support from the state. Making clear reference to the power enjoyed by his adversary Augustine—who had previously sent a threatening letter, summoning Felix the Manichean to his courtroom-like presence—the heretical teacher concluded: "The authority granted to a bishop is quite surprising . . . besides, I cannot resist the imperial laws."[16]

Augustine's care for the church at Hippo was certainly not limited to polemical discourses and the threat of political intervention. In fact, he traveled a great deal—often on the back of a mule and in harsh weather conditions—in order to visit the members of his diocese, to preach in his colleague's churches, and, especially, to take part in church councils. Around twenty times, he made the trip to Carthage—a 300 kilometer trip from Hippo on average—where most of the African church councils took place. In 421, he made one of his two longest trips and traveled to Tubunae (Tobna, near Barika) in the south of Numidia to meet with the African Count Boniface. From Carthage, this was a 600-kilometer journey.[17] In the summer of 418, at the age of sixty-five, he left from Carthage and traveled to Mauretania Caesarea, a journey of more than 1000 kilometers. In the same year, he covered more than 2200 kilometers on trips.

Augustine was also quite involved in appealing to the secular authorities on behalf of members of his flock. Though still a private citizen, the bishop in this period possessed a sort of "intercessory" prerogative before the authorities that allowed him to appeal to a judge for leniency, lobby for the humane treatment of prisoners, and seek justice against extorting tax collectors. He was also the natural protector of widows, orphans, virgins, the poor, and travelers. Finally, the bishop worked alongside his clergy to improve the moral climate of the society at large.

By demanding that its basilicas serve as places of asylum, a role previously played by pagan temples, the church became a refuge and defense for runaway slaves, for debtors being tracked down by powerful creditors, and for all citizens regardless of their class or distinction. At times this included actual criminals who were pursued by the authorities, and local officials or magistrates who were fleeing the fury of a "lynch-mob" that opposed an official decision. Augustine was very concerned about

16. Augustine *Against Felix* 1.1.12 [unless otherwise noted, all English translations of *Against Felix* are my own].

17. Cf. Augustine *Letter* 220.3, 12.

the basilica at Hippo remaining as a place of refuge. In a sermon, he commented on the subject: "There are three types of people who take refuge in the church: the good who are fleeing from the wicked; the wicked fleeing from the good; and the wicked who are fleeing from the wicked. How can such a knot be untangled? It's better to give sanctuary to one and all."[18]

While a bishop's intercession could certainly have an influence, this was generally not the case. In fact, as previously noted, the Catholic bishops had little influence before the magistrates and municipal leaders, many of whom were pagans, Donatists, or Donatist sympathizers. When Augustine made an official complaint to Eusebius, curator of Hippo, over a young Donatist fanatic who was beating and threatening the life of his Catholic mother, the municipal leader—probably a pagan who did not want to alienate the powerful Donatist community at Hippo—declared that he was unable "to render a judgment against the bishops."[19]

Due to the constant requests of church members, Augustine was regularly drawn into such intercessory work—appearing before local authorities to resolve issues, to seek a reduction in taxes, etc. Despite being the Catholic church's champion at the council of Carthage in 411, he still spent many mornings in waiting rooms, patiently waiting his turn, to have a brief audience with a local official. Often, even after a long wait, Augustine was still rebuffed. In a sermon, he communicated: "Let me be, let me not have to endure all that, don't let anybody force me to. Look, as a little concession to me, give me a holiday from this business. I beg you, I beseech you."[20]

Desiring to avoid a corrupt legal system that often resorted to torture, and wanting to avoid the expense of travel, attorneys, and court fees, many African Christians and pagans preferred to have their grievances quickly and impartially heard at the *audientia episcopalis* ("the bishop's court"). Based on a law passed in 318 that was clarified by a second law in 333, Constantine invested the bishops with the authority to serve as judges in all matters. All that was necessary was for one of the parties to bring the case before the bishop, including cases that had already been heard in the secular courts. Later, in 399, Honorius limited the bishops'

---

18. Augustine *Sermon Guelfer* 25 [English translation my own].

19. Augustine *Letters* 35.1 [English translation my own].

20. Augustine *Sermon* 302.

jurisdiction to religious issues, and all other cases were referred to the secular courts. In civil cases, including punitive judgments, the bishops were allowed to serve as arbitrators, and their interventions served as grounds for appeal. Hence, this "bishop's court" should be considered as an ecclesiastical institution somewhere between an actual tribunal and a simple forum for arbitration and reconciliation. In light of the fluctuating Roman legal system, this phenomenon can be best understood by considering some aspects of African social life.

Augustine often listened to cases all morning up until his mid-day meal. On fasting days, his "court" remained in session all day. Seated in a large room (*secretarium*) adjoining the basilica, he was assisted by members of his clergy—at times neighboring bishops—who functioned as notaries and assessors. Though Roman law was not excluded, the basis for the ecclesiastical tribunal's decisions was church law, canons articulated at church councils, and the bishop's own judgments. Large numbers of plaintiffs poured into the "bishop's court," seeking solutions for all types of problems: family problems, quarrels with neighbors, property boundary disputes, wills, debts, thefts, and a host of other legal issues raised by those in the city and countryside alike. As is typically the case, verdicts were often contested by those viewing themselves as victims, and there was no lack of complaints, especially from the rich. Augustine commented: "They have endless quarrels, they oppress the righteous, they laugh at our judgments, and they waste our time that could be devoted to divine things."[21]

Augustine regarded this role of hearing cases and making intercession as *angaria* ("forced labor"), which only resulted in pastors being distracted from their service to the church. The church did not fail to remind the state of its responsibilities. For example, during their council in 401, the African bishops asked the imperial authorities to appoint officials who would oversee the needs of the poor—a task previously carried out solely by the bishops.

Augustine spent nearly forty years serving as bishop of Hippo. He described his position by writing: "God gave me as a servant to the people of Hippo."[22] The morning began with a liturgical assembly in the Hippo basilica where the Scriptures were read from the apse by a deacon and

---

21. Augustine *Exposition on the Psalms* 118.24.3 [English translation my own].
22. Augustine *Letter* 124.2 [English translation my own].

then by Augustine himself. These readings were accompanied by chanting and followed by a sermon from the bishop. The sermons were varied and included themes derived from a feast day, short speeches, longer homilies, lessons based on current events, and commentaries on biblical texts. Regarding the latter, Augustine took an allegorical approach to the Old Testament, focusing on the "spiritual meaning" of the text, as he had learned from Ambrose. Augustine's 800 surviving sermons appear as improvised dialogues, and their simple form indicates that he was addressing audiences of simple, less-educated people. With catechumens excused at the beginning of the sacraments, Christians from Hippo and the surrounding area gathered before the altar in the nave to celebrate the Eucharist—though no African council had ever prescribed this. The members of the believing community surrounded the bishop as he prayed for the Eucharist and consecrated the bread and wine, which were distributed among the clergy and believers.

"To preach, to convince of error, to correct, to instruct—all of this for everyone. What a responsibility, what a weight, what a burden! Who would not want to relieve himself of such a burden?"[23] Augustine's pastoral responsibilities for the people of Hippo and the church at large included "correcting errors" of both leaders and victims of the schisms and heresies that disfigured the face of the African church. Augustine's career can thus be divided along three lines, each of which was marked by a doctrinal controversy: from 387 to ca. 405, his polemic against the Manicheans; 400 to 420, his battle with the Donatists; and 412 to 430, his anti-Pelagian campaign. These were not successive controversies, as each one overlapped significantly with the next. Up until his death, Augustine continued to battle against heretics, though some popes balked at following some of his positions—some of which were excessive. This was especially true in the fight against the teachings of Pelagius and his cohorts.

PELAGIUS, CAELESTIUS, AND JULIAN: "GREAT, SUBTLE SPIRITS"

While Christianity in Africa was being torn apart by disputes between Catholics and Donatists, in Rome cultivated laymen from respected families, including men and women who were in contact with the finest minds

---

23. Augustine *Sermon Frangipane* 2.4 [English translation my own].

in the church, gathered in communities to discuss Paul's epistles. They became ardent converts to a movement led by Pelagius, which centered on the doctrines of salvation and grace, renouncing worldly goods, living a celibate life, and living according to the Gospel's precepts. Born into a Christian family in Britain, Pelagius came to Rome around 380, where he spent thirty years. He became acquainted with theologians from all over the Mediterranean world in Rome—a center for theological inquiry and the origin of numerous theological and ecclesiastical disputes in this period.

Caelestius—another lay monk of British origin, though more dynamic than Pelagius—was the primary spokesperson for the Pelagian movement. In 410, after the Vandal sack of Rome, large numbers of Romans, particularly those from noble families, fled the imperial capital and sought refuge in the African provinces in cities such as Carthage.

One familiar example was that of Pinianus, who settled with his wife (the future saint Melanie) and his mother Albina in Tagaste, where the wealthy family made generous contributions to the local church.[24] As the rich nobleman was passing through Hippo, the local believers gathered in a thunderous demonstration—complete with terrifying screams and loud insults—in order to force Pinianus' ordination as a priest in the church. While Pinianus did not desire this vocation and even feared for his life, the church put pressure on Augustine to ordain him. However, the bishop replied: "I spoke to them about not ordaining Pinianus against his will—a promise by which I was bound."[25]

In reality, as Albina was convinced, the church members were probably more interested in Pinianus' fortune than they were in his pastoral abilities.[26] Pinianus' wife Melanie came from the powerful Valerian family and was described by the Latin historian Palladius as "the richest heiress in the Roman world."[27] For a number of years, she focused her attention on the region of Tagaste, where she owned a great deal of land, and helped to establish two monasteries—one for women and the other for men.

---

24. Cf. Augustine *Letter* 126.7.

25. Augustine *Letter* 126.1.

26. Cf. Augustine *Letter* 125.2.

27. [Cf. Palladius *Lausiac History* 61.1–7.]

It was Pelagius' ascetic ideals that attracted most followers to this monastic-like movement. In 410, the British monk arrived at Hippo but failed to meet Augustine, who was away from the city at the time. His abbreviated trip to Hippo was followed by a longer stay in Carthage, before he set out for Jerusalem in the spring of 411. Caelestius, however, stayed behind in Carthage.

Though it is beyond the scope of the present work to elaborate fully on the origins of Pelagianism and its developments over the course of the fifth century, it will suffice here to point out how the "crisis of piety" spread through the African church. Shortly after the controversy was ignited in Africa by Caelestius, the Africans moved quickly to confront the issue raised by Pelagius' spokesman. While on a visit to Carthage, the Milanese deacon Paulinus took the initiative to summon Caelestius before an ecclesiastical assembly. The pious layman, who had previously sought ordination in the church at Carthage, criticized the local tradition since the time of Cyprian in which children were baptized to wash away the taint of original sin. Caelestius also defended the movement's key teachings, especially denying that Adam's sin was transferred to his physical offspring. Though Adam was created mortal and experienced death because of his own sin, Pelagius had argued, "man, if he has the desire, can abstain from sin," and uphold the commandments of God through his own strength. In short, the Pelagians denied the necessity of grace. The African bishops never reached the point of excommunicating Caelestius for heresy at the council of Carthage of 411, because he fled Africa and sought asylum in Ephesus.

Overwhelmed with educating the African church about the decisions made at the council of 411, and continuing to deal with the Donatists after their condemnation, Augustine received only a brief report of the Pelagian developments at Carthage and the news of the local synod that implicated Caelestius. However, from this point on, Augustine began to confront these "great and subtle souls"—Christians thirsting for "perfection."[28] As many of them came from powerful Roman families, these ideas eventually influenced even the bishop of Rome.

In 412, before entering fully into this theological battle and waging a polemic against his Pelagian adversaries, Augustine addressed many Pelagian issues in his book *On the Merits and Forgiveness of Sins and on*

---

28. Cf. Augustine *Letter* 186.5.

Infant Baptism. In 414–415, Augustine began to preach sermons against Pelagian thought and to write additional polemical works such as *On Nature and Grace*, in which he argued that man was in need of God's grace for his justification and salvation.

While the African church leaders were denouncing Pelagian teaching, the movement was close to gaining support in the East. In fact, at the council of Diospolis (Lydda) in 415, fourteen bishops gathered under the leadership of the metropolitan bishop of Palestinian Caesarea. Communicating with much moderation, Pelagius managed to convince the bishops of his orthodoxy. After being acquitted of heresy and remaining in full communion with the church, Pelagius quickly wrote a triumphal report to his friends and supporters. This triumph, however, was short-lived. Despite the silence and procrastination of Pope Innocent I (Pelagius had many powerful supporters in Rome, including the priest and future pope Sixtus), the African bishops accepted the challenge of returning the church to its traditional doctrine.[29]

Two provincial councils met in 416 to confront the Pelagian heresy. One met Carthage under the direction of Aurelius, the primate of Proconsularis. The second met at Milevus and was presided over by the Numidian primate Severus, though Augustine dominated the council. Afterward, conciliar letters, in which the African bishops unanimously condemned the original Pelagian doctrine as it had been articulated by Caelestius during his testimony at Carthage in 411, were sent to the pope. However, news came from Rome of a group actively pressuring the pope to uphold the decision of the council of Diospolis and to rehabilitate Pelagius. Then, a third appeal was made to the pope in the form of a letter signed by the bishops of Carthage, Hippo, Tagaste, Uzalis, and Calama, with Augustine's work *On Nature and Grace* appended to the letter. Over the course of these years, the Pelagian crisis was not confronted by the bishop of Rome, but rather by his African colleagues.

Innocent's responses to the African bishops are preserved in Augustine's correspondence.[30] With prudence and without wanting to involve himself fully in the controversy, the aging pope was in general theological agreement with the views of his African colleagues and even declared that Pelagius and Caelestius should be expelled from the church. Though

29. Cf. Augustine *Letter* 191.1.
30. Cf. Augustine *Letters* 181–83.

Innocent considered the two men guilty of heresy, he was still not convinced of the danger that their movement posed to the church. In the eyes of the Roman bishop, jealous over his own position, the most important issue was that the African bishops needed to be careful about respecting his episcopal authority. Because of the authority granted to Peter—and those who inherit his seat—all decisions made by individual churches, though perfectly just, should be confirmed by the apostolic see. In short, Innocent I seemed more concerned about affirming his primacy as pope than confronting a lay monk and his fellow heretics.

Innocent died on March 12, 417. His successor Zosimus was not the most competent theologian, and, being of Greek origin, he was sympathetic to the support Pelagius had received during his time in the Holy Land. Hence, for the African bishops, Zosimus' stance only aggravated the crisis; for the heretics, it was an anticipated measure of favor. At this stage, Augustine had just written his work *On the Deeds of Pelagius* in which he made the observation that, despite Pelagius' acquittal at the council of Diospolis, the bishops had not "approved of his positions, which they certainly would have condemned if he had not retracted them."[31] Claiming that he was carefully studying the confusing controversy, Zosimus invited Pelagius and Caelestius to Rome to defend themselves against their accusers. The latter came to Rome and pled his case, and his responses were satisfactory to the pope. Exonerating Caelestius, Zosimus publically remarked at how surprised he was at the conduct of the Carthaginian fathers, who rushed to judgment and condemned Caelestius without a firm basis. However, out of respect for the African bishops, he allowed them the freedom to reexamine carefully the controversy and make their conclusions on the basis of "serious" evidence.

Pelagius responded to Zosimus' invitation by sending a written declaration of his position along with a letter of recommendation from Praylos, the newly appointed bishop of Jerusalem. The pope investigated the matter in a public session, which ended in Zosimus declaring that the accused were innocent of all charges. Though Heros and Lazarus, two bishops who had written letters opposing the decision at Diospolis, were available to testify against Caelestius, Zosimus essentially dismissed the testimony of these men who were also his political enemies. The case was heard and concluded. In a letter dated September 21, 417, the pope ad-

31. Augustine *Reconsiderations* 73.

monished the African bishops who had dared to oppose the faith of such a pious man: "How we were deeply moved. Hardly anyone in attendance could hold back their tears at the thought that such men of faith could be so slandered." As was expected, the false accusations came back on the accusers. However, such a decision reflected a lack of understanding of the African church and the authority of its leaders in the context of the global church. Observing the direction taken in this controversy, which posed a threat to sound doctrine, the African bishops communicated to Rome a passionate declaration, reaffirming their position against the heretical teachings of Pelagius and his followers.

These developments did not escape the attention of the Emperor Honorius. The Latin-speaking community at Jerusalem had reported that Pelagius' followers were involved in a bloody rebellion there. Also, Caelestius had gotten involved in disputes that had degenerated into violence. Guilty of instigating public disorder, he chose to flee the city in order to avoid being arrested. Thus, on April 30, 418, an imperial rescript ordered "Pelagius and Caelestius, those who have caused trouble for the Catholic faith," expelled from Rome, while those supporting them were also warned of an impending judgment. Interestingly, the emperor did not wait for Pope Zosimus' verdict before taking measures to condemn the heresy. In a letter sent to Carthage on April 29, Zosimus continued to communicate his indignation from the previous year in which he chastised the African bishops for angrily condemning such wonderful Christians. Despite acting arrogantly and getting sidetracked by the controversy's gridlock, Zosimus made no official decision about the Pelagians.

Following their fourth local council on the issue, the African bishops continued to stand firm in their opposition to Pelagius. On May 1, 418, 214 bishops from Proconsularis and Numidia gathered in Carthage for a plenary council. In a reaffirmation of Innocent's excommunication of Pelagius and Caelestius, the bishops drafted nine canons articulating orthodox teaching on original sin, baptism, and grace, and then sent the document to Rome.

Finally, in a type of encyclical, written in the months that followed the council at Carthage and signed by all bishops in the Roman world, Zosimus issued his *Tractoria.* The document was largely a restatement of the Carthaginian document, in which he articulated his opposition to the Pelagian heresy and condemned the errors of its proponents. In the *Tractoria,* Zosimus also expressed his appreciation and indebtedness to the African bishops. Isolated and often enduring difficult circumstances, the African church had managed to defend the Catholic faith. Twelve years later, the lay historian Prosper of Acquitaine emphasized this point when he wrote: "Africa, it is you who pursues the cause of our faith with the greatest zeal. . . . What you decided has been approved by Rome and followed by the empire."

After Zosimus' death in December, 418, and Boniface's subsequent consecration as pope, the Pelagian issue was far from resolved. The heresy spread to Gaul, Britain, and other areas—especially within Italy. After 420, the controversy took a new turn that was distinguished by the heated exchange between some strong personalities. Among the Italian dissidents, Julian, the young bishop of Eclanum (Campania) who would eventually take refuge in Sicily and then Constantinople, was a master of dialectics and became the fiercest defender of the condemned heresy. Without a doubt, in this latest and final phase of the Pelagian crisis, the main characters—pursued by the emperor and pope alike—posited themselves as confessors of the true faith. Because of their relationships with functionaries in the Roman administration, the African bishops were able to make effective appeals to the authorities about the Pelagians—though this support was taken to all sorts of extremes. For instance, Augustine was in communication with Count Valerius—to whom he dedicated *On Marriage and Concupiscence* and whom he congratulated for his Catholic faith and praised for his "terror that inspires the impious and new enemies of Christ."[32] Valerius refused to hear any appeals addressed to the emperor by the Pelagians and used coercive measures against those rebel bishops who refused to obey the emperor's rescript.

The Africans knew how to cultivate important contacts. In 419, Alypius, the bishop of Tagaste, was sent to Ravenna on behalf of the church. Having previously served in the Roman administration as a financial assessor, Alypius was aware of the best strategies for navigating the imperial palace's bureaucracy. According to Julian, Alypius took with him a gift of eighty horses, which incited the righteous indignation of the former bishop of Eclanum: "Why have you deprived the poor, fattened herds of horses from every part of Africa, to be driven by Alypius to Italy and offered to every tribune and decurion?"[33] In Africa, Augustine did

---

32. Augustine *Letter* 200.2 [English translation my own].

33. Augustine *Against Julian, an Unfinished Book* 1.42 [unless otherwise noted, all English translations of *Against Julian, an Unfinished Book* and *Against Julian* are my own].

not hesitate to admonish the local magistrates to live according to the orthodox faith as part of their civil duty: "They should live firmly rooted in this faith, and they should respond to enemies of the faith with chastisement and repression."[34]

The question of original sin and the related issue of grace, insurmountable stumbling blocks between Augustine and Pelagianism, also raised problems about the role of sexual relations within marriage. In 401, in his work *On the Good of Marriage*, Augustine challenged certain arguments condemning marriage. Adeodatus' father attempted to show that marriage was inherently good because "God created the sexes." In *City of God*, he added:

> But we, for our part, have no manner of doubt that to increase and
> multiply and replenish the earth in virtue of the blessing of God,
> is a gift of marriage as God instituted it from the beginning before
> man sinned, when He created them male and female, in other
> words, two sexes manifestly distinct.[35]

There were two main themes in Augustine's thought on sexuality: first, mastering the right of reason or allowing true love to triumph over the flesh's impulses; second, reproduction as the essential goal of sexuality. Later, for example in his work *On Marriage and Concupiscence*, he tended to regard sexual intercourse as an evil element of marriage: "Conjugal chastity makes good the evil passion used to procreate children."[36]

On the other hand, Julian, convinced that he was unscathed from physical or moral sins, was quite comfortable with "a legitimate physical union." Augustine responded by chastising him for "celebrating sexual instinct." He added: "Are you speaking of your own experience? Do you really not want a couple to refrain from this evil, which you call good, and prefer that they jump into bed each time they are overcome with desire, sometimes not even waiting for night to come? . . . If this is your sexual life, please spare us the details of your personal experiences in this debate."[37]

Hence, this theological controversy became a personal conflict between Augustine and Julian. From this point onward, the Pelagians

---

34. Augustine *Against Julian, an Unfinished Book* 1.9.

35. Augustine *City of God* 14.22.

36. Augustine *Reconsiderations* 2.79.

37. Augustine *Against Julian* 14.28.

focused their attacks solely on Augustine, their implacable enemy who needed to be soundly defeated. In a letter to Augustine in 418 in which he praised the bishop of Hippo for his stance against the Pelagians despite Rome's silence on the matter, Jerome, who did not have the habit of freely sharing compliments, wrote:

> For you have stood firm with the ardor of faith against the blasts of the winds, and you have preferred, to the extent that it depended upon you, to be set free by yourself from Sodom rather than to dally with those who are perishing. Your wisdom knows what I mean. Well done! You are famous throughout the world. Catholics revere and embrace you as the second founder of the ancient faith. And, what is a sign of greater glory, all the heretics despise you . . . in order to slay with their desire those whom they cannot slay with words.[38]

In passionately defending the primacy of divine grace against heretics who advocated man's complete ability to do good works and avoid sin, Augustine, who would not allow himself to be influenced by Julian and others, became quite entrenched in his views. These developments surely caused the bishop of Hippo to adopt some extreme positions on grace. This ultimately gave rise to a view of grace known as "Augustinianism," which was employed in the church's battle against "practical Pelagianism." It was further developed by the Protestant Reformers, and later in the seventeenth century by Jansen, St. Cyran, and their friends at Port Royal.

Though a complete survey of Augustine's theology of grace and salvation is beyond the scope of the present work, his doctrine was particularly articulated in three anti-Pelagian works—*On Admonition and Grace* (426), *On the Gift of Perseverance* (429), and *On the Predestination of the Saints* (429). In short, Augustine asserted that out of the great masses of men and women lost in original sin (*massa perditionis*), God has chosen—by virtue of his divine power, on account of his mercy, and without taking into consideration the personal merits of individuals—a certain part of the human race to be predestined to salvation. Due to the fact that no one deserves salvation, God's actions are in no way unjust. Because grace is efficacious and irresistible, and the believer is given the gift of perseverance, the elect are secure in their eternal salvation.

---

38. Augustine *Letter* 195.

On the other hand, lacking grace, the reprobate are assured of a certain condemnation.

During this period, the doctrine of predestination was especially troubling for the monastic communities. In Africa, Augustine responded to the concerns of the Hadrumetum monks by writing two books on the subject. These works were actually more offensive to the monks at Marseille, led by John Cassian, as well as those at Lerins. Despite this opposition, one of Augustine's greatest admirers was the Gallic layman, Prosper of Aquitaine. Also, in 431, a year after Augustine's death, Pope Celestin I, in prudent Roman fashion, communicated his praises for Augustine: "The life and merits of Augustine, of holy memory, will always be preserved by our community. A man never accused of the slightest suspicion of wrongdoing, he will be remembered by us as a man of great knowledge and who was always regarded by my predecessors as one of the great teachers."[39]

Augustine, who defended sovereign and divine grace while arguing against man's ability to make spiritual progress on his own, was continually attacked by Julian, whom Augustine regularly referred to as the "remarkable architect of the Pelagian system."[40] By making *ad hominem* arguments and in bringing up Augustine's past, Julian's main goal was to discredit Augustine. Through his books and an intense propaganda campaign, Julian sought to challenge the notion of original sin by purposefully confusing Augustine's teaching with Manichean dualism.

Despite the good relationship Augustine had had with Julian's father, the Pelagian bishop of Eclanum, a master of irony and sarcasm, attacked the "old man of Hippo" and the "king of donkeys" with the most injurious language. With further insults, Julian presented himself as a Roman patriot against "the African" and the "hard-headed Numidian." Through trite nationalism, which proved to be quite effective, Julian, making reference to the ancient wars with Carthage, attacked the "Punic polemicist" and his "bad Carthaginian faith" that corrupted the true Roman doctrine.

Julian offered a fierce closing statement against Augustine—the accused who had Faustus as a tutor, the hearer who was initiated into the "despicable sacraments," and the "faithful disciple of Mani." In short, Julian, who boldly declared that he was unable to tell a lie, claimed that

---

39. Celestin *Letter* 21 [English translation my own].

40. Augustine *Against Julian* 6.11.36.

Augustine was forever a resident of "Mani's brothel," and that "no wild herb could cure this infection." Throughout this exhausting controversy, Julian, through his monotony and exaggeration, posed as the Catholic church's advocate and herald. Indeed, his friends inscribed these words on his tomb in Sicily: "Here lies Julian, Catholic bishop." Until his death, Julian continued his offensive against Augustine. Despite his age and fatigue, the bishop of Hippo remained a fierce polemicist quite capable of delivering a solid blow with just a few stinging words. In short, Augustine put his young adversary—he who "wanted to make a name for himself by making a big fuss"—in his place.[41]

In the spring of 430, as the Vandals ravaged Hippo and as Augustine became weaker in the final months of his life, he continued to respond to Julian's admonition that he should stop being a Manichean. This battle ended tragically as Augustine died before being able to finish his tome against Julian, which he had set aside two years prior. It is significant that the final phrase of this incomplete work was still another response to Julian's charge that Augustine was a Manichean supporter—the last and greatest accusation by the Pelagian bishop.[42]

THE AFRICAN CHURCH IN THE FIRST THIRD OF THE FIFTH CENTURY

Though the African *catholica* was unique in that it could gather 300 bishops together in a church council where there would be unanimous agreement on the canons prepared by the church's doctors, the local churches continued to have fragile theological foundations. Augustine made many references to this "superficial nature of African Christianity."

In 388–389, after his return from Rome to Tagaste, Augustine, then a layman, published *On the Catholic and Manichean Ways of Life*. In the work, he painted an unflattering picture of African Christians, his fellow countrymen who were far from being exemplary in their faith. The habits of the clergy were also scrutinized by the church's critics, and scandals were not a rare occurrence. Church members were attracted to superstitious practices, while other believers remained entangled in some absurd practices that resembled pagan excesses. There were those who honored

---

41. Augustine *Against Julian* 4.15.75.

42. Cf. Augustine *Against Julian, an Unfinished Book* 6.41.

tombs and images, and others who made meals for the dead while having drunken feasts in the cemeteries. As previously mentioned, the *refrigerium* was a widespread custom in the provinces of the western Roman Empire. These memorial meals, which largely perpetuated a similar pagan practice, were especially popular in Africa.

In his *Confessions,* Augustine informs us that his mother Monica, who had joined him in Italy, was attempting to continue the *refrigerium* practice when she was forbidden to do so by the cemetery caretaker at Milan. He writes: Ambrose, "illustrious preacher and exemplar of piety as he was, had forbidden the celebration of these rites."[43] When Augustine was consecrated as bishop of Hippo, there were still remnants (*purgamenta*) that continued these practices, and he struggled in vain to purify his flock from such traditions. While the Christians of Hippo suffered from severe spiritual apathy, these traditional pagan practices remained alive.

During the final decades of the fourth century, the African church (*ecclesia transmarina*) grew significantly in its infrastructure, requiring the need for many "functionaries"—many of whom accepted the call to church ministry against their will. None of the African church leaders could make a claim to apostolic succession. The worldly power that influenced the African ecclesiastical hierarchy actually resulted in an overall spiritual decline in the clerical ranks. Clergy, deacons, priests, and even bishops at times yielded to the temptations that came with ecclesial administrative authority. This was the case of Paul, the bishop of the village of Cataqua (Byzacena), who was confronted by Augustine over a tax matter.[44] A financial prospector who was riddled with debt, Paul acquired a piece of land and then put it in the name of the church in order to avoid paying taxes on it. He also abused his position by withdrawing money from the church treasury for his own expenses.

The canons of the African church councils are filled with teaching that confronted the potential worldly temptations of clergy. They were warned that they did not have the right to take another ministry position in a foreign city without the authorization of their bishop. It was also necessary to put limits on clergy traveling to the imperial court, a particular habit of African clergy. While the clergy gained admirers among secular

---

43. Augustine, *Confessions* 6.2.2.

44. Cf. Augustine *Letter* 96.2.

leaders, such compromises with the authorities rendered the church leadership vulnerable. Despite restrictions on such travel to Italy, the decrees from the African councils in 393, 397, 405, and 407 that continued to address the issue were proof that they were hardly heeded by the clergy.

The same canons also forbade bishops and priests from authorizing private dealers (*conductores*) with the right to manage imperial land holdings or to develop the land in the name of the prince (*procurators*). These clergy were informed that that they were not permitted to give their time to such business negotiations that took them away from their ministry duties or required them to travel. Such disciplinary rulings from the councils revealed the stagnation that existed in some dioceses due to the negligence and incompetence of some clergy who preferred to perform their duties more as business leaders than as pastors. Hence, the conciliar decisions rendered at Carthage show that, from the middle of the fourth century, the African church began to resemble a governing body.

In many cases, church properties were becoming so large that it was necessary to develop a managing infrastructure to oversee the "heavenly manna." At Hippo, a team of clergy (*praepositi*) trained in accounting was entrusted with managing the church property. In some areas, church properties were so vast that more administrative help was required. The council of Carthage in 407 requested that the Roman government appoint official advisors (*advocate*), laymen who represented the church's material interests. Some churches possessed significant tracts of land, which were farmed by settlers (*coloni ecclesiae*) who also lived on the land.[45] Servants also worked these lands as the church was rather slow in liberating its slaves. This was evident during two councils at Carthage, in June and September of 401, when the practice of freeing slaves was introduced into the church (*in ecclesia*) as an official ceremony. Prior to passing this legislation, the African bishops seemed quite concerned to learn if this practice had been accepted in Italy and if the emperor had given his seal of approval to it.[46]

Indeed, the African believers contributed generously to the church needs. Augustine, who had donated his own family's estate to the church at Tagaste,[47] devoted a large part of a sermon praising his fellow priest

---

45. Cf. Augustine, *Letter* 35.4.

46. Cf. *Codex ecclesiae Africanae* c. 64; c. 82.

47. Cf. Augustine *Letter* 126.7.

Leporius, who had come from a wealthy family, yet had given away all of his inheritance in order to build a monastery and a hospital.[48] Despite such generosity, these contributions failed to meet the financial needs of the local African churches, which included the clergy's financial support and the community's material needs. Also, funds were needed to build and maintain numerous church facilities—basilicas, churches, chapels— as some cities had multiple locations for worship. A survey of the significant archaeological remains lead us to conclude that such construction and maintenance required a considerable amount of money.

Despite the African *catholica*'s continual growth since Cyprian's period, and especially since Constantine's peace, the clerical personnel largely came from modest, uncultivated backgrounds. We know of only half a dozen bishops from Augustine's day that did not fit this description. Apart from the bishop of Hippo, there was Bishop Aurelius of Carthage, Alypius of Tagaste, Fortunatus of Cirta, Possidius of Calama, and Evodius of Uzalis. Not counting those pastors who were illiterate—especially among the Donatists—most African church leaders possessed only a basic theological and pastoral training. During a church council in June of 401, Aurelius complained about the lack of educated clergy. The council of Hippo in October of 393 was an exceptional event as Augustine, a young priest who had been ordained for only a year, addressed the plenary council of bishops. Under the supervision of his own bishop, Augustine gave a theological lecture to the gathered bishops. His sermon was so interesting and instructive for his "areopagus" that, at the request of several bishops, he later published it under the title *On Faith and the Creed*.

Because of the rivalry between the Catholics and Donatists, the constantly multiplying Donatist churches, and a crisis in recruiting Catholic clergy, the choice of pastors during this turbulent period was not always favorable. The existence of the two rival communions in the majority of the cities caused a chaotic distribution of the clergy. Some cities like Carthage, which had around 500 clergy in 430, were at the point of saturation, while in other areas church leaders were virtually non-existent. The highest priority of the African clergy did not seem to be serving where believers were in need, regardless of location, or in carrying out the apostolic duty of opposing heretics. A further insight is gleaned from the

---

48. Cf. Augustine *Sermon* 356.10.

African church's refusal to follow the canons of the council of Sardica in 343, which established guidelines for promoting church leaders through the ranks of the clergy. Because of a lack of presbyters qualified for the office of bishop in the African church, it became possible for deacons to be promoted directly to bishop.

Considering further the disparity in the number of church leaders in different regions, there were some bishops, like those in Hippo and Tagaste, who were quite committed to setting apart new leaders. Possidius wrote that Augustine left behind "a very sufficient" number of clergy in Hippo, which included seven priests in 427.[49] However, this was not the focus of most African pastors. Even in the diocese of Hippo, there was a lack of clergy who could minister in Punic, the primary language of many of the rural villages.

Though numerous monasteries were founded in Africa (Augustine was not the innovator of African monasticism, though he contributed greatly to its development), the spiritual and theological capabilities of the monks were generally mediocre, and Augustine was hardly in favor of their ordination to the ministry:

> It is something highly deplorable if we raise monks up to such ru-
> inous pride and think that clerics, among whom we are counted,
> are worthy of grave abuse. After all, at times even a good monk
> does not make a good cleric if he has sufficient continence and,
> nonetheless, lacks the necessary instruction and the personal in-
> tegrity required.[50]

However, in 396–397 a decree from Emperor Arcadius communicated the expectation that the church would ordain monks. Yet the council of Carthage of September 13, 401, forbade bishops from consecrating monks who had deserted their monastery because, at this time, some of the most mediocre monks were leaving their monasteries in hopes of being ordained to the priesthood in another diocese.

Though certain monks ambitiously pursued a career in church leadership, there were other clergy who sensed the call to serve in the lesser clerical orders, such as the diaconate. Here they were entitled to ecclesiastical immunities, and the material benefits of the church, while not having to be burdened with the pastoral duties of a presbyter or bishop. In the

---

49. Possidius *Life of Augustine* 31.
50. Augustine *Letter* 60.1.

420s, a canon from an African church council stipulated that those clergy who refused to accept a higher clerical rank in response to the church's needs would be dismissed. In a letter to a Donatist priest, Augustine does not hide his convictions concerning Paul's words: "He who desires the episcopacy desires a good work (1 Tim 3:1), and yet so many are forced to accept the episcopacy against their will. They are led off, imprisoned, kept under guard, and suffer so much that they do not want until they have the will to accept that good work."[51]

This stagnant state of the Catholic clergy further explains why the church, following the council of Carthage of 411 and the death of Donatism, began to welcome ex-schismatic clergy into the ranks of its leadership. By 401, the legislation that banned apostate clergy from continuing in the ministry was no longer being applied. We observe here the Catholic church's desire to realize the celebrated "unity" of African Christianity. Though encouraged in this direction for nearly a century by the imperial authorities and the church at Rome, the African *catholica* seemed most motivated to assimilate these clergy because of the great needs of its growing churches.

Despite its weaknesses and failures, the African church, since the time of Tertullian and Cyprian, had demonstrated some level of sensitivity to the often awkward interventions of the bishop of Rome. It seems that the pope, in order to strengthen his position, was often predisposed to offer a favorable judgment to those who sought absolution, often making this decision without listening to the arguments of the opposing party.

At the end of 418, the controversy involving the priest Apiarius illustrated the conflict between the African and Roman jurisdictions. The priest from Sicca Veneria, who had been excommunicated by Bishop Urbanus for misconduct, appealed to the Roman bishop. Nothing could have been more injurious for the Africans and more agreeable to Rome. Once again, we meet Zosimus, a very confident pope who had managed to alienate a portion of the clergy in his own city. The pope acceded to Apiarius' request and sent three legates to Carthage. One of them, Faustinus of Potenta, rather arrogantly informed Urbanus that he must rehabilitate his priest or face excommunication. This course of action was, of course, contrary to the African practice that had just been reviewed at the coun-

51. Augustine *Letter* 173.2.

cil of Carthage of May 1, 418. That is, under threat of excommunication, it was forbidden for priests and lesser clergy to appeal a decision already pronounced by their bishop to an overseas authority (i.e., the pope). The matter, however, could be referred to neighboring bishops, to their primate, or even to an African church council. In upholding his decision, Zosimus appealed to some alleged canons of the council of Nicea.

While waiting for more information on the matter, a council met at Carthage in 419 and decided that Apiarius, after seeking and receiving pardon for his sins, could be readmitted to communion. Though not allowed to return to the ministry at Sicca, he was permitted to serve in another church that accepted him. A few years later, in 423, Apiarius fell into even deeper sin and he was again excommunicated. Knowing the way to Rome, he did not hesitate to return there, and, once again, his case was heard. The new pope, Celestin I, also sent Faustinus to inform the African bishops of his decision to absolve Apiarius. Appearing before an African plenary council, where Bishop Aurelius ultimately emerged victorious, Faustinus proved to be more violent than in his previous mission, and, in the name of the pope, he forcefully declared that Apiarius was exonerated. However, after three days of discussion and Faustinus' vehement defense, Apiarius actually confessed to his crimes, which forced the legate to abandon his mission and leave Carthage in much confusion. A final judgment was rendered by the African bishops, and Apiarius' excommunication was made permanent.

During this confrontation with Rome, the African bishops succeeded in gaining the upper hand. From the couriers who came from Alexandria and Constantinople with official copies of the canons of Nicea, they learned that the canons used as the basis of Zosimus' decision—which Faustinus claimed were authentic—had nothing do to with Nicea. On the contrary, the fifth canon of Nicea forbade any bishop, including the bishop of Rome, from receiving into communion a priest who had been excommunicated by another bishop. Any appeals needed to be settled by a council of bishops. For the Africans, this provision also applied to an excommunicated bishop, which eliminated any possible recourse to the bishop of Rome. Aurelius and fourteen of his colleagues responded by offering some timely advice to their Roman colleague: "In the church of Christ, one must act with simplicity and humility, refraining from the arrogant behaviors of the present day." The African bishops clearly communicated their position and, alluding to the alleged conciliar canons falsely invoked by Rome, they referred to the actual decrees made by the fathers at Nicea:

> The canons of Nicea very prudently and justly decreed that all matters should be concluded in the very place that they originated. The grace of the Holy Spirit is not lacking in any province where priests are at work in the administration of justice . . . so that no one will believe that God has entrusted into a single person—whoever he might be—the standard for justice, while ignoring countless numbers of bishops united together in council. . . . Please do not send us any more accusing clergy . . . because, regarding our brother Faustinus (not to mention the disgraceful Apiarius, already separated from the church of Christ for his wicked deeds), we are sure that he will not be tolerated for very long in Africa.[52]

In 425, the African church found itself once more in conflict with the bishop of Rome over maintaining its traditional autonomy—not unlike the harsh conflict that arose between Cyprian and his colleagues with Pope Cornelius and Stephen and the lively dissensions between Augustine and the Roman bishops during the Pelagian controversy. These episodes were characteristic of papal policies that sought to extend Rome's authority into provinces that had escaped its complete control.

The Africans took advantage of these controversies and the difficulties that accompanied Zosimus' accession to the papal seat (including the election of a rival pope), to draw up several conciliar decrees that established their identity within the *catholica*. The affair with Apiarius was the ultimate manifestation of the African church's need for autonomy. Soon afterward, however, the Arian Vandals would invade the African provinces, and the "earthly city" would develop as the "city of God" declined. This was the fleeting glory of the "great church," which, like a fragile mirage, would quickly dissolve and fade away.

ADDITIONAL RESOURCES

Bonner, *Saint Augustine of Hippo: Life and Controversies.*
Brown, *Augustine of Hippo: A Biography.*
Chadwick, *Augustine.*
Decret, *Aspects du manichéisme dans l'Afrique romaine.*

52. Mansi *Conciles* III.839; IV.1516 [English translation my own].

Decret, "Augustin d'Hippone et l'esclavage."

Mandouze, *Saint Augustin: L'aventure de la raison et de la grace.*

Marrou and Bonnadière, *St. Augustin et l'augustinisme.*

O'Meara, *Young Augustine.*

Perler, *Les Voyages de Saint Augustin.*

Plinval, *Pélage, ses écrits, sa vie et sa réforme.*

Trapé, *Saint Augustin, l'homme, le pasteur, le mystique.*

Van der Meer, *Augustine the Bishop.*

10 The Final Stages of the African Church: From the Vandal Invasion to the Arab Maghreb

THE VANDAL CENTURY

A seasoned traveler, Augustine wrote: "the ultimate voyage—death—is the only one that should occupy our thoughts."[1] Amid the misfortunes of the mid-fourth century, Augustine personally wished that this ultimate journey would not be delayed. In his biography of Augustine, Possidius recounted:

> On one occasion he said, as we sat with him at table and were dis-
> cussing these matters: "You know that during our present disaster
> I pray God to deliver this city from the enemies that surround it
> or, should he decide differently, to make his servants strong in
> accepting his will or at least to take me from the present world to
> himself."[2]

At the end of May or beginning of June in 430, the Vandals laid siege to Hippo. In the midst of the onslaught, which lasted fourteen months, Augustine received his wish and died alone in his small monastic cell on August 28, 430, at the age of seventy-six. Possidius added: "He did not make a will because as a poor man of God, he had nothing to leave."[3] With Augustine buried on the very day that he died, the African church also experienced a precarious fate following the end of Roman Africa.

Augustine, however, had not shared the sentiments of his colleague Jerome, who, after learning about Alaric's conquest of Rome in 408, wrote: "the whole world perished in one city."[4] For Augustine, Rome's history was merely a chapter in the history of salvation. It would ultimately cease

---

1. Augustine *Letter* 1.2.
2. Possidius *Life of Augustine* 29.1.
3. Possidius *Life of Augustine* 31.6.
4. [Jerome *Ezekiel* preface (English translation is from *NPNF* 2.6).]

to exist and would not have a place in the "city of God." He added: "Are you astonished at the world going to pieces? You might as well be astonished that the world has grown old. The world is like a man; he's born, he grows up, he grows old . . . the world has grown old; it's full of troubles and pressures . . . Don't be eager to cling to an aged world."[5] Nevertheless, as the empire was under siege in August of 410, Augustine still held out hope that this "world," the Roman Empire, would survive.

Following the Vandal conquest, Jerome expressed his own confusion over the state of things: "If Rome can perish, what can be safe?"[6] However, Augustine chose to regard the imperial capital as more than palaces and triumphal arches: "Perhaps Rome isn't perishing, if Romans aren't perishing . . . What is Rome, after all, but Romans? I mean, we are not concerned with bricks and mortar, with high apartment blocks and extensive city walls."[7] Hence, Augustine saw the city of Rome—a spiritual heartland for him since his youth—as an ideal symbol of "civilization" par excellence that could be experienced and shared by all of humanity.

Augustine was not at all surprised by "all the spoiling, then, which Rome was exposed to in the recent calamity—all the slaughter, plundering, burning, and misery." This was simply a natural part of "barbarian savagery." On the other hand, he did find it admirable that Christians, who had taken refuge in the basilicas, were spared by the Vandals. However, he observed: "Whoever does not see that this is to be attributed to the name of Christ, and to the Christian temper, is blind; whoever sees this, and gives no praise, is ungrateful; whoever hinders any one from praising it, is mad." Augustine added that though the Vandals acted with compassion in this case, they should not be credited with what only God can do. That is, he alone is capable of bringing some civility, even for a moment, to their "fierce and bloody minds."[8] Like many of his contemporaries, Augustine reacted to Rome's fall with mixed feelings. On one hand, he was repulsed by the brutal acts of terror. On the other, he felt pity for the savage and brutal persecutors, who were strangers to basic human decency (*toto orbe terrarium*)—Roman culture and values. These "hordes," of course, descended upon a large part of the North African population.

5. Augustine *Sermon* 81.8.

6. [Jerome *Letter* 123.16. English citation is from Peter Brown, *Augustine of Hippo: A Biography*, rev. ed. (Berkeley: University of California Press, 2000) 288.]

7. Augustine *Sermon* 81.9.

8. Augustine *City of God* 1.7.

In a previous letter to the African Count Boniface, Augustine had made mention of "African barbarians."[9] Such rugged peoples had settled in the African interior or in the mountainous regions of Kabylia, the Aures, or the Ouarsensis. Others formed semi-nomadic tribes that hovered around the southern boundaries of Roman Africa—areas not controlled by the Roman army or administration and which were hardly touched by the church. Augustine, however, had no dealings with the new European "barbarians," who would dominate "barbarian" Africa for the next century.

Originally from the Baltic shore region, the Vandal tribes had immigrated toward more fertile areas. In 409, they arrived in Spain and, twenty years later in May, 429, they crossed the Straits of Gibraltar. Under the leadership of a true military commander, Genseric, some 80,000 men, women, and children headed for the African coast. Though they conquered Carthage in 439, the Vandals were able only to secure a small part of the African provinces, which included portions of Numidia and the Mauretanian coastline. The conquered region amounted to around 100,000 square kilometers, less than one-third of the territory of the former provinces. The remaining areas were divided up into autonomous territories and Berber "kingdoms." From the perspective of the empire as well as the church, these losses were immense. While Rome lost the essential foundation of its economy, the church was without its typical base of support against the Vandals, who, since the third century, had been Arians and opposed the divinity of Christ. We observe here the extent to which state and church interests had overlapped, and, when the state collapsed, the church alone was forced to preserve the legacy and culture of both the church and state.

Even more than the local and provincial officials who administrated the towns and provinces in the name of the emperor, the African clergy—as church leaders and as Romans—completely rejected Vandal rule. They opposed what they saw as a double evil—the domination of barbarians and heretics. In response to this radical opposition, the Vandals demanded complete allegiance to their rule and their Arian faith.

From the moment of their arrival in Africa, the Vandal conquerors put these policies to work. The king not only named his leading counselors and officials, he also appointed the highest ranking Arian clergy—leaders of a church that he controlled through the Carthaginian patriarch. It is

9. Cf. Augustine *Letter* 220.7.

difficult to determine if persecution against the Catholics began during Genseric's reign because he did not appear to have a specific religious policy in place. Nevertheless, the African *catholica* did suffer the consequences of political changes during this period.

Some of the religious measures adopted by the Arian king were probably not opposed by the Catholic clergy. For instance, those who engaged in public brawls—a regular occurrence between fans of opposing sides at the circus (the "greens" and the "blues")—were severely punished. Some were sentenced to hard labor in the government mines, while others had their ears cut off or were burned alive. Other measures focused on social morals. Brothels were closed, and the prostitutes were forced to get married. Men and women accused of adultery were threatened with the death penalty. Prostitutes were captured during raids in Carthage and shipped off to the countryside to prevent them from returning to the capital. In short, the Vandals put an end to the *dolce vita,* the Epicurean mode of living summarized by an inscription recovered at the forum in Thamugadi:

> *Venari/Lavari, Ludere/Ridere, Occ [sic] est/Vivere*
> The hunt, the baths, the games, the pleasure, this is the life.[10]

Regarding economic interests, the Vandals, not without reason, subjected the church to the same policies of confiscation endured by all large landowners: land was taken and assigned to new owners, while all other belongings—from buildings to jewelry to slaves—were also confiscated. Church property (buildings, land, and sacred vessels) was given to the Arian clergy. Genseric only granted favors to those he had good reason to suspect of collaborating with the former Roman government. That is, though he granted some concessions to the church, it was ultimately to gain an advantage over his enemies. For instance, in 454, the year before he raided Rome and sacked the capital once more, he authorized the election of a Catholic bishop in Carthage, a position that had been vacant for fifteen years.

When Huneric (477–484) succeeded his father, the Vandal religious policies quickly worsened. Initially, the new king seemed willing to curry favor with the Catholics. For instance, from 477 he began a bloody suppression of the Manicheans, which, according to Victor de Vita, was welcomed by most Catholic leaders. However, this was little more than a scheme by a fanatical tyrant who was about to unleash his real plan.

---

10. *Corpus des Inscriptions latines* VIII.17938 [English translation my own].

Huneric's initial approach was to focus his attack on property instead of people. He forbade non-Arians from holding any public position. Since the Vandal conquest, Catholics and others had still been allowed to serve in such roles. Those officials refusing to convert to Arianism had their belongings seized and were transferred to Sicily or Sardinia.

However, Huneric soon resorted to other tactics. Victor de Vita recorded that some nuns in one convent were tortured and suffered despicable humiliation—measures intended to force their conversion to Arianism. Several of them died from the attacks, while others were left crippled for the rest of their lives. We are also aware that close to 5000 clergy and laymen were deported at this time. As most were from Proconsularis, they were transported in caravans to Hodna, in the Saharan region, where those who survived were most likely enslaved by the Maures.[11]

The Arian clergy also undertook its own propaganda campaign, which had little difficulty arousing the king's zeal. In an attempt to offer a legitimate basis for his heinous crimes, Huneric summoned a council of Arian and Catholic leaders in which each side could present and defend its position. The Vandal king communicated, "In order to avoid scandal in the lands entrusted to us by God, we inform you, with the consent of our bishops, of our decree for you to come to Carthage on February 1, 484. Attendance is compulsory and failing to appear will result in a most unfortunate consequence for you." Forced to appear at the council, the Catholic bishops in attendance numbered 466 and included: fifty-six from Proconsularis; 107 from Byzacena; five from Tripolitania; 125 from Numidia; 120 from Mauretania Caesarea; forty-four from Mauretania Sitifien; and eight from Sardinia and Balearas. The gathering was little more than a masquerade, and, despite their discourses, the Catholics, not unlike the Donatists at the council of 411, were condemned before the meeting began. The Vandal king then issued an edict with reprisals against the Catholics, which he presented as the logical outcome of the council.

From this point on, persecution against the Catholic "heretics" was given legitimacy and carried out openly. Based on an initial decree of February 7, 484, Catholic worship services were banned in all basilicas, which were now Arian property. A second edict, issued February 25, 484,

11. Cf. Victor de Vita *History of the Vandal Persecution* 2.24–27.

forced all Catholics to convert to Arianism by June 1. Fines began to be levied, according to the person's social and economic status, while dissidents were exiled and had their belongings confiscated. Members of the royal court were branded with a dishonorable seal and listed among the state's chief criminals. The civil governors were warned to enforce the edicts faithfully or they would also be subject to the law. In all, 500 clergy from Carthage were denounced and sent into exile and, generally, the African Catholic leadership suffered much brutality: 334 pastors were exiled or dispersed; others were sent to Corsica to cut wood for the royal fleets, while another 90 leaders died in the two years following the council.

Though this was the most severe persecution endured by the African Catholic church, the Vandal king simply copied the anti-heretical legislation that was previously employed by the Romans. Hence, it was forbidden for Catholics to open their basilicas, to hold worship assemblies, to distribute the sacraments, and to ordain priests and bishops. There were certainly a large number of confessors, and every social class was included in this drama that shook the church. There were also apostates, including members of the clergy—that is, bishops, priests and deacons who agreed to be baptized as Arians and renounce their Catholic baptism.

Huneric's death marked an end to this period of violent persecution. He was succeeded by his two nephews—Gunthamund (484–496) and Thrasamund (496–523)—who prided themselves on being men of culture and liberal thought, and who pursued a rather clever plan for "Arianization." This included excessively burdening Catholic clergy with taxes and fines. Also, Thrasamund sent 120 bishops into exile, 60 of whom were sent to Sardinia.

Under Hilderic (523–530), the situation finally calmed down. Exiled bishops began to return, and the large number of vacant episcopates, such as Carthage, began to be filled and the churches were to be re-opened. According to the *Summary of the African Provinces and Cities,* in 484 the Mauretanian provinces and Numidia still had a large number of bishops—123 in Numidia, 42 in Mauretania Sitifien, and 126 in Mauretania Caesarea. As the *Summary's* text has some defects, these figures should be accepted with caution. Two regional church councils took place in 523, followed by another in Byzacena in 525, and then a general council in Carthage in February, 525. The latter council was attended by just 61 bishops and was something of a failure. This outcome can be explained by some unfavorable circumstances in the assembly itself, and by the fact that many of the independent-minded bishops of Byzacena and Numidia were not eager to meet with their colleagues from Proconsularis, including the primate of Carthage. With the turbulent period now behind them, the African *catholica*, despite the fact that many of their number joined the Arians, was able to carry on its traditions. This was largely due to a developed Christian culture and a church that had become deeply rooted in Africa.

The greatest amount of upheaval to the African church in the early church period was brought on by the Vandal conquest. Eventually, however, the Vandal territories were attacked by nomadic camel-herding tribes from Tripolitania—the same land that had been surrounded by independent Berber kingdoms that had amassed a significant fighting force. These kingdoms had been dismantled from within by those who benefited from the Roman *felicitas*, and by those who longed for the ancient landowning class and a Catholic church hierarchy. In short, the stage was set for a new conqueror to come and deal a death blow. The "reconquest" culminated in 533 with the Byzantine General Belisarius' campaign. After his victory at Tricamarum (south of Carthage) and the surrender of the Vandal usurper Gelimar, Roman power was restored in Africa. Despite its victory, the Byzantines still faced a small but ever-present movement of "re-Berberization."

THE AFRICAN CHURCH UNDER "GREEK" CONTROL

With the "barbarians" defeated and the empire restored, many Catholic church leaders were tempted by the potential of having renewed influence as allies of the state. Indeed, it was the end of the "hundred years of captivity," as the period of Vandal domination was called. In 534, the year after Justianian's armies emerged victorious, Bishop Reparatus of Carthage convened a council of 220 bishops to examine the challenges facing the *catholica* in this era of renewed hope. On the other hand, the Arian church was quickly fading into oblivion.

We have a fairly good idea of Africa's state when the Byzantines arrived in September of 533. The Vandals had not succeeded in creating a new civilization or even integrating with the cultures of this occupied region. Rather, Africa's social landscape was quite splintered. The populace, whether Romanized or not, was comprised of rival groups representing different and opposing cultural traditions.

Belisarius' victory overturned Genseric's conquest, and Vandal Africa was taken over by those who boasted of being Rome's legitimate successors. However, Africa had gone through quite a bit of change in the previous century. Efforts to re-establish the ancient southern boundaries of Africa, as constituted by Diocletian, ended in failure. Though the Byzantine administration tried hard to divide the territory into seven regions, as it had been in the fourth century, it basically inherited a region that the Vandals had ransacked. As a result, they controlled an unstable territory that was no larger than what their predecessors controlled. This included what is now Tunisia and eastern Algeria and extended, at least for a brief period, to the region of Sitifis that surrounded the Aures, and to some cities on the Mauretanian coastline. Thus, the Byzantines were unable to gain control of the majority of the African territory, which included one-third of modern Algeria and all of Morocco. Mauretania Tingitane was essentially reduced to the city of Septem (Ceuta), and Mauretania Caesarea was comprised of Caesarea and a couple of towns along the coast. The latter were fortified by their inhabitants and were only accessible from the sea.

The "re-conquest" also brought an unexpected set of circumstances as Catholic bishops were placed in the position of carrying out the will of the Byzantine authorities. One example is the "three chapters" affair—an improper designation to be sure—which brought opposition between groups of bishops and the official state church. Since the time of Nestorius, who was appointed bishop of Constantinople by the emperor in 428, there was a significant doctrinal controversy over the human and divine natures of Christ that captivated the attention of the councils of Ephesus in 431 and 449 and Chalcedon in 451. Convinced by his wife Theodora (a former dancer with a questionable past who had been converted to a life of theological speculation) that answering these theological debates came under his jurisdiction, the Emperor Justinian wanted to impose his own heretical view on the issue. Pope Vigilius, who was indebted to the empress for his position, had a deplorable attitude throughout the controversy and changed his position multiple times, which nearly caused a schism between Rome and the African church. As per usual, the African bishops refused to comply with the emperor's wishes and argued that the emperor should uphold the canons of the church, not try to determine them. Justinian reacted strongly to the Africans, enacting capital punishment and exiling his strongest opponents. As the most defiant church leaders were replaced by men devoted to Justinian, the African church was forced to obey the emperor.

Submitting to the Byzantine authorities, the African *catholica* regained its former privileges. Property and goods seized by the Vandals were returned. Church buildings were restored and many new ones were built, and monasteries were also founded. The bishops also recovered the practice of gathering on a regular basis for councils in order to strengthen episcopal unity that had been affected by the previous century's events and to renew a deteriorated sense of ecclesiastical discipline. As noted, in 534, the day after Byzantine authority was re-established, 220 bishops gathered for a council. Though the surviving lists are incomplete, we do know that plenary councils took place in Carthage between 525 and 646. Despite this lack of evidence, some observations can be made. The episcopate was particularly strengthened in Proconsularis as the number of bishops doubled from 48 at the council of 525 to nearly 100 who attended in 646. Tripolitania maintained five bishops during this period. On the other hand, the neighboring province of Byzacena, where the population greatly diminished since the Berber rebellions against the foreign authorities, went from 125 bishops at the council convened by Huneric in 484 to 43 in 646. Due to limited evidence, it is difficult to determine the status of the church in Numidia and Mauretania at this time. An episcopal list, which probably dates to the beginning of the seventh century, mentions but 15 bishops and churches in the central and western Berber regions. Though a few churches existed in the interior, such as Sitifis and Lambida (Medea), the rest were scattered along the coast and included Caesarea, Cartennae, Tingi and Lixus (near Larache on the Atlantic coast).

It should be noted that Donatism resurfaced as a threat in this period, particularly in Numidia. Benefiting from the support of local officials, these heretics took over former Catholic churches and continued to re-baptize Catholics, who joined their ranks in increasing numbers.

Justin II (565–578) essentially continued the religious policies of his father; however, he went even further by placing the bishops in a role of supervising the state's functionaries. This produced some internal disputes between the clergy—some of whom inflicted corporeal punishment on other church leaders—and conflict between the clergy and the laity. The primate of Carthage and the African church councils were no longer responsible for ruling on questions of church discipline; rather, all of these cases were referred to Rome. Simony and corruption, a veritable "gangrene," began to develop within the ranks of the clergy, and Gregory the Great (590–602) was continually called upon to settle disputes. Unfortunately, his intervention failed to motivate "lukewarm" church leaders. Gregory's letters provide some insights on such developments: the bishop of Tigisis was selling ministry positions within his diocese; the bishop of Lamiggiga (Seriana, north of Batna) accepted bribes from the Donatists; and, in order to escape condemnation, the primate of Byzacena purchased protection from the provincial governor for a large sum of money.[12]

As Byzantine Africa continued to sink into stagnation and become more fragile, this context fostered an atmosphere of insurrection among sedentary tribal confederations, including the Berber and Romano-Berber kingdoms. Cherishing their hard-fought independence, they were quite hostile to the "Greeks"—the term they used to describe the Byzantine functionaries who claimed to represent Rome—but were quite aware of the new empire's power. Within this depressed context, the Berber tribes submitted to the new administration, in which they were pressured by crushing taxes and forced to offer bribes to the local governors. In this sense, the Berber kingdoms regretted the demise of the Vandals, under whom they had suffered less hardship. The time had come, however, for a new power that would come from the East.

AFRICAN CHRISTIANS: *DHIMMI* IN AN ARAB MAGHREB

Marked by eight campaigns directed by different leaders who experienced victories and defeat, the Arab conquest of North Africa unfolded over the course of a half-century, beginning in 649. It began with an initial raid against the "unbelieving country that misleads and deceives." These words were attributed to the Caliph Omar by the early Arab historian Ibn Abdel Hakam.[13] Around 705, Musa Ibn Nucayr's troops arrived at the shores of the Atlantic. It is, of course, not our purpose here to retrace fully the steps of this conquest. However, during the course of this great metamorphosis in which North Africa's identity went from being west-

12. Cf. Gregory the Great *Letters* 12.28–29; 1.82; 11.27.
13. Cf. Hakam, *Conquest of North Africa and Spain.*

ern, Roman, and Christian to being the Maghreb—the "sunset" of the eastern, Arab-Muslim world—what happened to African Christianity?

The conquest was carried out in the spirit of *jihad* ("holy war"), and battles were waged in order to convert the African peoples to Islam. The African Christians viewed this newly imported religion as a Christian heresy, something to which they were quite accustomed in Africa. This explains in part why many Christians converted to Islam. Driven by fear or greed, these converts simply viewed themselves as adherents to a different type of Christianity.

Conversion to the new religion was most keenly observed in the massive recruitment of Berbers into the ranks of the victorious Arab army. As war or *jihad* was a religious act, conversion was necessary, and it was largely a formality among the Berbers. Very early on, Arab leaders established centers for religious training in places like Kairouan in modern Tunisia. Taking the name *ribat* (from which the modern Moroccan capital of Rabat takes its name), these centers functioned as military bases and Islamic teaching centers. Truly, it is impossible to assess fully the significance of this movement of conversion to Islam as Africa was coming under Arab control.

Christians who refused to convert to the new religion were subjected to *dhimmi* ("protected") status and were forced to pay the *djizya* ("tax"). In exchange for this permanent status of inequality, the Muslim authority, which promised to respect the Christians, recognized their right to live on Islamic soil and guaranteed their legal protection. However, it was impossible for a Christian to hold any place of public service.

Having *dhimmi* or dependent status constantly reminded the Christians and Jews that they were minorities. However, this did not mean that they were marginalized in a Muslim society. Indeed, daily life in urban society brought Arabs and Christians into frequent contact. While the majority of Christians were merchants, others also worked as artisans. In fact, it was only puritanical groups like the *fuqaha* that forced the *dhimmi* to be segregated and feel the brunt of a sectarian attitude.

It is certain that a large number of Africans, refusing to accept *dhimmi* status, immigrated to Sicily, Sardinia, or Italy during this period. The African economy suffered as a result, and the Arabs were forced to recruit artisans and specialists to replenish this depleted labor pool, especially in the area of ship building.

During this "landslide," the African church was able to persevere for a period of time. However, the centuries of the great *catholica* were over. In two letters written in 1053, Pope Leo IX reminisced about the days when hundreds of African bishops would turn out for a church council. By Leo's day, only five bishops could be counted in all of Africa (*in tota Africa*). In a letter from Pope Gregory to Bishop Cyriacus of Carthage in 1076, we learn that Cyriacus was the last remaining bishop in Africa. While the African church continued to have a prominent place in the Western Christian tradition, it was merely the memory of the church that survived. Indeed, the church of Tertullian, Cyprian, and Augustine had disappeared.

Though the African episcopal hierarchy had disappeared, some indigenous Christian communities continued—two of which have been confirmed through archaeological research. Between 1913 and 1925, twelve funerary steles were discovered in En-Gila, a region fifteen kilometers south of Tripoli that has now been overcome by the desert. The funerary monuments, dating from 945 to 1003, were erected in remembrance of three who had died—Andreas, Petrus, and Maria. One of the deceased was referred as *judex*, which was probably an indication of his role as a leader in the Christian community in En Gila in the second half of the tenth century. Other inscriptions included simple eulogies and prayers for the deceased:

> *Requiem aeternum det tibi Deus et lux perpetua luceat tibi.*
> May God give you rest in eternal life and may perpetual light
>   shine upon you

> *Orate pro me, sic habeatis Deum protectorem in diem iudicii.*
> Pray for me and may God protect you in the Day of Judgment.

Other inscriptions, distinguished by a "barbaric" Latin, reveal a vague understanding of the Scriptures, which were probably cited from memory. Some biblical texts that can be recovered include:

> *In te Domine speravi, non confundar in aeternum.*
> In you Lord, I have put my hope, that I will never be put to shame
>   (cf. Ps 31:2).

> *Ossa arida resurgetis et vivetis et videbitis majestatem Domini.*
> Dry bones, you will rise up, you will live and see the glory of the
>   Lord (cf. Ezek 37:3–6).

O vos omnes qui transitis per viam, aspicite et videtis si est dolor,
quails est dolor meus.

Oh, all of you pass by the way, look and see if there is a pain like
mine (cf. Lam 1:12).

Read in their context and in light of the African church's destiny, these inscriptions, rescued from the desert sands, have a striking intensity about
them.

Three other epitaphs, also written in poor Latin, were discovered between 1928 and 1961 in Kairouan. These documents, dated 1007, 1019,
and 1046, provide evidence for a Christian community with a leadership
structure in North Africa's leading Islamic city four centuries after the
Arab conquest. One stele commemorates the life of *senior* Peter, probably
a leader in the local community. Another inscription mentions Firmus
who served as a *lector*, the first rank in the lower orders of the traditional Catholic clergy. The inscription from 1007 (of the Dionysian era)
also mentions the date 397 *anno infidelium* ("in the year of the infidels"),
which of course refers to the Muslim "year of the Hejira."

This double reference to the Christian and Muslims eras suggests
that the last African Christian communities had integrated and finally
disappeared into the Muslim society of their day. When the Ummayad
Caliphate of Cordoba came to an end in 1031, the last Christians at
Kairouan—the last vestiges of the glorious African church—had disappeared into Islam.

ADDITIONAL RESOURCES

Berthier, *Les Vestiges du christianisme antique dans la Numidie centrale.*
Courtois, "Grégoire VII de l'Afrique du Nord: Remarques sur les communautés
chrétiennes d'Afrique au IXe siècle."
Courtois, *Les Vandales et l'Afrique.*
Diehl, *L'Afrique byzantine.*
Lapeyre, "La politique religieuse des rois vandales."
Mahjoubi, "Nouveau témoignage épigraphique sur la communauté chrétienne de
Kairouan au XIe siècle."
Marçais, *La Berbérie musulmane de l'Orient au Moyen Age.*
Paribeni, "Sepolcreto cristiano di Engila."
Seston, "Sur les derniers temps du christianisme en Afrique."

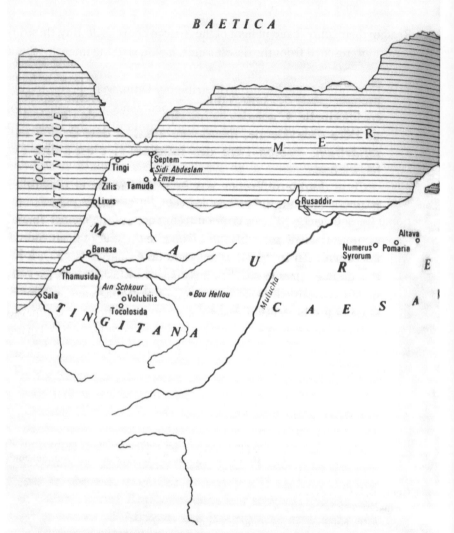

Source: François Decret with Mhamed Fantar, *L'Afrique du Nord. Des Origines au Veme siècle*, 1981, 350–53. The map was designed by André Leroux, and reproduced here with the kind permission of Éditions Payout.

General Map

Banasa Roman town/city   *Sidi Abdeslam* Modern town/city

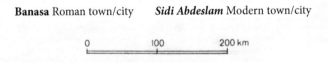

0   100   200 km

of Roman Africa

MER MED I

Hippo Diarrhytus
Chullu
Thabraca
Utica
Thuburbo Minus
Carthago
Rusicade
Hippo Regius
Clupea
Igilgili
Maxula
Ampsaga
Bulla Regia *Bagradas*
Simitthu
Sutunurca
Siagu
Curubis
Cirta
Calama
Thuburscu
Uthina
Neapolis
Cuicul
Thagaste
Thugga
Bure
Pupput
Sitifis
Thubursicu
Numidarum
Sicca Veneria
Thuburbo Maius
Pheradi Maius
Madauros
Furnos Maius
Abthugni
Assuras
Zama Regia
Hadrumetum
Lamasba
Mactaris
Lepti Minus
Lambaesis
Thamugadi
Althiburos
Thysdrus
Thubunae
Ammaedara
Calceus Herculis
Mascula
Theveste
Sufetula
Vescera
Aurasius Mons
Thelepte
BYZACENA
Acholla
NUMIDIA
Thaenae
Macomades
Minores
Cercina
Gemellae
Capsa
Chott Melrhir
Syrtis Minor
Chott el-Fedjedj
Tusuros
Tacape
Nepte
Meninx I.
(Djerba)
Chott el Djerid
Turris
Tamalleni
Gighthis
Bezereos
Pisida
Tisavar
Talalati

Si Aoun

Great Western Sand Sea

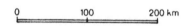

0   100   200 km

Cidamus

General Map

204

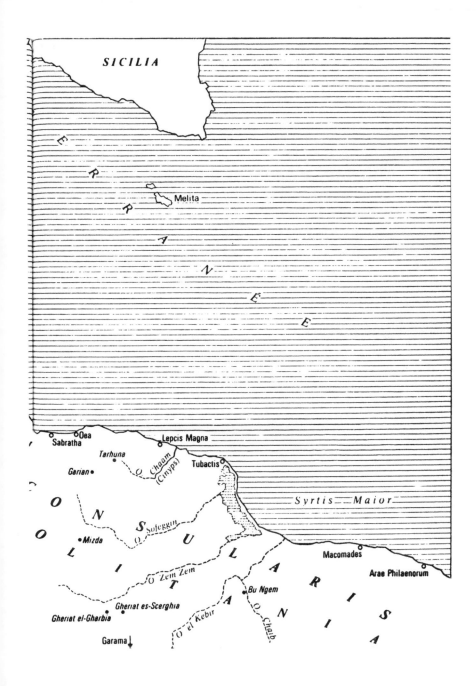

of Roman Africa (*continued*)

Chronology

North African Church History	Dates	Political, Religious, and Social Events
	111	Trajan establishes a precedent for Christian offenders.
	180–192	Commodus is emperor.
Twelve martyrs from Scilli (Proconsularis).	180	
Tertullian's *Apology*.	197–198	
Tertullian's *Prescription Against Heretics*.	c. 200	
	202	Rescript from Septimius Severus banning all Christian and Jewish proselytizing.
At Carthage, six Christians, including Perpetua and Felicitas, are martyred.	203	
Christian soldier condemned at Lambaesis. Tertullian's *Letter to Scapula*.	c. 211	
	211–213	Scapula is proconsul. Persecution.

North African Church History	Dates	Political, Religious, and Social Events
	212	Caracalla's edict extending citizenship to all in the Roman Empire.
Tertullian becomes a Montanist.	c. 213–214	
Bishop Agrippinus of Carthage convenes church council.	c. 220	
Ninety bishops gather in a council under Donatus of Carthage.	236–240	
	238	Gordian's revolt in Africa.
Cyprian is bishop of Carthage.	249	
	End 249	Decius' edict of persecution.
Fabian of Rome martyred.	January 250	
Violent persecution in Africa with large numbers of martyrs.	250–251	
Cyprian leaves Carthage to avoid arrest.	250	
Cyprian's *On the Lapsed*.	251	
Cyprian oversees seven councils in conflict with Rome on re-baptizing the lapsed.	251–256	African plague (252–254).
Schisms with Novatus, Felicissimus, and Novatian at Carthage and Rome.	252–255	
Cyprian sent into exile at Curubis (Corba).	257	Valerian's first edict against Christianity.
Cyprian martyred.	258	Valerian's second edict.

North African Church History	Dates	Political, Religious, and Social Events
	284–305	Rule of Diocletian and the Tetrarchy (293).
Two Christian conscientious objectors executed at Tingi and Tebessa.	295–299	
	302	First edict against the Manicheans (twenty-one more will follow under emperors between 372–445).
Forty-nine martyrs in Abitina; large numbers of apostates among clergy and believers.	303–304	Four edicts of persecution published against Christians, including the death penalty for offenders (304).
Crispina, martyred at Tebessa.	End 304	
Toleration granted to Christians in Africa.	305	Diocletian abdicates.
Mensurius of Carthage dies at Rome.	306–307	Maxentius and the restoration of the African church.
Consecration of Silvanus of Cirta. Caecilianus is elected and consecrated bishop of Carthage, then deposed by Secundus, primate of Numidia, who consecrated Majorinus in Caecilianus' place.	307	
Beginning of the Donatist schism.	308–310	Domitius Alexander, usurping emperor in Africa.
	312	Constantine's victory over Maxentius at Milvan Bridge.

North African Church History	Dates	Political, Religious, and Social Events
Donatus succeeds Majorinus at Carthage.	313	Constantine intervenes in the Donatist controversy, responding to the Donatists' appeal.
Council of Arles.	314	
	316	Constantine takes action against the Donatists.
	321	Constantine issues an edict of toleration.
Council of 270 Donatist bishops at Carthage.	c. 336	
	337	Constans rules in the western empire.
	337–345	Circumcellion movement, led by Axido and Fasir, emerges in Numidia.
Donatist martyrs.	347	Mission of the imperial legates, Paulus and Macarius. Massacres in Numidia. Wave of suicides among the Circumcellions. Constans issues an edict of unity, favoring the catholic church.
Augustine born at Tagaste.	354	
Parmenianus succeeds Donatus, who dies in exile.	c. 355	
	361–361	Julian's reign; his edict of toleration; the Donatist church reacts by appealing to the emperor for support.

North African Church History	Dates	Political, Religious, and Social Events
Optatus of Milevus writes his treatise against Donatism.	c. 365	
Donatist Bishop Rogatus of Cartennae initiates a schism.	c. 370	Firmus' revolt.
Augustine becomes a Manichean.	372–375	
	380	Emperor Theodosius declares Christianity the orthodox state religion.
	376–399	Constant reinforcement of the anti-Donatist legislation that benefits the catholic church.
Augustine leaves for Rome, then is named rhetor for Milan.	383–384	
Augustine is baptized in Milan (May 25, 387), then returns to Africa.	387–388	
Optatus is the Donatist bishop of Thamugadi (Timgad).	388	
Augustine ordained presbyter in Hippo.	391	
Augustine's public debate with Fortunatus the Manichean.	392	
Aurelius and Primianus are elected respectively as the catholic and Donatist bishops of Carthage.	391–392	

North African Church History	Dates	Political, Religious, and Social Events
Donatist council of Cabarsussa. Maximianus and his colleagues initiate a schism against Primianus.	393	
Council of 310 Donatist bishops at Vaga.	394	Death of Theodosius.
Augustine consecrated bishop of Hippo.	395	
Catholic councils at Carthage (June 26 and August 28).	397	
	397–398	Revolt by the African Count Gildo.
Augustine writes his treatise against Bishop Petilianus of Cirta.	401–405	
Catholic councils at Carthage (June 15 and September 13).	401	
Catholic council at Milevus (August 27).	402	
Attack against Maximianus of Vaga. Catholic council (June 14–29) asking the emperor to take measures to end the Donatist schism. Public debate between Augustine and Felix the Manichean.	404	

North African Church History	Dates	Political, Religious, and Social Events
Primianus, Petilianus and other Donatist bishops are sent into exile. Catholic council meets in Carthage to thank the emperor.	405	Honorius issues three edicts; Donatism is condemned as a "heresy"; there is a new edict of unity.
Catholic councils (June 16 and October 13) to demand radicals measures against heresy; bishops are sent on a mission to the imperial court.	408	Rigorous sanctions are handed down by the Proconsul Donatus.
Protests from African bishops; delegation sent to Ravenna.	409	Stilicho's murder. Alaric declares Attalus emperor. Honorius abandons his religious policy favoring the catholic church.
A catholic council meets in Carthage (June 14) asking Honorius to convene a conference where Donatists and catholics are required to attend.	410	Alaric sacks Rome (August). Honorius' edict of toleration is reversed. Marcellinus is designated (October 14) the organizer of the conference at Carthage.
Pelagius visits Africa.	410–411	
Conference (June 1–3, 8) with 286 catholic bishops and 284 Donatist bishops. First council of Carthage against the Pelagians (October/November).	411	Marcellinus rules in favor of the *catholica* (June 26); Donatism is banned and its properties confiscated.

North African Church History	Dates	Political, Religious, and Social Events
	412	Imperial edict issued definitively condemning Donatism (January 30); Donatists are Circumcellions are deemed outlaws. Resistance by blocks of Donatists in Numidia and Mauretania. New wave of suicides among the Circumcellions. Eight new laws issued supporting the edict.
Marcellinus is executed at Carthage.	413	Revolt of the African Count Heraclianus.
Councils at Milevus and Carthage condemn Pelagius' teachings. Pope Innocent I shows ambiguous attitude toward Pelagianism. African bishops make new appeals to Rome over Pelagianism.	416	
Pelagius and Caelestius are invited to Rome by Zosimus; their defense is favorably received.	417	

North African Church History	Dates	Political, Religious, and Social Events
Another council meets at Carthage. Crisis develops between the African church and church at Rome. The pope accepts the African bishops' judgment on Pelagius; Caelestius is excommunicated.	418	Honorius issues rescript expelling Pelagius and Caelestius from Rome and condemns them as heretics.
Augustine writes *Against Two Letters of the Pelagians*.	419–420	
Councils at Carthage concerning the priest Apiarius that brings opposition between Carthage and Rome; the Africans win their case.	419 and 421	
Beginning of a long and harsh debate between Augustine and the Pelagian Bishop Julian of Eclanum.	420	
Augustine's *Against Julian*.	421–422	
The scandal with Antoninus of Fussala. Council at Carthage.	422	
	424–427	Revolt by Count Boniface of Africa.
Augustine's last work, *Against Julian, an Unfinished Book*.	428–430	
	429	The Vandals enter Africa led King Genseric.

North African Church History	Dates	Political, Religious, and Social Events
Augustine dies (August 28).	430	Hippo is sacked.
"Arianization" policies. Catholic church property confiscated and given to Arian clergy.	439	Carthage is sacked.
Genseric authorizes the election of a catholic bishop in Carthage.	454	
	455	Vandal landings in Italy; Rome is captured and pillaged; numerous well-known captives are taken to Africa.
Catholic clergy and nuns tortured and deported.	477	Huneric succeeds his father (477–484). Bloody persecution against the Manicheans.
	484	Huneric convenes (February 1) a council of catholic (466) and Arian bishops.
Condemnation of the catholic church.\n\nFebruary 7 decree: worship banned; churches reserved for Arian use only.\n\nFebruary 25 decree: catholics required to convert to Arian faith; large numbers comply; 500 clergy from Carthage sent into local exile; bishops exiled.\n\nCatholic worship re-established; bishops regain their places of ministry.	484–496	Gunthamund's reign.\n\nPeriod of toleration.\n\nThrasamund's reign.

North African Church History	Dates	Political, Religious, and Social Events
	496–523	Berber tribes constitute independent kingdoms.
Return of exiles; election of new bishops.	523–530	Religious toleration.
Regional and general councils.	523–525	
	530	Gelimer, Vandal usurper.
The catholic church regains its power and its possessions.	533	Byzantine General Belisarius victorious at Tricamarum; end of the Vandal domination in Africa.
Fulgentius of Ruspe dies. Council of 220 bishops at Carthage.	534	
The "three chapters" controversy between the African bishops and the emperor. The African church has conflict with Pope Vigilius.	544	
Bishops receive new privileges. Crisis and corruption in the clergy. Renewal of Donatism.	565	Justin II succeeds Justinian. The "reberberization" movement is accelerated in Africa and the independent kingdoms are strengthened. The Djeddar dynasty rules in Mauretania.
	578	Tiberus II. Insecurity grows in the country.
Numerous African church councils.	591–595	

North African Church History	Dates	Political, Religious, and Social Events
Final council of Carthage.	646	Byzantine governor of Africa rebels. Breakdown of central power; conflicts between the church and state.
	647	Arab raids against Ifriqiya. Gregory killed and the Byzantines troops are crushed at Sufetula (Sbeitla).
	670	Founding of Kairouan.
	697	Arab conquest of Carthage.
Christians not converting to Islam are given *dhimmi* status (subject to a "protection" tax with no political rights). Fading away of Christian communities.	c. 705	Musa Ibn Nucayr's troops reach the shores of the Atlantic.
Leo IX notes that North Africa had no more than five bishops.	1053	
Cyriacus is the only African bishop.	1076	
Christians graves (dating 945–1003) are discovered near Tripoli and others (dating 1007–1046) at Kairouan.	10th/11th centuries	

Bibliography

Apuleius. *Metamorphosis or Golden Ass.* Translated by Thomas Taylor. London: Robert Tripphook & T. Rodd, 1822.

Augustine, Saint. *The Works of Saint Augustine: A Translation for the 21st Century.* Edited by John E. Rotelle. Brooklyn, NY: New City, 1990–.

Aziza, Claude. *Tertullien et le judaïsme.* Paris: Belles Lettres, 1977.

Barnes, Timothy D. "The Beginnings of Donatistism." *Journal of Theological Studies* 26 (1975) 13–22.

———. *Tertullian: A Historical and Literary Study.* Oxford: Oxford University Press, 1971.

Berthier, Andre. *Les Vestiges du christianisme antique dans la Numidie centrale.* Algiers: Maison-Carrée, 1942.

Birot, Pierre, and Jean Dresch. *La Méditerranée et le Moyen–Orient.* Paris: Presses universitaires de France, 1953.

Blumkenkrantz, Bernhard. *Die Judenpredigt Augustins: Ein Beitrag zur Geschichte der jüdisch–christlichen Bezeihungen in den ersten Jahrhunderten.* Basel: Helbing & Lichtenhahn, 1946.

Bonner, Gerald. *Saint Augustine of Hippo: Life and Controversies.* Philadelphia: Wesminster, 1963.

Braun, René. *Approches de Tertullien. Vingt–six études sur l'auteur et son œuvre (1955–1990).* Paris: Institut d'études augustiniennes, 1992.

Brisson, J. P. *Autonomisme et Christianisme dans l'Afrique romaine de Septime Sévère à l'invasion vandale.* Paris: Boccard, 1958.

Brown, Peter. *Augustine of Hippo: A Biography.* Berkley: University of California Press, 1967.

Chadwick, Henry. *Augustine.* Oxford: Oxford University Press, 1986.

Charles-Picard, Gilbert. *La Civilisation de l'Afrique romaine.* Paris: Etudes Augustiniennes, 1990.

Congar, Yves. "Introduction générale." In *Traités anti-donatistes.* Paris: Bibliothèque Augustinienne, 1963.

Courtois, Christian. "Grégoire VII de l'Afrique du Nord: Remarques sur les communautés chrétiennes d'Afrique au IXe siècle." *Revue historique* 195 (1945) 97–122; 196–226.

———. *Les Vandales et l'Afrique.* Paris: A.M.G., 1955.

Crespin, Remi. *Ministère et Sainteté: Pastorale du clergé et solution de la crise donatiste dans la vie et la doctrine de saint Augustin.* Paris: Études Augustiniennes, 1965.

Daniélou, Jean. *Les Origines du christianisme latin.* Paris: Seuil, 1978.

Decret, François. *L'Afrique manichéene (IVe–Ve siècles): Étude historique et doctrinale.* 2 vols. Paris: Études Augustiniennes, 1978.

————. *Aspects du manichéisme dans l'Afrique romaine: Les controverses de Fortunatus, Faustus, et Felix avec Saint Augustin.* Paris: Études Augustiniennes, 1970.

————. "Augustin d'Hippone et l'esclavage." *Dialogues d'histoire ancienne* 11 (1985) 675–85.

————, and Mohamed Fantar. *L'Afrique du Nord dans l'Antiquité: Histoire et civilization— des origins au V siècle.* Paris: Payot, 1981.

Delattre, Alfred L. *Gamart ou la nécropole juive de Carthage.* Lyon, 1895.

Delehaye, Hippolyte. *Les Origines du culte des martyrs.* 2nd ed. Subsidia hagiographica 20. Brussels: Société des Bollandistes, 1933.

Demoustier, Adrien. "Episcopat et union à Rome selon saint Cyprien." *Recherches de science religeuse* 52 (1964) 337–69.

————. "L'ontologie de l'Église selon saint Cyprien." *Recherches de science religieuse* 52 (1964) 554–58.

Despois, Jean, and Rene Raynal. *Géographie de l'Afrique du Nord-Ouest.* Paris: Payot, 1967.

Diehl, Charles. *L'Afrique byzantine: Histoire de la domination byzantine en Afrique (533– 709).* Paris, 1896.

Duquesne, Luc. *Chronologie des lettres de saint Cyprien: Le dossier de la persécution de Dèce.* Subsidia hagiographica 54. Brussels: Société des Bollandistes, 1972.

Duval, Yvette. "Densité et répartition des évêchés dans les provinces africaines au temps de Cyprien." *Mélanges de l'Ecole française de Rome* 96 (1984) 493–521.

————. *Auprès des saints, corps, et âmes: L'inhumation "ad sanctos" dans la chrétienté d'Orient et d'Occident, du IIe au VIIe siècle.* Paris: Études Augustiniennes, 1988.

————. *Loca sanctorum Africae: Le culte des martyrs en Afrique du IVe au VIIe siècle.* 2 vols. Rome: Ecole française de Rome, 1982.

Février, Paul-Albert. "Aux origines du christianisme en Maurétanie Césarienne." *Mélanges de l'Ecole française de Rome* 98 (1986) 767–809.

————. "Martyrs, polémique, et politique en Afrique (IVe–Ve siècles)." *Revue d'histoire et de civilization du Maghreb* 1 (1968) 8–18.

————. "Religion et domination dans l'Afrique romaine." *Dialogues d'histoire ancienne* 2 (1976) 305–36.

————. "Toujours le donatisme, à quand l'Afrique." *Rivista di storia e letteratura religiosa* 2 (1966) 228–40.

————. *Approches du Maghreb romain: Pouvoirs, differences et conflicts.* 2 vols. Aix-en-Provence: Edisud, 1989–1990.

Fredouille, Jean Claude. *Tertullien et la conversion de la culture antique.* Paris: Études Augustiniennes, 1972.

Frend, W. H. C. "Circumcellions and Monks." *Journal of Theological Studies* 20 (1969) 542–49.

———. *The Donatist Church: A Movement of Protest in Roman North Africa.* Oxford: Carendon, 1985.

———. "Jews and Christians in Third Century Carthage." In *Paganisme, Judaisme, Christianisme: influences et affrontements dans le monde antique : mélanges offerts à Marcel Simon.* Paris: E. de Boccard, 1978.

Guignebert, Charles. *Tertullien: Étude sur ses sentiments à l'égard de l'Empire et de la société civile.* Paris: Leroux, 1901.

Julien, Charles-Andre. *Histoire de l'Afrique du Nord.* Paris: Payot, 1994.

Kriegbaum, Bernhard. *Kirche der Traditoren oder Kirche der Märtyrer? Die Vorgeschichte der Donatismus.* Innsbrucker theologische Studien 16. Innsbruck: Tyrolia, 1986.

Lancel, Serge. *Actes de la Conference de Carthage de 411.* Paris: Cerf, 1975.

———. "Les Débuts du donatisme: la date du 'Protocole de Cirta' et de l'élection épiscopale de Silvanus." *Révue des Études Augustiniennes* 25 (1979) 217–29.

Lapeyre, G. G. "La politique religieuse des rois vandales." *L'Ancienne Église de Carthage* 2 (1933) 11–151.

LeJay, P. *Les Origines de l'Église d'Afrique et l'Église romaine.* Liège: Kurth, 1908.

Mahjoubi, Amor. "Nouveau témoignage épigraphique sur la communauté chrétienne de Kairouan au XIe siècle." *Africa* 1 (1966) 85–96.

Maier, Jean-Louis. *Le Dossier du donatisme.* Berlin: Akademie–Verlag, 1987.

Mandouze, André. "Le donatisme représente-t-il la résistance à Rome de l'Afrique tradive?" *Travaux du VIe Congrès international d'études classiques.* (1976) 357–66.

———. "Les donatistes entre ville et campagne." *Histoire de l'archéologie de l'Afrique du Nord* (1986) 193–217.

———. *Saint Augustin: L'aventure de la raison et de la grace.* Paris: Études Augustiniennes, 1968.

Marçais, George. *La Berbérie musulmane de l'Orient au Moyen Age.* Les Grand Crises de l'Histoire. Paris: Aubier, 1946.

Marrou, Henri Irénée. *St. Augustin et l'augustinisme.* Paris: Seuil, 1983.

———. "Survivances païennes dans les rites funéraires des donatistes," *Latomus* 2 (1949) 193–203.

Marschall, Werner. *Karthago und Rom: Die Stellung der nordafrikanischen Kirche zum Apostolischen Stuhl in Rom.* Stuttgart: Hiersemann, 1971.

Mesnage, J. *Le Christianisme en Afrique: Origines, developpement, extension.* 3 vols. Algiers: Jourdan, 1914–1915.

Monceaux, Paul. "Les colonies juives dans l'Afrique romaine." *Revue des études juives* 44 (1904) 1–28.

———. *Saint Cyprien.* Paris: Gabalda, 1927.

O'Meara, John J. *The Young Augustine: The Growth of Saint Augustine's Mind up to his Conversion.* London: Longmans and Green, 1954.

Paribeni, P. "Sepolcreto cristiano di Engila." *Africa Italiana* 1 (1927) 75–82.

Perler, Othmar. *Les Voyages de Saint Augustin.* Paris: Études Augustiniennes, 1969.

Plinval, Georges de. *Pélage, ses écrits, sa vie et sa réforme.* Lausanne: Payot, 1943.

Possidius, Saint. *The Life of Saint Augustine.* Edited by John E. Rotelle and Michele Pellegrino. Translated by Matthew O'Connell. The Augustine Series. Villanova, PA: Augustinian, 1988.

Powell, Douglas. "Tertullianists and Cataphrygians." *Vigiliae Christianae* 29 (1975) 33–54.

Roberts, Alexander, James Donaldson, Philip Schaff, and Henry Wace, editors. *Nicene and Post-Nicene Fathers.* Series 1. 14 Vols. Peabody, MA: Hendrickson, 1994.

———. *Ante-Nicene Fathers.* 10 Vols. Peabody, MA: Hendrickson, 1994.

Romanelli, Pietro. *Storia delle province romane dell'Africa.* Rome: Istituto Italiano per la Storia Antica, 1959.

Sage, Michael M. *Cyprian.* Patristic Monograph Series 1. Cambridge, MA: Philadelphia Patristic Foundation, 1975.

Salama, Pierre. *Les Voies romaines de l'Afrique du Nord.* Algiers, 1951.

Saumagne, Charles. "La persécution de Dèce à Carthage d'après la correspondence de saint Cyprien." *Bulletin de la Société nationale des antiquaires de France,* 1957 (1959) 23–42.

———. *Saint Cyprien, évêque de Carthage, "pape" d'Afrique (248–258): Contribution à l'étude des "persecutions" de Dèce et de Valérien.* Paris: Editions du Centre national de la recherche scientifique, 1975.

———. "Autonomie africaine et primauté romaine de Tertullien à Augustin." In *Il primato del vescovo di Roma nel primo millenio: Ricerche e testimonianze,* edited by M. Maccarrone, 173–217. Atti e documenti 4. Vatican City: Vatican Library Press, 1991.

———. "Mort et culte des morts à partir de l'archéologie et de la liturgie d'Afrique dans l'œuvre de saint Augustin." *Augustinianum* 18.1 (1978), 219–28.

———. *Morts, Martyrs, Reliques en Afrique chrétienne aux premiers siècles: Les témoignages de Tertullien, Cyprien, et Augustin à la lumière de archeology africaine.* Paris: Beauchesne, 1980.

———. *Saints anciens d'Afrique du Nord.* Vatican, 1979.

———. *Vie liturgique et quotidienne à Carthage vers le milieu du IIIe siècle: Le témoignage de saint Cyprien et de ses contemporains d'Afrique.* Vatican City: Pontificio Istituto di archeologia cristiana, 1969.

Seston, William. "Sur les derniers temps du christianisme en Afrique." *Mélanges d'archéologie et d'histoire* 53 (1936) 100–124.

Shaw, Brent D. "The Passion of Perpetua." *Past and Present* 139 (1993) 3–45.

Simon, M. "Le judaïsme berbère dans l'Afrique romain." *Revue d'histoire et de philosophie religeuses* 26 (1946) 1–31; 105–45

Tengström, Emin. *Donatisten und Katholiken: Soziale, wirtschaftliche und politische Aspekte einer nordafrikanischen Kirchenspaltung.* Studia Greca et Latina Gothoburgensia 18. Stockholm: Almqvist & Wiksell, 1964.

Trapè, Agostino. *Saint Augustin, l'homme, le pasteur, le mystique.* Translated by Victor Arminjon. Paris: Fayard, 1988.

———. *Saint Augustine: Man, Pastor, Mystic.* Translated by Matthew J. O'Connell. Spirituality for Today 4. New York: Catholic Book Publishing, 1986.

Van der Meer, Frederick. *Augustine the Bishop: Church and Society at the Dawn of the Middle Ages.* Translated by Brian Battershaw and G. R. Lamb. London: Sheed and Ward, 1961.

Warmington, B. H. *The North African Provinces from Diocletian to the Vandal Conquest.* Cambridge: Cambridge University Press, 1954.

Index

BV - #0039 - 230724 - C0 - 229/152/13 - PB - 9780227173565 - Gloss Lamination